The Craft of Copywriting

This book could not have been written without the constant help of Almighty God

The Craft of Copywriting

June A. Valladares

Response Books
A division of Sage Publications
New Delhi/Thousand Oaks/London

First published in 2000 by

Response Books
A division of Sage Publications India Pvt Ltd
M–32, Greater Kailash Market–I
New Delhi 110 048

Sage Publications Inc
2455 Teller Road
Thousand Oaks, California 91320

Sage Publications Ltd
6 Bonhill Street
London EC2A 4PU

Published by Tejeshwar Singh for Response Books, lasertypeset by Innovative Processors, New Delhi, and printed at Chaman Enterprises, Delhi.

Library of Congress Cataloging-in-Publication Data

Valladares, June A., 1948–
The craft of copywriting/June A. Valladares.
p. cm. (cloth). (pbk.)
Includes bibliographical references and index.
1. Advertising copy I. Title.
HF5825.V35 2000 659.13′2—dc21 00–021782

ISBN: 0–7619–9416–5 (US–HB) 81–7036–897–9 (India–HB)
0–7619–9424–6 (US–PB) 81–7036–898–7 (India–PB)

Production Team: Chandana Chandra, Radha Dev Raj, Richard Brown and Santosh Rawat

Dedicated with affection to the memory of
Mr Subhas Ghosal
champion of copywriters

Contents

Foreword

At first, I made an energetic effort to resist June's request to write the Foreword to her book. I argued that I was no longer active in advertising, indeed haven't been for years. But June would have none of it.

She said she owed such a deep debt to me that my absence from the madding *'ad*-ing' crowd didn't matter. In fact, she had already prepared the semi-final draft and it already included the words, 'Foreword by Cossy Rosario'.

Eventually, I capitulated and I'm glad I did. It gave me a chance to be among the first to look deeply into her very instructive, stimulating and *motivating* book.

Exploring June's book was (for me) like time travelling. I met former colleagues such as Gerson and Alyque in its pages. Not the Gerson and Alyque of today (I haven't had the opportunity to read the pieces they're specially writing for the book), but the Gerson and Alyque of those days. Some of my friends, like Mubi Ismail (later Mrs Mubi Pasricha) and Balwant Tandon, have passed, alas, into the realm of death. The fact lent a touch of poignancy to my reading of the book. Certain references brought back vivid memories of June's own early days as a *cub*, bewildered by the mysteries of copywriting, unable to understand the difference between a sentence and a headline, a headline and an advertising idea, yet full of words (a veritable thesaurus of them) and willing to experiment and keep on trying to *my* heart's content.

June didn't stay a cub for long, not because of my greatness as a trainer but because of her own insatiable appetite for professional knowledge, her systematic maintenance of files of work and exercises (something she exhorts her readers to be faithful to), her making the most of gifted colleagues to evaluate her work and guide her to the heights.

I was both touched and impressed by June's use of her own mistakes and failures as object lessons for her readers (not many authors admit to any imperfections, even transient ones!).Having climbed over her gaffes and faux pas to well-merited triumphs, she has used these incidents (and accidents) to help aspirant writers surmount their own inevitable failures and fiascos.

Endowed with that personal touch that breathes life into dead text, June, the writer and trainer, comes across as the person she is: honest, loveable, humble yet thoroughly professional. She evidently has a profound love for young people and it is they who will particularly benefit from reading and working through this book.

As her first trainer, and possibly the one who made the deepest impression on her, I have just this to say to the author, "June, you've done me proud!"

Cossy Rosario

Preface

This book has been a long time coming. I have wanted to read a book on the craft of copywriting by an Indian ever since I became aware that foreign books on the subject were few and also very expensive. But to date, I have not come across any book of this nature. This then is a modest attempt to set down the disciplines I have learned in the course of practising the art of '*salesmanship in print*'.

This book also tries to answer some questions I have been asked about agency life and how to survive the rough and tumble. If you have picked up this book, it means you are interested, whether you want to be a copywriter or not.

- How do you define a proposition?
- How do you get the feel of a product/job fast enough to meet a deadline?
- How do you handle three jobs at a time?
- Is it absolutely necessary to believe in the product? Or is it enough to believe in crafting a good ad?
- Do you write for yourself or the creative director?
- What if a product does not live up to its advertising?
- When do you leave an agency?
- How do you stay interested in your career?

In doing so, I have departed slightly from my original intention of producing a no-frills how-to-write-copy manual to include some personal experiences. This was supported also by my observations about creative people of the 'now generation'.

- They seem to be more *competitive.*
- *Money* is the main motivation . . . followed by success (i.e., promotions, status).
- There appears little or *no loyalty* to the company.
- The old guard constantly bemoans the *lack of values* in the younger set who in turn regards the oldies as 'drips'!
- There seems to be a great deal more *insecurity* and tension among young creatives.
- The high salaries and shortage of real talent have bred a sort of *know-it-all* air.
- They are more *secretive.* Brainstorming and teamwork are not in vogue.
- They have *no time* for any good old-fashioned *fun.*
- However, they *respect professionalism* when they meet it.
- Under the tough exterior, they are *just like we used to be!*

For these reasons, I think new writers will welcome a book like this one. The only way to deal with insecurity is to master your craft, which I hope this book will help you do.

It is primarily a workman's book. It will show you how to think, how to 'ideate', and finally how to write and evaluate good copy—for press ads, for hoardings, for radio, for films/TV/audio-visuals, for direct mailers. It tries to give you almost everything I have learned from other people, and a few tricks of my own.

From the outset, I must admit there is nothing original in this book. I am merely doing what copywriters the world over are doing every day of their lives—

Saying it differently.
While trying to say it memorably.
That for me is the essence of copywriting.

My advertising career began more than 25 years ago when one could count the number of ad agencies in Bombay (now Mumbai) without drawing breath. I was fortunate to learn my craft (writing copy is as much a craft as an art) under the deft guidance of such 'geniuses' as Cossy Rosario, Alyque Padamsee, Mubi Ismail, Gerson da Cunha and Noel Godin, who were all shining in the firmament that was Lintas India. Indeed, it was an environment where creativity crackled and sizzled. Everywhere you turned you met a star. It was enough to give you an indelible inferiority complex—or impel you to become a star yourself. It was a question of swim for your life or become breakfast for sharks.

On the client servicing side were strong personalities like Deep Kaul, Bulbul Singh, Shakti Maira, Raj Jagga and others with whom I was only on nodding acquaintance, because I was too junior to be spoken to. Gyan Bahl headed Media. Chief art director Raj Arjungi could draw a perfect circle freehand. And Balwant Tandon wrote brilliant lines for the press and jingles for the radio in Hindi.

I worked for about five years with Lintas, in three stints. The first time I left the agency was to oblige Gerson da Cunha who told me that Mr Subhas Ghosal and Ram Ray (at the time managing director and account supervisor respectively of Hindustan Thompson Associates) had asked for me by name. HTA was going through a rough patch and all their writers had left. I returned to Lintas briefly in 1977 on loan from HTA, as some Lintas writers had gone on leave simultaneously. This is unusual, and Shunu Sen—then marketing director at Hindustan Lever—once asked me at a meeting, "June, where are you coming from now?" (I am still trying to answer that question!). The third time round, in 1980, Alyque invited me to join Lintas as Creative Group Head. HTA found me dispensable, so I went.

The seven delightful years with my 'other agency', Hindustan Thompson Associates, are possibly even more deeply etched in memory than my time with Lintas in the '70s. Both agencies have changed since, in size and perhaps even in character . . . but when I think of my career in advertising, I think of Lintas and HTA as they lived and breathed and performed under the exciting stewardships of Gerson, Alyque (Lintas) and Mr Ghosal (HTA).

Copywriters then were reared on such staple fare as Rosser Reeves, Aesop Glim, John Caples, Stephen Baker, Otto Klepner and David Ogilvy. The books written by some of these giants may be hard to come by now. But when one is out to learn a craft, it is better to get back to the source—or as close to the source as possible.

Advertising was young enough in the '70s, so that when Julian Watkins (1959) listed "The 100 Greatest Advertisements", you could really believe they were so. Each ad was a classic. They stuck in your mind like so many burrs. I can never forget "They laughed when I sat down at the piano, but when I started to play . . ." (John Caples), or Odorono's "Within the curve of a woman's arm" by James Webb

Young of JWT, or the famous Sherwin Cody ad written by Max Sackheim, "Do you make these mistakes in English?" Those were all long-copy ads, so unfashionable in today's instant world, but I devoured every word. Some have been reproduced in this book and should be learned by heart.

HTA had its share of stars too—Ivan Arthur, Niko Nair, Sudhir Deokar, Damodar Warrior, Bahadur Merwan: all superb creative people with a terrific mastery of their craft. Ram Ray, the highly creative account supervisor who went on to head JWT San Francisco, before starting his own shop (Response India) was also a world-class photographer and the most 'unordinary' advertising person I have ever worked with. Roda Mehta was a bright young media planner and we became friends. When I left mainstream advertising in the '80s to follow a dream, I missed the challenge of pitting my mind and imagination against these touchstones. However, life offers enough challenges to go on with and so one has not been left entirely bereft.

I was 33 when I left Bombay and mainstream advertising to pursue my diverse interests in gentler environs. I have never regretted the decision. I believed then (and still do to a large extent) that copywriting is a young person's profession. A young body, physically fit, is better equipped to take the strain of long hours at work, the daily commute, the almost continual flow of adrenalin, the high pressures of deadlines and coping at all times with a hundred different egos daily.

I recognised early that I was not cut out for corporate life on a long-term basis. Ram Ray gave me important advice, "Learn to be a self-motivator", which I have tried to follow. It has borne much fruit and helped me cope in an ever-changing and dynamic world.

From 1982 to 1984, I kept in touch with my profession by writing an advertising column for the *Telegraph*, Calcutta, stopping when I went to Australia for six months. Here I got in with a Sydney group of poets and novelists who taught me much about the craft of poetry/fiction writing. Thanks to their efforts, my poems are aired on Radio Australia from time to time, and have been accepted by Nissim Ezekiel for P.E.N.

When Ivan Arthur asked me to rejoin HTA as creative director of the Madras office in 1989, computer graphics was changing the face of advertising. Being little exposed to this, I hesitated to accept the post. I am glad Ivan overrode my trepidation; Madras taught me a valuable lesson about advertising creativity:

> **Technology may become more sophisticated, but there is no substitute for IDEAS, and these can be generated only by the human mind.**

Thank heaven for that!

Restless in harness, I soon quit Madras and returned to my home—and freedom—in Poona. Here I donned the mantle of creative consultant and copy trainer.

The adage goes, "Those who can, do—and those who cannot, teach." I have never shrunk from sharing my professional knowledge with others. Teaching is the other side of learning and I enjoy interacting with young people. It is mainly for these—bright, enthusiastic and caring—that I write this book. I am grateful for this opportunity to give back to my profession, in some small part, what I took out of it.

Copywriting has brought me a few awards and many rewards.

Professionally, I have always been in the right place at the right time. My first lucky break came in 1971 when I was picked up by Lintas, Bombay, to be trained by copy chief Cossy Rosario: three hours a day for a whole year. There will always be writers who are more talented and who are better sellers than I shall ever be. However, I challenge any creative person in the industry to say that he or she received three-hours-a-day coaching in copywriting for a whole year by the incomparable Cossy. Whatever has remained with me about writing copy is due solely to his unstinting efforts to bring order to my chaotic mind. He was patient, witty, highly inventive and never dull. There were times I hated him for the discipline he imposed on me, but he bore that too, good-humouredly.

To him, and all those wonderful folk who gave me their pearls to harbour, my inadequate thanks.

June A. Valladares

Acknowledgements

- Cossy Rosario for his constructive scrutiny of the manuscript and generous Foreword
- For sharing their vision and wisdom:

  Ivan Arthur
  Seema Bakhshi
  Gerson da Cunha
  Shirley de Souza
  Roda Mehta
  Bahadur Merwan
  Alyque Padamsee
  Anita Sarkar
  Frank Simoes

- Lakshmi Pennathur, Patsy Fernandes, Anita Sarkar and Kevin de Almeida for many many hours of cheerful and affectionate labour over the final draft.
- Devashis Bhattacharyya and his team at Design Workshop for the art aid and cover design. Arindam Ganguli, Seema Bakhshi and Chandra Bhattacharyya for everything else.
- My prayer group and uncountable friends (particularly Suneel Kapur, Freny Tayebjee, Violet Bajaj and Sunita Rebello) for their unswerving belief, timely aid and unflagging encouragement.
- Sajid Peerbhoy who provided grist for the mill and Benjamin Borges who got it going.
- Most of all, Ranjan Kaul.

■ *With special thanks to Bahadur Merwan for the cartoons* ■

JAV

1

So You've Joined an Ad Agency, So What?

Jerry della Femina once said, "Advertising is the most fun you can have with your clothes on." Copywriting is the most fun you can have with pencil and paper!

When I joined Lintas as a cub writer in February 1972 I was totally confused. Everyone looked so important rushing about on some urgent job that was wanted yesterday. The only unoccupied person was me. I would mooch around the cabins housing the Great Creative Brains and beg to watch them work. Sometimes I was allowed. It is unlikely that cubs today get to say "Good morning" to creative directors in their agency.

But the '70s were different.

As were the '80s.

And the ’90s.

And the millennium is sure to be.

The trouble with trainees is that someone has to train them. And no one wants to. Usually I was loaded with a pile of proofs and sent on my way. It took me a while to figure out that if I did not stand up and be counted I would perish in the wash.

For the first six months in Lintas I was miserable. I could not tell an artwork from a hole in the ground. There were so many things to learn. The creative ‘pool’ was where I was dumped, but gradually I began to meet the account executives, the media people, the research bunch, the film and TV lot, the production ‘guys’, the model coordinator, the lunch boys, and a heap more. It was months before something went *ping* in my mind and I could sort out who was doing what to whom and when.

My poem, published in *Solus*, the Bombay Ad Club’s journal (vol. 8, no. 1) in January 1972, reveals how perplexed I was—even after a year!

Adqueries

Should barnacles wear billycocks or bowlers?
Should a donkey take a breather in the park?
Should a salamander bow to a solitary cow
If he meets her on the causeway after dark?
(adapted from an old rhyme)

May I put my thoughts in order with a question?
Do copywriters stand, a breed apart?
Is it only their mentality, their bubbling creativity,
Or their flambashy ties that make them all so smart?

Is it ideas, ideas, ideas all day long?
What happens when imagination fails?
Do THEY let you be a while, or do they forget to smile,
And ride you out of Bombay on a rail?

There are some things that I really have to ask;
Is the ad game as simple as it seems?
All that soap and beauty milk, and things of similar ilk,
To make you the woman of his dreams!

Will Brand Image stay as elusive as it is?
And "gestalt" always be a foreign word?
As for all those Propositions, with manypossiblexpressions,
They're things of which I wish I'd never heard!

How d'you make a headline do what you want it to?
Do you roll it in the mud and see it squirm?
If the ultimate result is a series of collapses,
Wouldn't you, sir, feel rather like a worm?

—JUNE VALLADARES

It takes a while to get the feel of your new workplace. Smile at everyone and ask questions—even if it means being a pest. Most agency folk are tolerant of newcomers bent on learning the job.

Never be too proud or too shy to ask, ask and ask questions.

And finally, *keep a notebook and take notes.* Do not trust your memory. Make lists, write aide memoires and tick things off as you go along. You will be glad of this when you are working on more than one campaign at the same time.

It Helps to Know an Agency's Set-up

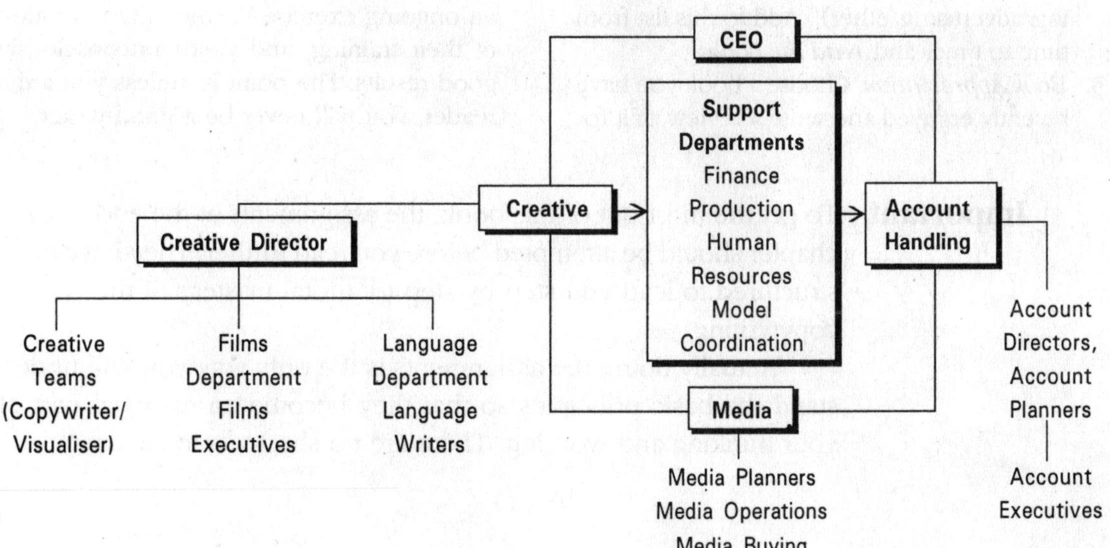

Get to know everybody, their names and designations. It helps to speak to people in the language they are most comfortable with. Write in English if that is what you are being paid for, but communicate with artists, printers and suppliers in Hindi, Marathi, Bengali or Tamil. You will find the work going smoother.

In an agency, everybody is working for someone else, and the whole shop is working for the client. Advertising is a service industry, however professional we are. The client pays the salaries, he tells us what to say. Our job is only to tell him how to say it.

There is a wide world out there besides the agency. Advertising is only one of the arrows in the client's marketing quiver. He has equally powerful ones like pricing, sales policy, a distribution network, packaging, research and development, to name a few. To become a rounded advertising person, make it a point to read about allied fields beyond the scope of this book.

Workout

1. Start a file of the assignments you do from this book. As far as possible, type your assignments, except where visuals are needed. Save everything you write. Even the lists.
2. Open a page on 'Books to Read' (marketing/advertising/other). Add to this list from time to time, and *read the books!*
3. *Book Appreciation:* Choose a book you have recently enjoyed and write a review of it for a hypothetical literary magazine. I ask my trainees to read three books a week. Fiction by an English author, fiction by an American writer, and one professional book on any aspect of advertising they like. This is an ongoing exercise for the entire duration of their training, and yields unconsciously good results. The point is, unless you are a reader, you will never be a good writer.

Important To get the most out of this book, the assignments at the end of each chapter should be attempted before you read further. They have been structured to lead you step by step to a total mastery of the craft of copywriting.

Actually doing the assignments is the only way you will understand the basic principles so that they become an essential part of your thinking and working. There are no shortcuts to success!

2

The Creative Spark

In Lintas everyone spoke of something called *spark*. Apparently some people have it and others do not. In the creative department, everyone had *spark* to a greater or lesser degree. Even the copy typist was considered to have *spark* because of the manner in which he typed: quickly, efficiently and with a minimum of fuss.

When I give wannabe writers a *Copy Test,* I look for spark—that indefinable ingredient. If they have it, they are considered trainable; if they do not, that means they may show their *spark* in some other field, and so this in no way brands them as inferior to those who were chosen for their copywriting potential.

For copywriters two qualities are essential:

- *a good command of the language*
- *imagination*

To this add a third: curiosity, which cannot really be discerned through a mere copy test. A person with these qualities is considered teachable. Whether the copywriter will make it in the tough, rough world of advertising depends on stamina, grit, resourcefulness, readiness and other characteristics. Agency life has a way of weeding out those who do not make the grade.

You Might Enjoy Doing this Copy Test

This copy test is devised for college graduates or those who have attended a course in communications which teaches the basics of advertising. Choose a quiet place, arm yourself with paper and pen, and away you go. This test must be done without help from anyone else. No cheating! You should be through in about three hours. Good luck!

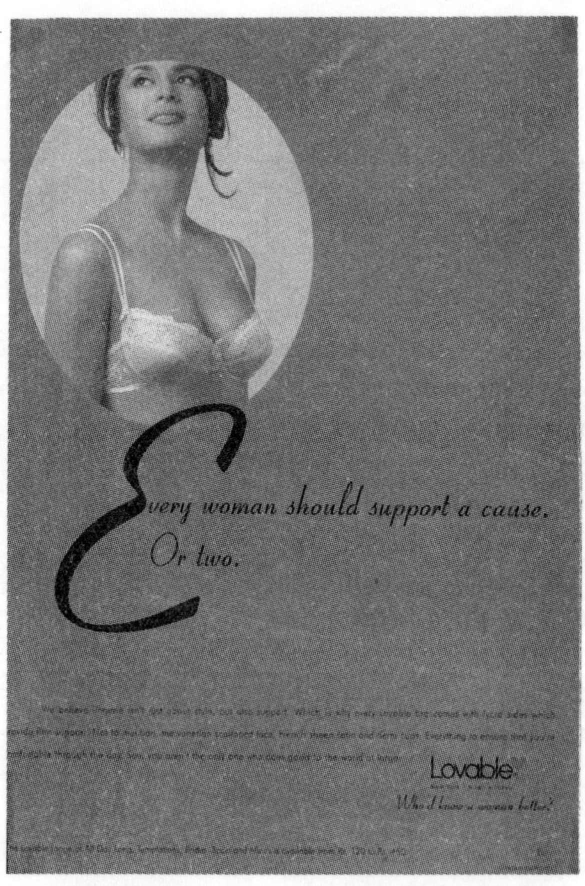

Every woman should support a cause.
Or two.
Lovable

Your Time Starts Now

Copy Test

1. Three advertisements for *Loveable Bras* are given here. They are part of a series. Study them carefully. Then write a fourth ad, making sure it fits in with the other three. Also, describe the visual idea you have thought up.

Be firm at work.
Our All Day Long bras have underwiring for support, a curved back which stays down, stretch side panels, a special fabric to help your skin breathe and lycra straps that don't back bite. Unlike people at work.
All Day Long by
Lovable
New York • Milan • Tokyo
Who'd know a woman better?

If our bra doesn't make you feel comfortable on the job, we suggest you change it.
The job, that is.
Our All Day Long bras are styled to give you what people don't: support. They have specially knit fabric to help your skin breathe, a touch of lace, stretch side panels, a curved back which stays down and lycra straps that don't dig into you. So after a hard day's work if you feel something snap inside you, rest assured it won't be your bra.
All Day Long by
Lovable
New York • Milan • Tokyo
Who'd know a woman better?
Regd. Trademark of "The Lovable Co.", Fifth Avenue, New York.

2. Write a story-article for *The Reader's Digest* (up to 500 words) on 'My Most Unforgettable Character'.
3. Write a dialogue between Mr Mehra and Mrs Mehra. Mr Mehra is driving the car through heavy traffic, while his wife is describing a terrible accident she witnessed that morning. Work in the following points as smoothly as possible *using dialogue only.*
   a. Mr Mehra suffers from high blood pressure.
   b. Mrs Mehra wears a hearing aid.
   c. The car is a 1967 Ambassador.
   d. Their two children attend local colleges.
   e. They are late for a wedding reception.

   These points can be introduced in any order. Take care not to force them into the conversation.
4. Rewrite the following story as imaginatively as you like. Give it atmosphere. Then continue the story to an interesting conclusion.

Shekhar and Rohan, young account executives, sit drinking beer in a local pub. It is a Saturday evening. Shekhar asks Rohan to telephone Natasha, a girl who has just joined the creative department in their agency. He refuses, saying he hardly knows her; that he had acted in a college play once with her, when she was the star and he had a role as a waiter; she would not remember him. Shekhar insists, so Rohan makes the call. Natasha has forgotten him completely!

So the men go alone to a dance at a nearby club.

Just that morning, Rohan's mother had said it was time he thought of getting married. But Rohan is too shy. He believes he cannot attract the kind of girl he would like to marry.

Now, at the dance, Rohan notices a plain-looking girl in a corner. She seems hurt and lonely. Suddenly her partner returns after dancing with another girl, a beauty. Rohan overhears the plain girl quarrelling with her 'date'. Then she turns and quickly walks away to the lobby outside.

Rohan notices a tear sliding down her cheek. He follows her into the lobby and catches up with her. "Sorry for intruding," he stammers, "but I couldn't help overhearing you and your friend. Can I see you home?"

5. Write a short, crisp headline for each of the news items set down here. They should be provocative—the type that will attract readers of *Time* or *Newsweek.*

News item #1

VIENNA: Austria's second biggest city of Graz will pay foreign beggars 3,500 Austrian schillings ($260) each per month to stay off its streets, officials have said. Instead of preying on passers-by in the picturesque city centre, up to 40 beggars will be sent by Graz's social service department to local parishes where they will receive financial help in return for performing odd jobs.

"We're not talking about regular work. Legally that is not possible as foreigners would need a work permit," the head of Graz's social services said. The project will run for several months before it is reviewed. Most of the beggars are believed to be gypsies from neighbouring Slovakia.

News item #2

HAMBURG: Many more women in western industrialised countries have difficulty bonding with their babies than is generally believed, a British psychiatrist claimed.

In extreme cases this has even cost children their lives, psychiatrist Ian Brockington told an international congress on child and youth psychiatry in Hamburg, northern Germany.

"Motherly love is not inherited. The bond between mother and infant has to be worked at very hard," he said. Mr Brockington has observed women who have difficulty in bonding with their children at his clinic in Birmingham, central England, since 1975. He said their rejection of their children often begins during pregnancy, especially when they are unplanned.

But he said most women can be helped through regular talks with social workers and by mother and baby play therapy, which has a "success rate of nearly 100 per cent."

Psychiatrists say one cause of psychological disorders in children and youth is the breakdown of the traditional nuclear family consisting of a mother and a father. In Germany, for example, 40 per cent of preschool children live with single parents.

News item #3

NEW DELHI: If you look at the 12-inch long box supported by what looks like legs at the front and legs-on-wheels at the back, you might think it is a toy that runs on batteries. It does not look like the conventional robot, but for its Bangalore-born inventor, Prof. Kumar Ramohalli of the aerospace and mechanical engineering department, University of Arizona in Tucson, the biological robot is the robot of the future. He hopes to send BiRoDs to Mars and other distant points in the solar system, where they will probe, dig, photograph, analyse and generally explore the planets, moons and asteroids.

"Look under BiRoD's hood and you'll see it doesn't have gears, servos and other complex mechanical systems," he says. "We are trying to imitate biological systems." Inside the new robot are thin, shiny wires and springs. When connected to a battery, they contract mechanically, mimicking the actions of muscles. The current flowing through muscle wires causes their molecules to rearrange themselves in a smaller space.

Muscle wires make the BiRoDs lighter, less bulky, insensitive to dust and other enemies of mechanical systems, and they also respond in milliseconds, can carry 17,000 times their weight, and go through millions of cycles without failing.

The prototype BiRoDs, which could revolutionise robotics, has infrared vision that enables it to avoid obstacles in the dark. Unlike other robots, BiRoDs can produce bursts of power, so they can store energy slowly and expend it suddenly.

News item #4

WASHINGTON: The United States of the 21st century will belong to Hispanics, according to an article in *Newsweek*. With a population growing at a rate seven times faster than the general population, Hispanics are changing the face of America.

The turning point came with the "bloodless coup of 1992, when salsa outsold ketchup for the first time." Since then, Hispanics have become 31-million strong and account for 11.4 per cent of the US population, according to the US census bureau.

News item #5

LUEBECK: The human tongue is a small miracle of engineering, consisting of muscles, mucous membrane and nerves. We use it constantly, for speaking, chewing, swallowing and tasting. Luckily, there is hope for people who have lost this important organ after a tumour operation.

Doctors at the ear, nose and throat clinic of Luebeck Medical University, in northern Germany, use a method of reconstructing the tongue from neck muscles, complete with nerves and blood vessels. The technique, which was developed by the clinic's deputy director, Stephan Remmert, makes use of the infrahyoidal muscles found to the right and left of the larynx, to replace the wholly or partially missing tongue tissue.

---

6. Correct the mistakes in grammar and spelling in the piece that follows.

Marie knew that ernie was the kind of guy who liked to smell super cooking when he came home to the apartment even though marie got home from work only a little time before he did sometimes she wondered how women with children even managed t get a meal on the table; at other times she wished she had a chance to find out but in six years it hadnt happened.

"Hi Ernie said this evening as always when he came into the foyeur and changed his lunch box down by the telephone. Marie heard it where she say :in one of the fat armchaires in front of the red living room drapes there was a magazine in her lap which she closed when Ernie came in.

Baby? Ernie said, don't you feel good, there was no smell of supper cooking.

Marie raised her head. she had a thin sweet face and her brow was surounded by brown curls. Hi she said softly "I was reading" she helod to him the magazine with a blue cover across the top i t said: Descant A Magazine of poetyr

What's that Ernie asked what the hell is that?

"It was on the subway this morning when I went to work. It was just lying there so I picked itup for something to read, she added I've been sort of reading it all day.

"Poetry?" Ernie said, in that voice which could reconise. it was the same voice in which he had said, "your father?" when he first met mr.walters who wore vests and twinkled at ladies and got drunk at the wedding.

Marie smiled tentatively at her husband. "I didnt have anything else to read. Dow you want supper."

"Of course I want supper" Ernie said but he sad down on the othre fat arm-chair under the velevet drapery of the valance. His motion stirred nothing in the small warm living room. I knew you always read funny stuff like essays like that but are you sure you feel Ok? I mean, who reads poetry?

Marie threw the magazine down to the white-velvet footstool on which no one ever put his feet. She said in a quite voice I feel fine and stood up. She went toward the kitchen saying, down down into the brine. Sleep of sharks.

"Zott!" Ernie mutered pretending to shoot himself in the head.

When you are done, type your assignment and state how many hours it took to complete it. Put your name on every page. Do not ask anyone for help, and do it at one sitting. Remember, if you cheat, you are only cheating yourself!

If You Want an Evaluation

Show your copy test to your creative director or copy chief and ask for an assessment. If this is not possible, you are welcome to send your *original effort* (preferably typed or neatly handwritten) to me at the following address:

June Valladares
Witsend
28 St Patrick's Town
Pune 411 013

The fee is Rs 250 (cheque or Demand Draft) and you will get a response within four weeks of receipt of your test . . . if you include a self-addressed envelope. Tests will not be sent back, so you might want to keep a photostat copy for your own reference.

(By the way, this sort of ploy when used in a press ad is known as a *buried offer*. It is one way to measure the effectiveness of your message. The publisher of this book is responsible for letting me know how many copies sell, but your response will give me an idea of how persuasive its contents really are!)

There is very little communication that does not seek to gain some sort of response. True or false?

The Copywriter's Attitude

Many people are drawn to advertising because of its perceived glamour and high salaries. The behind-the-scenes grind and the nitty-gritty of daily chores come as a rude shock. It is best to be prepared. The high salaries are justified. They are earned with blood, toil, sweat and tears.

Alyque Padamsee was fond of saying, "I have only two favourites in this agency. They are Talent and Industry."

So talent by itself is not enough, just as simply working your fingers to the bone is not enough if you are doing all the wrong things. Subhas Ghosal, who started his career as a copy trainee in J. Walter Thompson under the guidance of Edward J. Fielden, believed that all copywriters are constipated. Things come out in a rush at the last minute.

Sometimes a copywriter appears to be doing absolutely nothing. You might just be leaning back in a swivel chair with eyes closed and biting your lips like Rex Stout's great fat detective, Nero Wolfe. This does not mean you are asleep, but merely letting the wheels of your mind turn preparatory to writing your deathless words. (If you have not read Rex Stout, you have a treat in store. Besides, his word pictures are something else again.)

As you grow as a writer, you learn to do your thinking in not such an obvious way. Perhaps your serious thinking is done while you are busy with some other chore which is partly mechanical or which does not require too much mental effort. You learn that your brain is capable of thinking creatively and providing solutions while you are doing something quite unrelated—like having a swim or even while checking proofs or reading a book.

I need to sleep on things. After filling my mind with facts and data for a particular campaign, I stop thinking about it and switch off, turning to a totally different subject (it might well be the data collection for another product). My brain is set on auto-think for the first campaign idea. Hours later I press the ON button and sit down before my typewriter (or computer). And, hey presto, my fingers fly and the ideas just keep coming.

At first I used to get anxious when I could not come up with an idea fast enough to meet a deadline. However, a little tension is good because it gets the creative juices flowing. But too much tension and anxiety can sap energy and lead to poor performance. The thing is to find the right balance. All this takes time and practice. You will soon learn to be gentle with yourself, but not too gentle!

A Craft as Much as an Art

It was John E. Kennedy who defined copywriting as salesmanship in print. You will have to put away any dreams of being a John Grisham or a Guy de Maupassant in the interests of *selling your client's product*. If you can take the craft of writing to an art form of selling, you will not only win awards but earn your client's undying admiration. Accounts have moved from one agency to another with creative people who know how to sell. And that is the bottomline, the almighty dollar. The sooner you grasp this concept the less likely you are to be disappointed with the grease behind the glamour of advertising.

Another thing, because copywriting is a craft, the quality and style of the craftsmanship is bound to differ. Copywriters are like good carpenters who go to work turning out tables, but the size and shape and design of each table will be as various as the carpenters' expertise . . . even when they are all working to the same brief. There is also something to be said for the carpenter's calibre. Some are noted for their functional, hardworking tables. Others consistently produce beautifully wrought tables which are also as strong as steel. But whatever the design or form of the table, it must be a table at the very least, or the client may be justified in hiring another carpenter . . . uh, copywriter!

Only time will tell which sort of copywriter *you* are!

The Copywriter's Temperament

Like Christmas gifts, copywriters come in all shapes and sizes. They also come in all ages and from varied backgrounds. The less likely your background, the more likely you are to become a good copywriter. I have often wondered why this should be so and have concluded that successful copywriters are those who are exposed to life, who love people, who enjoy living, who will try anything (almost) once, who have enquiring minds, who empathise easily.

This is what makes agency life so exciting. You get to meet all sorts of interesting people—especially if you are young and unattached. Some love affairs lead to marriage—but agencies often insist on one spouse leaving the shop if this happens.

There is never a dull moment. Even the breaks between jobs are fun. One writer at HTA would play his flute while dreaming up a deathless headline. After that, the rest of us took up flute playing during office hours, much to the chagrin of the creative director! Creative people may slip out to have a coffee, or catch a matinee, or just walk the streets in order to recharge their grey cells. I personally think this is permissible as, on the whole, they are responsible people who meet deadlines and give of their professional best under all kinds of pressure.

As a copywriter you have to be a little of everything. Artist, writer, reader, manager, psychologist, salesman, diplomat, politician, entertainer, showman, mother figure, father figure, nurse, manipulator, linguist, acrobat, to name a few! That is why creative people stay interested in the profession longer than if they were slicing onions in a pickle factory. The pace of agency life demands that your mind jumps easily from one subject to another. In the process, you learn to computerise your brain and switch smoothly from one job to another. You learn to switch from C to A to B drive in less than a microsecond—and access information in milliseconds.

This does not mean that agencies abound in musical grasshoppers. Temperaments vary; there are writers with mercurial natures who work side by side with dour, taciturn types—and both kinds win awards for creativity in advertising.

Copywriter: Part of a Team

The copywriter's partners in crime are the visualisers and art directors. In most agencies, the art department is made up of men and women whose native language is not English. For obvious reasons, you the writer are expected to be fluent in English and hopefully have another language or two under your belt. (Solely Indian language copywriters also exist, and with the spread of advertising, are doubtless more numerous today than ever before.)

Since ad campaigns are the product of teamwork, language barriers must be sensitively broken down. Great ideas can spring from a visualiser or art director as much as from the copy side.

It might irritate you when art people just sit back and wait for you to think of the headlines for them to illustrate. Establish enough rapport with your art partner so you can come up with a headline that serves as a sign-off to a great visual idea—if that is what is needed. The main thing is to respect your partner and foster a good working relationship, recognising mutual strengths and weaknesses.

I do not know the current figures of how many copywriters, visualisers and art directors there are in India today. However, it can be safely said that these professionals are more recognised now than a few decades ago, when people thought a copywriter was some sort of typist. Advertising in this country has come into its own and there is no looking back.

John O'Toole (1981) in *The Trouble with Advertising* writes: Advertising people are . . .

> fascinated with human behaviour: what makes us tick, how we act and react in groups and in society. They have an unquenchable thirst to find out why people do what they do, to plumb the enigma of their infinite individuality and essential similarity, to get out and listen to them and understand them—even the ones very different from themselves. I've never known a successful advertising person who wasn't a closet social psychologist . . .
>
> Successful advertising people are also compulsive communicators. They've done a lot of writing simply because they had something that needed saying—or taken photographs or drawn drawings because there were images that had never been seen from quite that point of view before. Early on they knew they had to get their thoughts, feelings and ideas before others. Most, therefore, are quite verbal, though not always in terms of the spoken word. A number of fine advertising men I've known have had severe stuttering problems but superb writing skills. Some others, articulate and eloquent, couldn't write anything worth a damn. Those who aren't verbal are graphic communicators, and a few satisfy the compulsion through music . . . .
>
> This absorption in poetry, which continued over the years with an occasional appearance in obscure magazines, was immensely helpful in adapting to the disciplines of advertising writing. Synthesis of conception, economy of expression, the lyricism that contributes to memorability—these skills that are so essential to good advertising are the basic tools of the poet.

Should a Copywriter Read?

As a writer you must surely have a passion for reading. I have never met a writer who did not love words and the way they are put together, or not been interested in the meaning of words, the roots of words, the history of words. If you do not have a passion for the written word, you may become king in a mediocre agency, and you may even win a few awards, but you will never be really great. Not in my eyes anyway.

There seems to be a tendency in India today to minimise the knowledge of English and its spelling and grammar. You can never express your ideas in the best possible way unless you understand the nuances of a language. This means it is also a tremendous advantage to be bi-lingual and tri-lingual. More strength to you if you are master of more than one language. You will be able to empathise and communicate with varied consumers better. But whatever the language you speak, try and have as idiomatic a command over it as you possibly can. Recently, language mixing has become *au courant*, Hindi words being written in the Roman script. Some popular headlines of this nature:

- *Daag dhoondte reh jaoge* (Surf Ultra)
- *Isme kaddu zara nahin* (Volfarm ketchup)
- *Hamara Bajaj* (Bajaj scooter)
- *Zara chak ke dekho* (Monginis)
- *We are like this only* (V Channel)
- *Humko Binny's Mangta* (Binny potato chips)
- *Karta hai sabko mad* (Monginis slice cakes)
- *Yeh dil mange more* (Pepsi)
- *Palmolive da jawab nahin* (Palmolive shaving cream)
- *Young ho ya old, sab ki pasand Merrigold* (Merrigold margerine)
- *Thodi se pet pooja* (Perk chocolate)

Check Your Reading Habits

1. Are you a member of a library? Which one?
   The British Council • USIS • Circulating • Any other • College • Town Hall
2. How many books do you read in a month?
3. Which newspapers do you read?
4. Which English writers have you read?
   Tick from the following:
   William Shakespeare • Jane Austen • John Milton • Graham Greene • Anthony Trollope • George Elliot • Alfred Lord Tennyson

• William Makepeace Thackeray • Oliver Goldsmith • Charles Dickens • Jonathan Swift • Harold Pinter • Lytton Strachey • Tom Stoppard • E.M. Forster • Rudyard Kipling • D.H. Lawrence • James Joyce (Irish) • Daphne du Maurier • John Fowles • Charlotte and Emily Bronte • John Bunyan • Joseph Conrad • H.E. Bates • Lewis Carroll • G.K. Chesterton • H.G. Wells

5. Which of the following American writers have you read?
   Eudora Welty • Sinclair Lewis • J.D. Salinger • Scott Fitzgerald • John Cheever • Ernest Hemingway • Henry Miller • Harriet Beecher Stowe • Margaret Mitchell • Walt Whitman • Nathaniel Hawthorne • Ralph Waldo Emerson • Rex Stout • Dorothy Parker • Edgar Allen Poe • Ray Bradbury • Isaac Asimov • William Faulkner
6. Which of the following world-famous writers have you read?
   Doris Lessing • Gabriel Garcia Marques • Milan Kundera • Salman Rushdie • R.K. Narayan • Anita Desai • Satyajit Ray • Morris West • Mohandas Karamchand Gandhi • Edward Lear • Ogden Nash • Tennessee Williams • Arthur C. Clark • Premchand • V.S. Naipaul • Ved Mehta • Kamala Das • Nirad Chaudhari • Vikram Seth • Rabindranath Tagore
7. What non-fiction do you read?
8. Have you had anything published—in your school magazine? In your university journal? Anywhere else?
9. Do you like poetry?
10. Do you write poetry? Secretly? Published?
11. Who are your favourite authors/poets?
12. Which is the last book you read? When?
13. How much do you read of writers with an Indian background? Translations? Or in the regional language?

This is not a test. It is just a yardstick of the amount of reading the average copywriter ought to have done by age 25 or so. I suspect the bulk of a lifetime's reading for the sheer pleasure and excitement of discovery gets done by this age. After that, all or most reading falls into two categories—job-related or for relaxation.

Especially so when your job deals essentially with *words, words, words*. Like Eliza Doolittle you want to cry out, "I'm so sick of words!" In case you are on a book-hunt, you might chance upon these helpful titles . . . on the pavements of Mumbai's Flora Fountain!

Professional Books

Stephen Baker	*Systematic Approach to Advertising Creativity*
Rosser Reeves	*Reality in Advertising*
Aesop Glim	*How Advertising is Written and Why*
John Caples	*Tested Advertising Methods* (Prentice-Hall, 1975)
John Caples	*Making Ads Pay*
David Ogilvy	*Ogilvy on Advertising: Confessions of An Advertising Man*

Jerry della Femina	*Those Wonderful Folk Who Gave You Pearl Harbour*
Otto Klepner	*Advertising Procedure*
J. Nath	*Advertising Art and Production*
Alex Osborn	*Applied Imagination/Your Creative Power*
Philip Ward Burton	*Which Ad Pulled Best?*
	Advertising Copywriting

A few of these books may be out of print or considered old hat. But sometimes the Old Hats work the Hat Trick!

Magazines and Journals

Today there is so much more written about advertising and marketing than ever before. Every economic/financial newspaper carries some sort of supplement in which there could be a feature on advertising. The *Economic Times* has 'Brand Equity'; the *Financial Express* has 'Brandwagon'; the *Times of India* has 'Response'; the *Business Standard* has 'The Strategist'. Besides, business magazines have regular columns on marketing, advertising and media.

There also exist several new glossies on the subject.The widely read *A&M* magazine, priced at Rs 50, is brought out bi-monthly. Other advertising journals are *The Brief, Solus, Ad Review,* to name a few. It might be worthwhile to lay your hands on some foreign advertising magazines, such as America's *Advertising Age,* Australia's *b&t* and the UK's *Campaign.*

Advertising Courses

These are mushrooming all over the country. At the very least they give the student an overall picture of the industry and its varying disciplines. They generally offer diplomas or degree courses. Contact the 3As of I for details.

Television Programmes

Zee TV had a weekly programme called *The Dream Merchants,* which dealt with advertising and marketing. There may be similar programmes being aired currently. A great deal of coverage is also given these days in *India Business Report.* Check out your BBC and Star Plus weekly programmes.

International Show Reels

Most agencies with foreign affiliations have access to what is being done in offices outside India. There is generally an exchange of information available to writers and artists. Ask to see the video cassettes of the best TV commercials.

Also see the Cannes films, Clio award winners, shows by IAA, and BA's, Quarterly AdIndex.

A Copywriter's Luggage

The Dictionary

Because this book is about writing in English, arm yourself with dictionaries published by *Collins*, *Random House*, *Chambers*, *Oxford* or *Webster*. Correct spelling and grammar make all the difference between excellent and mediocre writers. When in doubt, open the word book.

But even if you are writing in Hindi, Marathi or French, the rules are the same. Master them, before you break them. I know that the trend today is to use a mixture of English and Hindi idiom, and that is fine because it shows that language is alive and well and kicking in India, but you still cannot get away from plain old Queen's English. I have still to see a press release or an instruction manual written in 'Hinglish'.

The Thesaurus

I use the reliable Roget's. There are others just as good. Make the thesaurus your working Bible. It is indispensable when it comes to searching for a useful phrase or alternative word, a great aid in writing good body copy.

The Proof Reader's Guide

This humble sheet of paper is probably the most valuable tool in your day-to-day working kit. Master the signs and symbols and you will be your printer's friend for life.

How to Mark Your Proof Corrections

Cancellation

Delete, or take out, character or ~~the~~ word marked.

Insertion

the / Insert word, letter, or punctuation mark written in the margin.

Spacing

Insert space between words, letters, or lines

Close u p, or take out the space.

Close up, but leave some space.

Position

Turn a reversed letter.

Carry further to the left.

Carry further to the right.

Move down a letter, character, or word.

Move up a letter, character, or word.

Indent one em.

Straighten a crooked line.

Straighten lateral margin of printing.

tr Transpose of order words or letters.

Correct uneven spacing.

Paragraphing

¶ Make a new paragraph.

no ¶ No paragraph.

Miscellaneous

Push down a space or quadrat that prints.

(?) Question to author. Is this right?

stet Allow to stand as it is.

first/ This is the ~~foremost~~ example in this table.

e/ The press proofs of these documents have bean received and corrected.

new/ This is an example for insertion of matter.

Figures and abbreviations, such as (100) and (Oct.) which require to be spelt out in full are encircled.

under letters or words to be altered.

under letters or words to be altered.

Kinds of type

l.c. PuT in lower case.

caps Put in ~~capitals.~~

u use a capital.

s.c. ~~Put~~ in small capitals.

ut ~~Put~~ in small capitals.

rom. Put in *Roman*.

ital Put in ~~italic~~.

b.f. Put in ~~bold face~~.

e put in **bold face**.

w.f. Wrong font (wrong size or style).

a/ Superscript a.

1/ Superscript 1.

2 Subscript 2.

× Type is broken or imperfect.

Punctuation

Period.

, Comma.

; Semicolon.

: Colon.

' Apostrophe.

" " Quotation marks.

=/ Hyphen (-)

en One-en dash (–).

1/m One-em dash (—).

2/m Two-em dash (——).

(/) Parentheses.

[/] Brackets.

A Professional Library

If you cannot as yet afford to build up your own stock of professional books, make sure you have access to them. Most good agencies have a library where you can refer to graphics and art books, international and award-winning ads, books on art direction, copywriting, research, marketing and sales techniques.

Read up as much as you can about the work you love to do, and you will create work that your clients will love.

Something to Write On

This could be an old-fashioned portable typewriter (yes, these are still around!) or a computer, or just plain paper and pencil. Choose the weapon that gets those little grey cells whirring. I like my trainees to hand in typed assignments; they are neater, speedier and more professional. However, thumbnail sketches and roughs are all part of the day-to-day work. Learn the rules before you break them.

A Grammar Book

My publisher considers *Wren & Martin* out-dated; so find a more current grammar book, if you can.

Encyclopaedias

Make certain your agency library contains at least one good encyclopaedia, the *Britannica* or the *Columbus*, or at least a good book of facts (Isaac Asimov has compiled two fairly decent-sized volumes).

Quotation Books

We learn a great deal from reading the thoughts of wiser minds than ours. So keep browsing through quotations by experts in every field of human endeavour. They come in handy when you are stuck for an idea.

The Internet

More and more agencies are providing their people with computers—and hooking up to the Internet. This is the age of the information blitz. Go for it, baby!

Fowler's Book of Modern English Usage

An absolute must—and you might also like to see Hobson Jobson's dictionary of Anglo-Indian words. And Eric Partridge's *English: Usage and Abusage.* The list is endless.

Here is proof. Ivan Arthur, head *honcho* (creative) of Hindustan Thompson Associates (HTA) shares his thoughts on . . .

The Ultimate Advertising Bibliography

by Ivan Arthur

John Caples, Rosser Reeves, James Webb-Young, David Ogilvy, Leo Burnett, Jack Trout, Al Ries, Stephen King. These and other big names proudly walk through the corridors of your advertising library. You go to them with reverence and intellectual gluttony and you are not disappointed. You find them professionally sustaining and useful, handing you excellent ready-to-use packets of insight from the homely art of copywriting to the more impressive science of brand building and agency management. You use these 'packets' on the job, as guides to producing advertising; for presentations, to impress clients and sell campaigns, or as training course material.

My bibliography is a little different, however. You will not find the books I am talking about under 'Marketing' or 'Advertising', nor will they provide you with those ready-to-use packets of insight on advertising. These are the books that enlightened me about creativity and advertising beyond the staple wisdom of the classics on the subject.

Two books helped me during my first years as a copywriter. One was an old, anonymous little masterpiece called *The Cloud of Unknowing*, and the other was *The Collected Works of St. John of the Cross* (1979), a 16th century Spanish poet and Christian mystic. Both these books trace the journey of the soul towards God and they express the longing to be one with Him. In one of John of the Cross' poems, *The Dark Night*, he describes, what to me seems like the creative process of a copywriter.

One dark night
Fired with love's urgent longings
—Ah, the sheer grace!
I went out unseen,
My house being now all stilled.

The last line, which in the original Spanish reads, *estando ya mi casa sosegada*, became for me a mantra and a working formula whenever I was stuck for an idea. It is not easy, especially after a confusing brief, to transform the crowded, messy rooms of one's mind into a *casa sosegada*; and then to walk out into that *noche oscura*, the dark night, and discover the object of the brief's 'urgent longings'. But when one did—ah, the sheer grace!—things happened!

Another great textbook of advertising for me has been Leonard Bernstein's *The Joy of Music*, a collection of essays and exciting analyses of well-known classical pieces. The book includes an engaging critical appreciation of Bach's *St Matthew Passion*, some rare and surprising insights into Beethoven's *Eroica* and *The Fifth Symphony,* and a delightful journey through the innards of jazz. This last essay, which brings alive the concepts of syncopation, the blue note, improvisation and the jam session has been for me a perennial source of inspiration, and I have borrowed extensively from it for presentations on advertising creativity.

I enjoyed reading Salman Rushdie's *Midnight's Children*, first, of course, as a novel, and later as a lesson in industrial advertising. Remember the first chapter of the book—the part where the protagonist-doctor has to examine the young lady through the nine-inch hole in a white sheet? Part by throbbing part, the doctor was able to see and touch every inch of shimmering skin on that female anatomy, but he was not able to see the face of his patient. So, though he had seen almost all of her, he did not really know her! I thought that was a wonderful metaphor for industrial advertising in India, and we used that punctured veil as a model to plan and present a breakthrough industrial campaign for one of our clients. Later we borrowed the 'punctured veil' model for a textile advertising campaign which went on to win advertising awards and sell kilometres of printed fabrics.

The books of Mrs Henry Wood, Barbara Cartland, Masters and Johnson, Havelock Ellis and the *Kama Sutra* are founts of knowledge on how advertising works. The roles for advertising, the spectrum of consumer responses, the management of brand-consumer relationships and the variety of advertising stimuli—all these you will find in the red-hot pages of romance and sex. The dynamics of courtship, love-making and marriage; the mental, emotional and physiological stages in the fine art of seduction and wedlock are amazingly good teachers of marketing and advertising. They not only bring the subject of advertising alive, they help the student see vividly the more complex concepts of commercial persuasion and brand building.

Wild life, mythology, fairy tales, physics, mysticism—these are the books I go to for my lessons on advertising.

My most actively used 'book', however, has been the city of Mumbai itself and its fabulous circulatory system—the suburban train service. As I walk through the city's streets, I visualise my feet shuffling through the pages of a continuously updated textbook on advertising. The sales strategies and patter of the roadside salesman are probably the best course in copywriting available anywhere. Long have I stood at street corners and on pavements listening with rapt attention to the compelling eloquence of the pavement magician, the tight-rope walker and juggler, and the aphrodisiac vendor. They have provided me with examples of the most vivid demonstrations and metaphors, of the most imaginative use of USP, AIDA, positioning, preemption and all the other learned concepts of commercial communication—far greater than any training course or international seminar on advertising could give me.

The master communicators of the road are, to my mind, the beggars of Mumbai, and I have marvelled at their instinctive feel for consumer behaviour; their clever and imaginative designing of stimuli and the finesse of their executions. There is no doubt that what we are witnessing in Mumbai is designer beggary, an industry worth millions of rupees every day, masterminded by some brilliant marketing minds and highly creative art directors and copywriters. Their storylines have been scripted with flair. Their jingles are artfully stolen compositions expertly delivered. The casting, costuming and art direction are perfect and the individual performances brilliant.

Very often I am tempted to think that our trends in marketing and advertising are anticipated on the streets by the pavement salesmen and beggary industry. Study what is happening on the streets today and you will know what will happen in the market tomorrow. My recommendation to you is to read this book carefully. When stuck, take a walk down the road or buy yourself a second class return ticket from Churchgate to Virar. By the time you return to your table in your office, you will have got your idea.

And what about the other books I have mentioned? Do I recommend you buy and read them all? Not really. Those just happened to be the books that found connections in my personal unconscious, which in turn was able to process those connections into advertising insights. There may be other books that may do the same for you, depending on your sphere of interest. While the classical texts on advertising have their utility, the most rewarding insights are those you manufacture on your own by making connections. I believe that everything is a metaphor for everything else. Everything is a teacher of everything else. The more interests and experiences you have outside advertising, the larger will be your library of advertising inspiration.

Read Caples and company. They are good.The ultimate bibliography, however, is one generated by what moves you personally.

Take yourself seriously when it comes to learning your craft and practising it faithfully; but do not take yourself too seriously when you come up against criticism.

Workout

Choose an ordinary item, like a clothes hanger, or hairbrush, or shoehorn—an everyday object. Hold it in your hands for a while, and examine it minutely. Take note of its shape, size, the material it is made of, its colour and texture. Then, spend a few minutes imagining what life would be like without this item. Write down what you would have to do in order to get the same results (i.e., clothes being hung, hair getting brushed, etc.) using alternative means.

As a corollary: when you have finished this part of the exercise, do the following using the same items. Close your eyes and start feeling the clothes brush/hanger/shoehorn/whatever. Take special notice of its feel, smell, shape and contours. Take your time feeling each object. Then open your eyes, and get out a sheet of paper. Write down whatever thoughts come to mind about the object you have just handled.

3

The Principle of Show, Don't Tell

Advertising is all about persuading people. It needs the skills of selling to be translated to the right medium, whether paper or celluloid. People tend to believe what they can *see*. The trick is to write the type of copy which brings your client's product to life before your customers' eyes, even if they are sitting in their own homes. In a shop, customers get a chance to *see* what they are buying. Notice how people behave in the supermarket or the bazaar. If the product is not packaged, they tend to handle the tomatoes, squeeze the fruit to judge freshness and firmness; they *smell* the mangoes or papayas, they *look* and *look* and *look* and *ask* and *feel* before they decide to buy! This sort of behaviour annoys the shopkeeper, but customers are not daunted.

On my first visit to a supermarket in London, I was roundly told off by the floor manager for poking at some tomatoes. ("Don't squeeze me until I'm yours!"). Never before had this country bumpkin seen fruit and vegetables all nicely sorted and graded and pre-packed in cellophane cartons. You can see but cannot touch. However, you are fairly well assured that the stuff is fresh and of good quality.

But to get back to the point: people want to see/touch/smell/taste the products they are buying. It is the copywriter's task to make them believe they are doing so—by reading your press ad, viewing your film or television commercial or hearing your radio spot.

You may ask, what is so difficult? I will just tell my prospective customers all about my client's product and that should be enough. If that were so, you would not be reading a book on copywriting!

You have to trust the person you are learning from. Sometimes you are asked to do an assignment which you think you are unprepared for. It is like a non-swimmer being asked to jump into the deep end of a swimming pool. No matter how nervous you feel, go ahead and jump. Remember your swimming coach is there to dive in and save you. At least while doing the copy assignments, you will not get wet!

Read the story that follows, then attempt the assignment that follows.

THREE MARRIED COUPLES were neighbours and good friends. Sunita was married to Gerry, Anne to Bob, and Seema to Arindam. These six and their kids did everything together when they were not actually working. Bridge, golf, PTA meetings, picnics, like any ordinary suburban couple living in a large metropolis.

Sunita was an expert at baking cakes and biscuits of all kinds—but her oatmeal cookies were especially delicious. "As good as Sunita's cookies" had become the byword for excellence in the area where they lived.

One day a neighbour asked Sunita to make her three dozen cookies—and she would pay for them. "It's to be a very special gift for my parents on their wedding anniversary—please oblige me, Sunita!" So Sunita agreed to make the cookies if the lady supplied the materials. She joked, "I can't take money from you—I'm not in the biscuit business, you know!"

That afternoon, when Anne and Bob came over to play bridge, Sunita mentioned the episode. Bob said, "But shouldn't we make money on this? Let's all go into the biscuit business!" So it was agreed that Bob (who was a good cook himself) would help Sunita make cookies at night and on weekends. Seema and Anne would be the packaging department. Gerry would be the business manager and purchasing agent (for instance, buying the sugar, butter and oatmeal at wholesale rates), and Arindam would be the sales manager. He had the gift of the gab.

THREE MONTHS LATER they were fully in business. Sunita and Bob were making cookies in great batches. Seema and Anne had worked up attractive cellophane-wrapped cartons. Gerry had found out the most economical places to buy sugar in large quantities. And Arindam had hired some university students to work as his sales staff!

And here is how they did their selling. After lecture hours, a young student would ring a doorbell and present a sample of Sunita's Cookies to the housewife. The sample consisted of two cookies wrapped in a see-through envelope. "We're not asking you to buy, just to TRY our cookies. WE think they're good. If you like our cookies, you can buy them at Asifali's department store on Main Street."

Meanwhile, Arindam had been to Asifali's department store and spoken to the manager about Sunita's Cookies. "Will you keep a dozen cartons of our cookies on your counter? You don't have to pay for them unless you sell them. But we know it's good stuff and we'll try and get customers to buy from you."

SIX MONTHS LATER Gerry, Bob and Arindam had quit their former jobs and were working full time on Sunita's Cookies. Arindam was travelling all over the state, organising his teams of student-salesmen. He no longer told storekeepers they could pay when they sold the cookies. Department store owners had heard of the quick popularity of Sunita's Cookies—spreading from town to town like a bush fire. They were only too happy to get the cookies and pay for them on normal terms.

And then what? One night the six business partners were playing bridge. It was hard not to talk shop when they met. Arindam said, "I wish we could find a less expensive way to do the sampling. College students can't spare all day doing this—they have to study. And I feel I'm spending too much time and money trying to locate and train new students. Is there a cheaper way to get people to try our cookies?"

Bob said, "Let's try advertising. Let's start with our town, and if it works, we'll try another town."

Gerry had another idea. "Take one town where we now have sampling, stop the sampling, and run some ads. But let's also run the same ads in a town where we have not had any sampling before and compare the results."

The story of Sunita's Cookies is based on an example given by Aesop Glim, about whom you will be hearing more.

So we come to the question—*What is advertising?*

If you can write the right copy for Sunita's Cookies, you know the answer.

We will assume that the college student method of door-to-door sampling produced a new customer for Sunita's Cookies at a total sales cost of Rs 1. Profits usually come from repeat sales, rarely from the first sales, in the case of most low-priced or medium-priced products.

Advertising produces the first sale—the quality of the product produces the repeat sales.

If the product is not good enough or worth the money—no repeat sales. (The consumer is not a moron.) No repeat sales—no more advertising, no reason to advertise in the first place. For high-priced goods (consumer durables like fridges, washing machines and television sets) the repeat sale is frequently through a recommendation to a friend by a satisfied customer.

On all products you must have satisfied customers or you are out of business. Remember, advertising alone cannot sell poor products at a profit to the advertiser. If door-to-door selling produced new cookie customers at Rs 1, will your advertising copy produce new customers at 50 paise a piece? Obviously, Sunita and Company would be very happy if it did.

Workout

Try your hand at writing a headline and a piece of copy to sell Sunita's Cookies. Your copy should be 100-150 words in length.

Take your time. Imagine in fullest detail, the college student—a pleasant, cheerful young man or woman. Picture the housewife coming to the door . . . the offer of a free taste of delicious cookie . . . the taste of the cookie itself.

Now write the message that will make people go to Asifali's store and pay real money for a full box of Sunita's Cookies—without any sampling. Remember, your total equipment consists of a pencil and paper, the facts about the product, and your imagination. Your advertising message must create new customers at a lower cost than real-life representation and sampling.

This is the moment when you will realise that advertising is a substitute for sampling. It is your job as the copywriter to give the reader— with the aid of words alone—all the thoughts, sensations and desires formerly aroused by the pleasant, cheerful college student and the generous sample of truly delicious cookies! Your written message is a substitute for all this.

To Check Your Progress

When you have completed this assignment, file it away for future reference. As you add to your file, you will be able to see how far you have come from the writing of this first ad, without any real experience, to the kind of writing you will be doing when you are through with this book (if you care to do the assignments which accompany most chapters).

4

Sell the Sizzle, Not the Steak

Sell the sizzle, not the steak is another way of saying, "Show, don't tell." People are always more mesmerised by sleight of hand than a documentary. It is human nature to want to escape from the humdrum into fantasyland. Advertising offers people a reason to be so seduced. Sell them an idea, draw them a picture, invite them into Paradise, even for a moment. They will come down to earth again when they actually use the product!

Consumers subconsciously expect this to happen. Advertisers today have to try harder than ever to get into the consumer's mind. There are so many products clamouring for attention. The consumer's memory span may be very brief. So the advertiser tends to shout his wares loudly and dramatically in a bid to make immediate sales over a short period. He cannot depend on the consumer remembering him for too long.

The wiser advertiser goes slowly and steadily, calling the process *Brand Building*. He spends his money over the years and in carefully budgeted amounts. But every message he sends out ties in with the overall impression he wants to create for his product in the minds of his consumer. This way takes patience, money and good strategic thinking—and bears fruit in the long run. But how many advertisers can afford this approach?

Ever Eaten a Branded Egg?

You have probably not eaten a branded egg. Here is why.

Many years ago the farmers of Maharashtra approached a well-known agency to do some advertising for their eggs. They were to be helped in their efforts by a leading marketing company which was one of the agency's clients. Now, egg marketing in the state is a very delicate operation, the prices of eggs fluctuating wildly—from high in summer, to low in the monsoon, and lowest in the cool months. Check this out! To make things more complex, there are English eggs and *desi* or country eggs; vegetarian and non-vegetarian eggs; and fertilised and unfertilised eggs.

The agency was asked to unscramble these eggs and come up with an advertising campaign in sync with the proposed marketing goals: to stabilise the price of eggs, give them a branded identity, and back them up with the trademark of a Co-operative Farmers' Association. Till then, Bombay (or Mumbai as it is now called) had just one branded egg, Crown Eggs (unfertilised), which was sold at a few outlets in the upper crust areas. No one in the agency had heard of Crown Eggs, much less eaten one.

The client, who had an interest in animal feedstuffs, worked out a marketing strategy and directed the agency to think of an umbrella name for the eggs of Maharashtra, and how to sell them.

The audio-visual medium seemed the best way to present the creative ideas to the farmers who had had no previous advertising agency exposure. The agency was sure that a slide-n-sound show would zap the hay out of the farmers' ears.

The account supervisor on the job was a tall, burly Sikh whose hair and beard had been effectively erased by an American college education. His only concession to Sikhism was the thick *kadha* he sported on his massive wrist. He was bald, wore gold-rimmed pebble glasses, smoked pot, and was totally convinced that he was primarily a poet and a painter, and only accidentally an ad man. He approached the marketing of eggs with the same nonchalance with which he tossed off a page of poetry.

"January, February, May, *June*," he thundered from across the creative department to the juniormost copy trainee, "the Egg Show is on the 16th. Just get the stuff together, will you? I'll meet you in the auditorium at 6 o' clock. Pramod will organise the projector and I've arranged for a car to pick you up at 5 p.m." And he sauntered out of the agency, perhaps to paint a picture.

Thanks to the well-oiled machinery of a large agency, work on the Egg Show went on. The agency came up with a variety of suggestions, from car stickers to mobiles to leaflets. Our poet's brainwave was to distribute the leaflets to consumers via the medium of Bombay's *dabbawalas*, an ingenious idea which I have not seen used as yet.

The big day arrived. The agency presentation began with a five-minute audio-visual on the versatility of the egg, drawing on history (the first fried egg was laid by an Egyptian hen on a burning Sahara rock), literature (Omelet or the Prince of Denmark), and medicine (an egg a day keeps the doctor away), to drive home the salient points. The farmers sat stolidly through the show, but it did raise smiles among the client team.

Then the agency launched into the main story—showing the agriculturalists how to put all their eggs into one basket, brand them as Royal Eggs, and splash the new brand all over the major cities and towns of Maharashtra. This would certainly, the farmers were assured, inculcate the egg-eating habit even among the lower middle classes (who could resist a name like Royal?) and increase their per capita consumption. *Voila*, the more eggs eaten, the more the profits for them. The agency sat down smugly, and waited for the applause.

Furore among the farmers.

They were calculating at the top of their voices how many *paise* they would make per egg, after deducting the advertising costs, which they would have to bear. Each one came up with a different figure. The client tried to outshout the farmers while assuring them of surefire marketing and distribution strengths. *Royal Eggs* would reach even currently non-egg-eating families, and extra sales would more than offset the farmers' expenses. Sceptical arm-waving and more shouting greeted this view. The agency sat silently and watched its brilliant creative efforts crack up.

After an hour or more of heated debate the farmers left, never to be seen again. The client paid for the cost of the presentation and is now using it as educational fodder for management trainees. For my role in the affair, I was given a marble egg-shaped paperweight by the films chief Mubi Ismail—for being a good egg—which still sits on my desk. And eggs in Maharashtra still sell at different prices in different seasons. (*This is a true story.*)

Market research can establish beyond the shadow of a doubt that the egg is a sad and sorry product and that it obviously will not continue to sell. Because after all, eggs won't stand up by themselves, they roll too easily, are too easily broken, require special packaging, look alike, are difficult to open, won't stack on the shelf.

—Robert Pliskin (1963)

Test Your Brand Awareness

Can you think of some successful advertisers who have built strong brands in the following product categories?

Category	Brand Name	Advertiser
Toilet soaps		
Detergents		
Cigarettes		
Textiles		
Men's suiting		
Home appliances		

Category	Brand Name	Advertiser
Television sets		
Refrigerators		
Edible oils		
Cosmetics		
Shoes		
Lighting		
Earth-moving equipment		
Electronics		
Steel		
Automobiles		
Airlines		
Travel agents		
Hotels		
Tourist agents		
Banks		
Telecommunications		
Courier services		
Advertising agencies		

Why do you find these brands memorable?
Which campaigns do you remember?
Do you recall the visual? Or the slogan?
How long do you think these brands have been around?
Would your mother agree with your list?
How about your grandfather?

Looking for an Agency to Join?

Let us see how the principle of *Show, don't tell* works when you decide that copywriting is what you want to do with your life and you have to choose where to work. You look around the marketplace and make a list of the local ad agencies. Perhaps you list them by size. No agency is *telling* anything about itself, but they *show* you something by their ads, and by the type of people they hire. (You can tell a good company by the people it keeps!) Perhaps you know some friends who work in advertising.

What does your list tell you apart from the size?
Agency A produces highly visible and even shocking advertising.
Agency B builds brands in a workmanlike manner.

Agency C does mainly public service campaigns.

You poke around some more and talk to a few more people (handling the tomatoes). Perhaps you start looking out for recent campaigns produced by these agencies by studying the key numbers at the bottom of ads that strike you between the eyes.

Sooner or later you get the *feel* of an agency, though you might not have stepped inside it. You get to know it by its client profile, by reading about its performance in the trade journals, by talking to advertising people and adding to your store of information. You have not *tasted* the steak yet, but you can *smell* and *hear* its sizzle. And if you are hungry enough, you will follow your nose.

This is what happens to people who are exposed to the advertising of a product or service over a period. It is the sizzle that attracts and eventually impels them to buy the product or service (the steak).

Selling the sizzle is what advertising creativity is all about.

In the accompanying piece, Gerson da Cunha, former general manager of Lintas and prominent media and theatre person, shares his views on what creativity means to him.

Selling Spring

by Gerson da Cunha

'Creative' is a word much bandied about. But all too rarely does it go with a useful understanding of it. It is often used to describe a gimmick, difference for difference' sake, or statements so personalised, they are virtually doodles, or expressions that are basely exploitative in their effort to seize attention and interest. Innovation must make sense. Creativity must be relevant. (We speak here of the harnessed arts, not the explosive departures from convention and orthodoxy common in the so called 'fine' arts.)

A well-worn anecdote has helped me gain a better grasp of what creativity may be about. Two blind beggars, we are told, were seated on different park benches. Each had an upturned hat beside him soliciting charity. One beggar had a placard on his breast reading, "I am blind." The other man's placard said, "It is spring, and I am blind." The latter's hat overflowed with money. History is silent about the other hat.

The better salesman has defined creativity for me; it is the connection of two elements previously unrelated, creating something new, with meaning and purpose. Spring linked to blindness yields a new statement of great pathos and strength, all of it with a very clear objective, of course. On a different level, it's what poetry does, the surprise and stimulus of good poetry.

Now, this definition, or at least explanation, of the creative process suits a variety of uses. How to design a good piece of rhetoric, or an effective advertisement, how to find a solution to a resistant problem, even how to make certain life choices. Find the relevant as yet un-associated feature in the problem-solution.

I have often been baffled at the whimsical, sometimes mystic approach to creativity: the need for velvet-curtained dimness, communion with nature, the obligatory arrival of 'mood'. Much more important than any of this would be a few bouts of really intensive preparatory study or experience. I have found that immersion in the factually relevant often produces wonderful ideas. I am put in mind of an advertising campaign we once tackled in Lintas to promote the importance of protein in the Indian diet, especially for pregnant and lactating mothers. The scientist taking us through the technical background of the subject came up with the thought that eventually created a winning ad. An illustration of a pregnant young woman in profile went with a headline that read: *By the time your baby is born, he'll be nine months old already.* The ad went on to speak of the importance (for baby) of protein in Mummy's diet.

Another lesson this teaches is that, in writing, the content of what you say must be as creative as how you express it. We tend to forget baby's prenatal phase. In the ad, it was important to draw attention to it, creatively.

At the same time, *how* you put across a thought may be the golden content of it. A memory from trainee days in copywriting will serve to make the point. A creative director in a leading advertising agency was telling us that, in some ways, copywriters must aspire to write like poets. "For instance," he said, "I could say something like this, couldn't I, 'Beautiful women should produce many daughters, so that we may always be surrounded by beautiful women.'" It was a trite thought. Ah, but it's a different story, said our instructor, if you put it as Shakespeare does in the first couplet of his First Sonnet: *"From fairest creatures we desire increase that thereby Beauty's rose might never die."* Same thought, now made unforgettable.

Warm-up

It is important to get a tangible sense of your product. Use the following exercise as a springboard for your creative thinking. As you will see, facts are relevant.

Find an ordinary BRICK and study it carefully.

Then write down as many uses of the brick as you can think of.

You may add to the list below, then go on to do a similar exercise with other items of your choice.

Ordinary usage	*Extraordinary usage*
construction	sculpture/sculpting
weights	for etching
struts	as coloured powder
stepping stones	
goal posts	

Now think of five more items. For instance, a knife, a flower pot, a hammer, a pen. Do the above exercise for each of them.

When you are done, make a list of 55 more items.

See how hard it is even to think of them?

You have started to become a copywriter.

Cogito Ergo Copywriter

The more you think, the stronger and more flexible your brain cells stay. Copywriting is fun!

Workout

The *Deep Seeing* exercise which follows should be done after completing the assignment above. You will benefit most by doing the assignments in the order in which they appear. The exercises are like building blocks which aim to train while they entertain—so relax and imagine you are in copywriter Montessori class!

Deep Seeing

There are several important spin-offs to this interesting exercise. It sharpens your ability to focus, teaches the importance of perspective, teaches how to *show*, not just *tell*. I insist that my trainees do at least 15 Deep Seeing exercises ... which is probably why I have so few trainees!

What to Do Choose a picture that attracts you from a magazine/newspaper/book. *It must not be an advertisement.*

It should not be a Salvador Dali type painting. In other words, choose something real, something lively, something gripping and not stylised.

Study the picture intently for a while. Then write a description of the picture in under 500 words, reading as much as you can into the scene. When you are through, put the picture into an envelope and seal it.

Ask someone who has *not* seen the picture to read your piece. Then open the envelope and ask your friend if the mental image he/she has formed tallies with the picture revealed. The answer might surprise you!

Here is an example of a Deep Seeing exercise. The picture described is reproduced on p. 54. No peeking—till you have read the piece.

Step silently into a world where the present finds itself inextricably bound to the future. It's a small, dark world, illuminated only by a golden glow that reflects off the heads and torsos of two women, sole participants in an ancient ritual.

There at the little linen-covered table sits the woman who makes it all happen. In front of her rests the instrument of her profession—a crystal ball planted on a little gold base. Notice how she studies the palm of her client seated opposite her. She's no ordinary fortune-teller intent on making a fast buck. No, her bearing suggests majesty and the multi-layered pearl necklace around her indicates that she is a lady of some substance. She definitely looks it, large-made but graceful. No wrinkles crease the brow below which dark make-up heightens the intensity of her eyes. A golden turban decorates her head, while a black tunic covers her shoulders.

What about her following? She's not the type who accepts just anyone. Take the client seated across from her. There's an air of sophistication that graces her being too. She's clad in a rich black dress that reveals a triangle of bare back below her neck.

Her hair, soot black, is elegantly tied back. Definitely not the sort who has given up on life. She's barely thirty and her figure is trim and well-cared for. What fate has brought them together?

What does the future hold in store?

—by Benjamin Borges

(*Now see the photograph below.*)

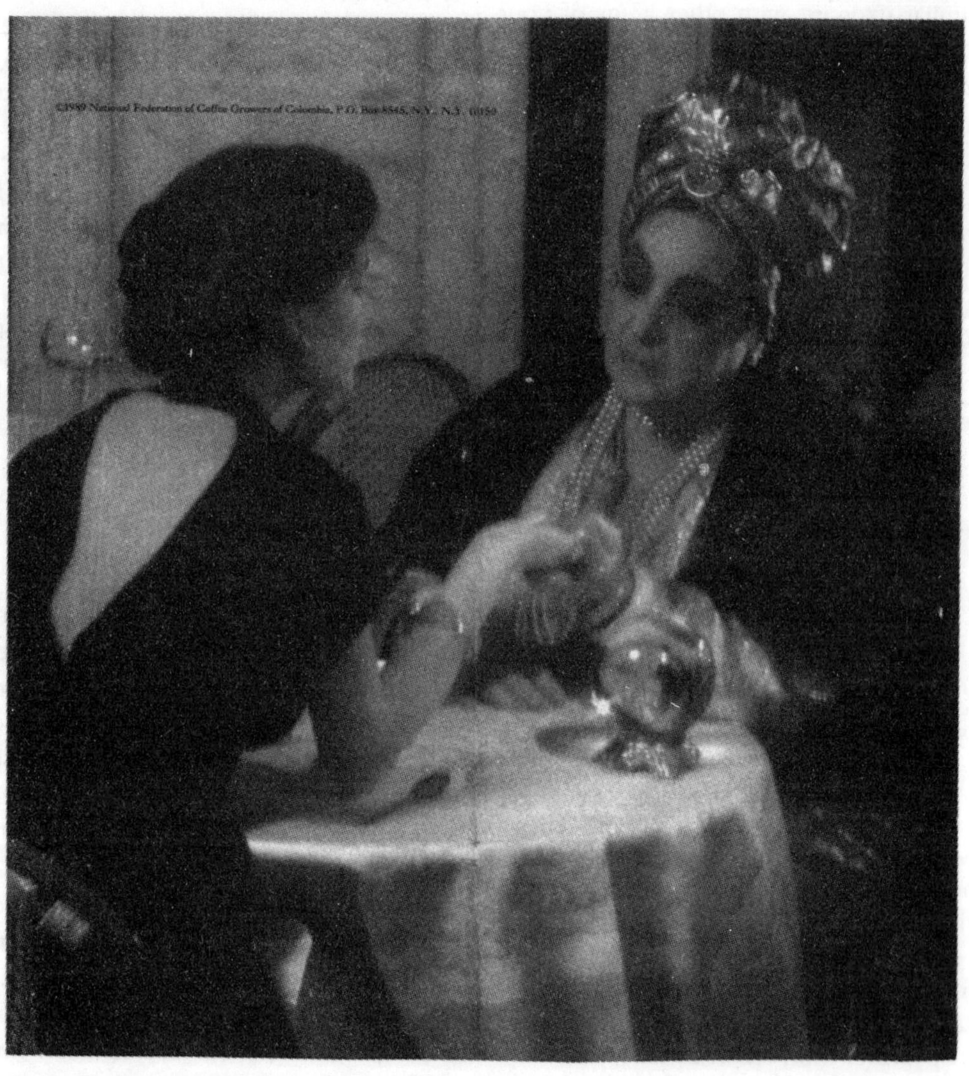

Do you think the Deep Seeing piece gave an accurate mental image of the photograph?

In what way do you think it has fallen short of being an accurate representation?

Does the writer penetrate deeply enough into the characters of the two women shown?

Attempt a Deep Seeing exercise on this same piece and show the result to a friend who has not seen the photograph.

Do a Deep Seeing Exercise as often as you can.

Each time, try out the result on someone and ask them to rate your efforts on a scale of 10. If you hit 9 on 10, you have begun to get the drift of 'Show, don't tell'.

5

The Anatomy of a Press Ad

A strong-minded head of an agency, who is also its creative director, once said to me in connection with training his writers, "I don't want them to write like me; get them to write like *The One Show!*" (Collection of award-winning ads.)

Although I was taken aback at the time, I decided to approach the creation of an advertisement through the study of these award-winning ads. It was a challenge to my own creativity . . . it meant, in a sense, working backwards. One had to dismantle the ad, as it were, and learn how to rebuild it.

Perhaps there is something to be learnt from this. But I still prefer the method of mastering the fundamentals of copywriting first, laying the foundation, and then building the structure. Since you have picked up this book, we will press on, regardless. One day you may be featured in *The One Show*, or even in the *Hall of Fame!*

I have learned that it is far easier to write a speech about good advertising than it is to write a good ad.

—Leo Burnett

Most people imagine they are experts on advertising. Ask your hairdresser what he thinks about a particular ad campaign and he will oblige whether he knows anything about advertising or not. And he is right to feel this way. Because ads are addressed first of all to the reader who just might be your hairdresser. We the practitioners and creators assault consumers from every newspaper, hoarding, cinema hall and even on TV in the privacy of their homes. So why should they not tell us what they think of our performance?

Even the man in the street will recognise an advertisement when he sees one. Very simply, a *Press Ad* can be divided as follows:

A. The headline
B. The visual
C. The text/body copy
D. The logo
E. The baseline
(See the Parker Pen ad on the next page.)

Marshall McLuhan (quoted in Fitzhenry (1993, p. 19)) called ads "the cave art of the twentieth century". Press ads can be in black and white, or in colour. They appear in different sizes, shapes, in magazines and newspapers. They may be purely typographical, or come with a drawing, illustration, photograph . . . with banners or without, with borders or without (bleed), but in whatever shape or size they come, they are immediately recognisable to the reader. People can also identify the logo or company symbol that signs off their advertising message.

CHOOSE
YOUR PARKER
LIKE YOUR WORDS.
CAREFULLY. **A**

The Ambre Laque is hand brushed with gold dust, giving each pen its own unique pattern

The silver Ciselé has its origins in a seventeenth century European snuff box design

B

The Firedance is a genuine Chinese Laque, with an 18k gold nib

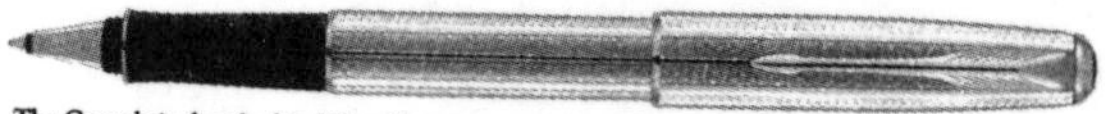

The Cascade is sheathed in 23k gold plating and aptly named for its fluid, rippling geometric design

PARKER SONNET IS NOW IN INDIA. Choosing one, however, is going to be difficult. Nevertheless, this very pleasant task can be accomplished at an outlet near you. There you can linger over the range. And when you finally choose your PARKER, remember, that its lifetime guarantee will ensure that it lives with you for ever. **C**

PARKER®
SONNET **D**

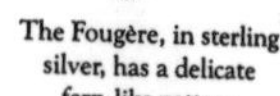

The Fougère, in sterling silver, has a delicate fern-like pattern

Your words are worth it. **E**

PARKER and SONNET are trademarks of PARKER Pen Products, U.K.

For trade enquiries contact : Delhi : 7514885, 7525156, 3554950, 3554746 • Mumbai : 8740129 • Calcutta : 250407 • Chennai : 4913823 • Bangalore : 2211646.

CITIBANK

COMPUSERVE

A Word About Logos

'Logo' comes from the Greek—meaning 'word'—and, truly, the logo says a great deal about a company in a *word.* If a picture speaks a thousand words, the logo or symbol stands for the entire spirit, culture and purpose of a company or institution. Who can fail to recognise these famous logos?

Press Ads

Have you ever thought about the number of press ads that readers are exposed to? It could be useful to try and categorise them. In an ad agency you will hear press ads and campaigns being referred to by type/category—as listed below. Most of these categories, you will see, are self-explanatory and easily recognised and understood. Some examples of press ads have been given as well. Study them carefully, paying special heed to placement of the headline, visual, baseline and logo in each case.

Type/Category of Ad

Industrial

Advertising for engineering and other industries, for OEMs (original equipment manfacturers).

Born and bred in India, he takes on the world.

He's your favourite Tyreman. And that's why you cheer him on.

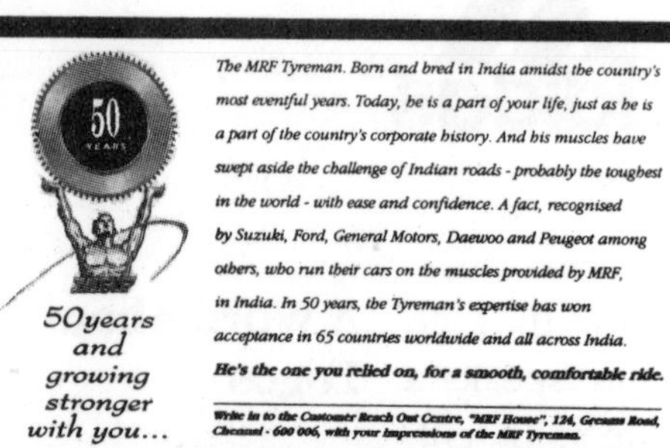

50 YEARS
50 years and growing stronger with you...
The MRF Tyreman. Born and bred in India amidst the country's most eventful years. Today, he is a part of your life, just as he is a part of the country's corporate history. And his muscles have swept aside the challenge of Indian roads - probably the toughest in the world - with ease and confidence. A fact, recognised by Suzuki, Ford, General Motors, Daewoo and Peugeot among others, who run their cars on the muscles provided by MRF, in India. In 50 years, the Tyreman's expertise has won acceptance in 65 countries worldwide and all across India.
He's the one you relied on, for a smooth, comfortable ride.
Write in to the Customer Reach Out Centre, "MRF House", 124, Greams Road, Chennai - 600 006, with your impressions of the MRF Tyreman.

Corporate ad for MRF

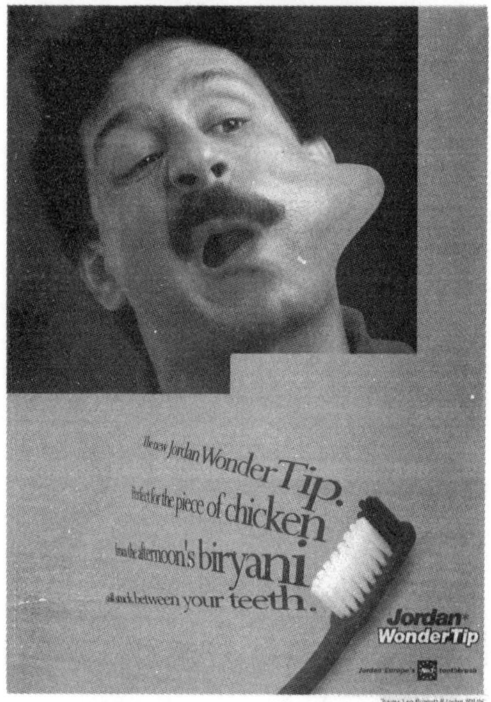

FMCG ad: Jordan toothbrushes

Corporate

Ads done for companies either through public service/good citizen campaigns, or even through their products, with the objective of creating an image.

Public Service

Campaigns sponsored by advertisers for causes, such as AIDS, road safety and anti-pollution.

Financial

Leasing and finance schemes, loans and deposit-raising, certain types of bank advertising, ads for life and other forms of insurance.

Public Issue

Ads to inform people of rights issues and to announce the results.

Classified

Small ads: for Sale/Help Wanted/Matrimonial/To Let/Job Offers.

Consumer Perishable

Ads promoting fast-moving consumer goods (fmcg), such as noodles, drinks, soaps and clothes.

Teaser

A series of ads that may appear in the same newspaper on the same day or on consecutive days, which reveal the advertiser's message in stages.

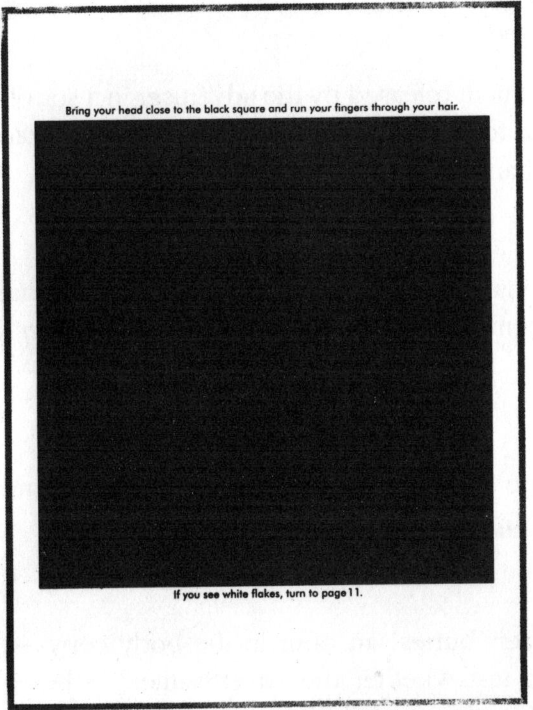

Bring your head close to the black square and run your fingers through your hair.
If you see white flakes, turn to page 11.

TAKE THE CLINIC ALL CLEAR WORLD CUP CHALLENGE

Shampoo every time India plays. Get All Clear of dandruff before the finals.

DHO DALENGE!

A two-ad teaser campaign for Clinic Shampoo

Cartoon Strip

These use a story/art direction technique which works very well, especially for children's products.

Consumer Durable

Advertising for products where the consumer has to pay out a substantial sum—washing machine, TV, car and house.

Promotional

Advertising meant to boost short-term sales, e.g., to clear stocks through a contest, free offer or banded offer.

Cartier
Pasha C watch
Solid steel
Automatic movement
Water-resistant to 100 metres
CARTIER BOUTIQUE : THE OBEROI, LOBBY LEVEL, MUMBAI TEL : (022) 2855976 / 2025757 EXT 6878 SHOWROOM : RAVISSANT, NEW DELHI. TEL : (011) 6837278 / 6831468 AUTHORIZED DEALERS : DANABHAI JEWELLERS AND SONS, MUMBAI. TEL : (022) 6494685 / 6494686 • TIME AVENUE, MUMBAI. TEL : (022) 6515757 / 6515858 • JOHNSON AND COMPANY, NEW DELHI. TEL : (011) 3321592 / 3731935 • KAPOOR & CO., NEW DELHI TEL : (011) 4693712 / 4627530 SOLE DISTRIBUTOR : FINEX DISTRIBUTION PVT. LTD. MUMBAI. TEL : (022) 6514367 SERVICE AGENTS : MARCKS & CO. MUMBAI. TEL : (022) 2670999 / 2676412 • TIME WATCH MAKERS, MUMBAI. TEL : (022) 4143898 / 4141610 • KAPOOR & CO., NEW DELHI. TEL : (011) 4693712 / 4627530 • DOSHI & DOSHI, CHENNAI. TEL : (044) 8533658

Consumer durable: Cartier watches

A promotional ad

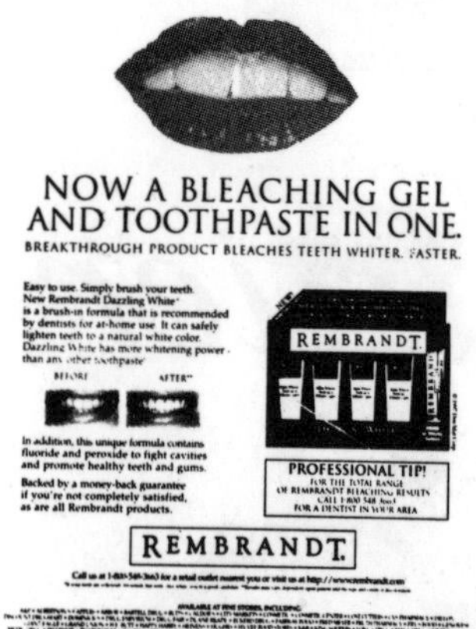

A launch ad

Souvenir

A token advertisement released by the advertiser in a souvenir or programme for a special event, e.g., a rock concert to raise funds for charity.

Advertorial

Advertising material presented in the form of an editorial message, as in many women's magazines or in the *Reader's Digest*.

Direct Response

Ads which require a 'direct response' from the reader and usually have a coupon to be filled in at the end.

Buried Offers

Here the advertiser 'buries' an offer in the body copy—a gimmick used to test whether the advertisement is being noticed and read by the target audience.

Launch

Advertising that introduces a new product or an improved one.

Important

Types/categories of ads should not be confused with the 'techniques' used in developing a press ad.

Creative Approaches

Any of the above types of ads could employ one or more of a number of creative approaches or techniques. For instance, in the Testimonial technique, an endorsement by a famous person could be used for a Launch ad, or even an Advertorial. Here are a few commonly used approaches.

The Testimonial Approach

Uses famous personalities, people in authority, or ordinary customers who are satisfied with the product, to testify to the brand's benefits.

The Lifestyle Approach

Where lifestyle is used as the main appeal—as in the case of many cigarette, textile and liquor ads.

The Problem–Solution Approach

Also known as the before-after approach, these ads work very effectively, especially on TV. A split screen is common usage, showing the situation before and after use of the product.

But whatever the type of campaign you are asked to work on, there is one highly imaginative (read creative) approach which you might bring to every job. I call it the *Bernbach approach*.

The Bernbach Approach

Turning Negatives into Positives

Sometimes things seem not to be going your way. There is nothing unique about the *product*. It is just one of those old me-too brands. Or perhaps you have been handed a lemon—a campaign no one else wants to touch with a barge pole. Hang in there. Or go out and buy a copy of *The Power of Positive Thinking*.

Bill Bernbach of Doyle Dane & Bernbach made advertising history by turning negatives into positives. His method was to take what seemed like a weakness of a product and turn it into a strength. The old Lufthansa ads and the Volkswagen ads are fine examples. It means you come straight out and tell the reader what your products apparent limitations are, but you offer them as an advantage. The Volkswagen was a small, ugly car—with a first-rate engine and a sturdy body. It also consumed less petrol. So the agency told it as it was—and won public sympathy and acceptance of the 'little bug'.

Lemon.

Here are three ads from my portfolio which serve as illustrations. Two of them won awards and the third was selected from an array of campaigns by no less than the then Prime Minister, Mrs Indira Gandhi.

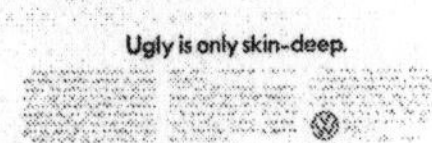
Ugly is only skin-deep.

World Wildlife Fund

This is the story of how a mere trainee (a negative!) won the Ad Club award for the Best English Press Ad 1972 (a positive!). It could happen to you. The copy chief, Cossy Rosario, was down with jaundice and I was left pretty much to my own devices. A client came to the agency, Zafar Futehally, who headed the World Wildlife Fund (India).

It is now called the Worldwide Fund for Nature. Mr Futehally wanted to save the tigers of India, which were being killed for their skins. There were just a handful left in the country. A 'public awareness' campaign was urgently required. The only snag was—*no money to pay for the advertising!* Alyque Padamsee agreed to do the job for free, and put the juniormost trainee to work on it as everyone else was too busy. He meant to oversee it himself.

So I set about thinking of ideas, and found a nice picture of a tiger's head. I stuck that on a sheet of paper and the visualiser drew cross-sights around it. There was a movie going on in town—*Born Free*—about a lioness called Elsa. That gave me the idea for the headline and Alyque helped me write the body copy. Yes, those were the days!

Mr Futehally liked the ad but there was *No Money.* It so happened that the chairman of Hindustan Lever dropped in and Alyque showed him the ad. He was impressed and agreed to pay for a single half-page insertion in *The Times of India.* The rest is history. Lintas entered it for the Ad Club awards and it won.

There are only 2000 tigers left in India.
How did this happen? Only 50 years ago, there were 40,000 tigers in India. But as hunting grew in popularity, the tiger population was drastically reduced.
Wildlife is part of our natural wealth. If we don't do something about it now, the only tigers our children may see might be in a storybook.
What you can do to save them
• Join World Wildlife—India. The membership fee is only Rs.10 per year (and you get a free newsletter).
BORN FREE
SENTENCED TO DEATH
• Stop buying animal skins and furs. Try and persuade your friends to do the same.
• Write to the Minister in Charge of Forests in your state, and urge him to set aside lands for game sanctuaries.
• Whenever you see an example of indiscriminate destruction of wildlife, report it to the Game Warden and send a copy of your letter to the Editor of your local newspaper.
By the time you finish reading this...it's possible that there will be only 1,999 tigers left in India. Act now.

JOIN WORLD WILDLIFE—INDIA,
Hornbill House, Prince of Wales Museum Compound, Bombay-1.

Ad Club Award Winner: 1972

It was the grandest evening of my young life. I still remember wearing the ankle-length black cotton skirt and blouse with sequins which my mother sewed for me for the occasion. Mubi Ismail and I swam in the Taj swimming pool while the advertising glitterati swanned around in dinner jackets and cocktail dresses. Someone poured champagne down Mubi's throat as she floated. Later, with damp hair and clothes, I was treated to my first drink in a bar by Alyque. A senior manager from Hindustan Lever actually spoke to me. And glory of glories, I saw myself receiving my award from the minister for information and broadcasting, Mr I.K. Gujral (later our Prime Minister for a while), on the fledgeling Doordarshan (television) evening news.

Note to the reader: My publisher thinks it is immodest of me to want my photograph put in this book, but these are the little rewards which make the advertising grind—and it is that for the most part—worth it. People do not just work for salaries, but also for satisfaction and appreciation. Incidentally, writing this book at all is a labour of love. So if I sound a bit full of myself, forgive me.

There were many more important 'awardees' at that Ad Club function but it was the juniormost writer's photograph that adorned the press report in *The Times of India* the next day. An astonished Gerson da Cunha asked, "June, how on earth did you manage that?" I grinned, "That's my secret." But the truth is, having been a journalist for a while, I knew all the press men and they were tickled pink at my success! So, now you know.

Miss June Valladares of Lintas India Limited who received the award for the best press advertisement in English from the advertising Club, Bombay, on Saturday.

Make advertising socially motivated: Gujral

By A Staff Reporter

Communications media could be effective instruments for social change, Mr. I.K. Gujral, Union minister of state for information and broadcasting, said in Bombay on Saturday.

The media could take up issues like environmental problems and maintenance of law and order, he said.

Mr. Gujral was addressing the Advertising Club at its seventh annual all-India awards function.

He said socially-motivated campaigns were being carried out mostly by governmental agencies, while the private sector was busy mainly with the promotion of commodities.

Mr. Gujral said the communications media should strive to co-relate socially motivated campaigns with the sale of consumer products. Otherwise, advertising might lead only to consumerism, which was undesirable.

The Advertising Club gave away 20 awards under 11 categories. There were no winners in the category "innovation in media." Two categories, "Outdoor advertising" and "Campaign as a whole," were added this year.

Mr. A.N. Sen, chairman of the awards committee, said the club received 728 entries from 52 organisations.

Air-India

Here is another example from my portfolio of a negative that became a positive. This one too won an award—from the Commercial Artists Guild (CAG), now known as Communication Artists Guild. This time the ad was 100 % the copywriter's idea—visual and all. The Air-India hoarding at Nariman Point, Mumbai, is changed every week. It is used not just to sell the airline but also to draw people's attention to anything topical, and also to charitable organisations. That week it was the National

This week's hoarding is for those who cannot see it.
National Association for the Blind. Flag Day Sep. 14

Air-India hoarding at Nariman Point, Mumbai

Association for the Blind which needed highlighting. This hoarding—created entirely without the aid of an art director!—was instantly approved in-agency and by the client.

20–Point Programme For Prosperity

Nobody liked the state of emergency declared by Mrs Indira Gandhi in 1975. But orders are orders and HTA was given the task of preparing the communication which explained some of the measures taken by the government. Four or five separate campaign approaches were shown to Mrs Gandhi personally in a presentation lasting fewer than five minutes. Without saying a word she walked around the table on which the ads were laid out and pointed peremptorily to the one reproduced on p. 67. This story was related to me by Niko Nair, then creative director of HTA, who was there. It made my day—even though I was not in favour of Mrs G's dictatorial behaviour. As things turned out, her government was ousted 18 months later, to make way for the Janata Party.

The objective: To inform the public that bonded labour, the bane of India's peasants, had been officially done away with. This ad would be one of a series dealing with the other subjects in Mrs G's proposed 20-Point Programme for Prosperity.

Here I must digress a little. While working on this book, I asked Bahadur Merwan (who has done all the cartoons for it) if he remembered this ad done in 1975 when we were colleagues in HTA. He looked at me quizzically and said, "June, I was the art director on the job! I took the photograph of this poor family at Bombay Central station!" This in itself would be nothing unusual, except that Bahadur had left the agency shortly after awards; our ways had diverged, and

Nation on the move

Born with a life sentence.

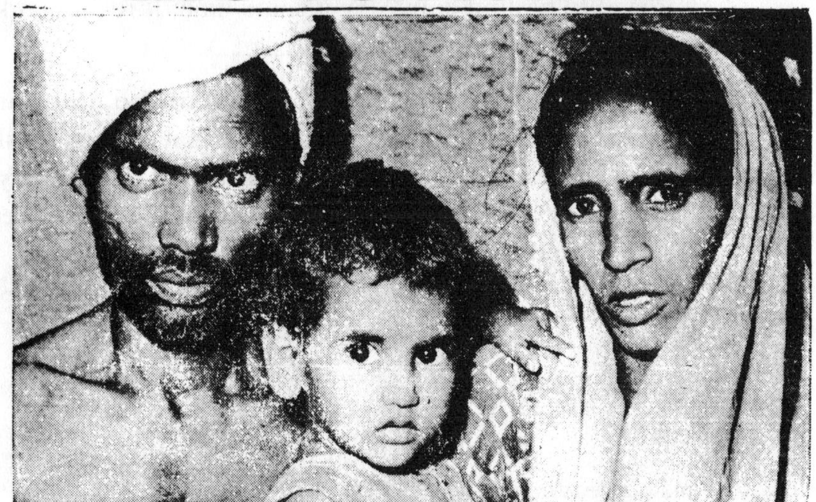

Set free on June 26, 1975.

All 200 million of them.

Rural indebtedness was like some giant monster with a stranglehold on millions of our poor farmers.

These unfortunate peasants were born in debt and stayed that way all their lives.

Now by a decree of Government, these men and women have been freed from the shackles of debt. They may now live with dignity–borrow money on reasonable terms from Rural Banks. The landless will be given land. Special sites will be reserved for building houses for them. Agricultural workers will be assured a minimum wage, and get better irrigation and power facilities.

Government has made the first move. But, now, we the people must help ourselves. Working together, striving together, we can remove all obstables to the nation's progress and help bequeath a future our children will be proud of.

20-Point Programme for Prosperity

- Reduction of prices, display of stock position.
- Agricultural land ceiling; redistribution of land.
- Housing sites in rural areas.
- Abolition of bonded labour.
- Liquidation of rural indebtedness.
- Minimum wages for agricultural labour.
- Better irrigation for greater productivity.
- More power for greater production.
- Development of handloom sector.
- Better cloth for more people.
- Socialisation of urban land.
- Property valuation; punishment for tax evasion.
- Confiscation of smugglers' properties.
- Liberalisation of investment procedures.
- Worker participation in industry.
- National permit scheme for road transport.
- Income tax relief to the middle class
- Essential commodities at controlled prices for students
- Controlled prices for text-books and stationery.
- Increased employment and training opportunities.

Let's get on with the job.

Mrs Gandhi's choice!

when I met up with him again in April 1999, I had not set eyes on him for almost 22 years!

So, even if you are dumped with a *me-too* product (where there is no particular distinguishing mark), or a campaign that no one else wants to touch, you would do well to meet the challenge and give your whole attention to it. Take a negative situation—whether in life or in advertising—and turn it into a benefit. That is the Bernbach Approach to writing copy. Try it some time. It really works!

Our job is to sell our clients' merchandise, not ourselves. Our job is to kill the cleverness that makes us shine instead of the product. Our job is to simplify, to tear away the unrelated, to pluck out the weeds that are smothering the product message.

—William Bernbach (1989).

Warm-up

Go through your favourite magazines and newspapers and look for striking ads. Keep a *separate file* for ads you think are good.

They will come in useful as we proceed in our study. After you read each chapter, examine your file of ads, looking for the principle you have just read about. Having read about the Bernbach syndrome, try and locate ads where you think a negative attribute has been turned into a positive benefit. The product may be an fmcg (fast moving consumer good), or an industrial product, or even a service (airlines, hotels).

Choose at least five such ads and follow the example.

Product	*Weakness*	*Strength*
AVIS car rental	No.2 to Hertz	Avis tries harder to please its customers, because they are small enough to give personalised service.

As you keep adding to your 'striking ads' file you will begin to see distinct techniques or approaches used by the creators of the ads. Sometimes the idea is *Copy* based. There are also ads where the *Visual* element holds the idea, and these too should form part of your file. At this stage, concentrate on becoming familiar with the Bernbach Approach—turning negative into positive.

There will be time enough for the others, as you read on.

Workout

1. Study the classified ads in your daily newspaper. How many types of classifieds do you notice? Write them down in the space provided below, and give an example of each. You may cut the ad out and stick it in the book.
   a. For Sale

   b. Obituaries

   c.

   d.

   e.

2. From your daily newspaper and old magazines cut out at least three more examples of the types of press ads listed in this chapter. Can you add to the list?
3. Ask a friend to cut out several interesting photographs from your newspaper or favourite magazine. The pictures must not be posed or taken from ads. They must be candid camera action shots. Try writing suitable, catchy captions for the pictures.
4. Write an account of your day. Highlight the times when you have acted in an imaginative or creative manner. Then count the number of times you have shown imagination in handling a situation. What is your score? Write it here:

   20 and above: Good
   15–20: Fair
   Below 15: Pull up your creative socks!

6

The Loch Ness Monster

For a long time after you have joined an ad agency you will wonder who or what this creature is. The *Client* seems to be another word for the Loch Ness Monster who lives in some dark deep place and is never seen, only heard of through terrified account executives, "Hurry and get that copy done, client meeting in 15 minutes." Or "Gosh, the client's not going to understand that." And after a meeting, "The client absolutely loved the stuff, but he wants us to change the headline, visual and body copy, and make a few alterations in the baseline." Comes a time when you are so curious—or frustrated—you feel you must meet this mythical creature for yourself.

In the course of your career you will run the gamut of all types of clients, so do not be in a hurry to meet them. Since clients are basically people, they will be as different as personality types. They will also reflect the corporate culture of the company for which they work. After a while you will be talking like a true advertising pro. "Client X—oh, they're such darlings, real gentlemen, they never touch your copy except to suggest the removal of a comma." Or "Those guys at . . ., can't stand the wretches, they're agency-baiters." Or, "Client Y, he's a tough cookie, but he's always right!" On the whole, the clients you will meet are just ordinary beings doing their job, which is to look after their company's advertising budget (adspend).

Some agencies have a policy of protecting creative people from the client. I have never figured out the reason for this, because sooner or later you are going to have to sit across the table from the client—often in the presence of a squirming account executive—to explain why you think the copy is the best thing ever written and why it is going to sell the client's product like it was going out of fashion. When you get down to it, there is an inverse relationship between how many times you see the client and how good an account executive you have on your team. The better the account executive is at selling an idea, the less interaction you need to have with the client.

When you meet the client for the first time make sure you

- are escorted by a senior colleague
- smile when you are introduced
- do not talk about the weather
- do not volunteer information; wait till you are asked
- do not slap the client on the back
- keep your opinions about the client, how the meeting went, and what the account executive ought to have said, for when you get back to the agency

---

I never tell one client that I cannot attend his sales convention because I have a previous engagement with another client; successful polygamy depends upon pretending to each spouse that she is the only pebble on the beach.

— David Ogilvy (1971, p. 52)

Client–Agency Relationship

It is the job of the account executive/supervisor to prepare the *Agency Brief.* This document contains all the essential information that the client wishes to divulge to the agency to get the advertising work done. The more a client tells, the better the agency sells, so it is in the interest of both client and agency to share as much information as possible.

One of the most frustrating things a copywriter has to put up with is securing a proper brief from an account executive. If it is off course, all your creative work gets shot to hell. A good creative brief in turn depends on client servicing to elicit a workable Agency Brief from the client. Sometimes the copywriter has to do this job for him, so it is best to be prepared. If your client is a good marketing man, and knows his onions, you are lucky. If he hums and haws and is reticent about giving facts and figures, you are in trouble.

If a client has confidence in the agency, he will tell more; if the agency feels good about the client, it will produce better work. The agency has a different relationship with every client, depending on whether he is a new or old customer, his adspend, his status in the market, how good a paymaster he is, and even his behaviour pattern. Clients may also relate to their agency on these terms. *But in the final analysis, all clients stay with an agency because they are interested in the best deal for their advertising rupee.*

The bottomline then, is budget, not buddies.

I know half the money I spend on advertising is wasted, but I don't know which half.

—Lord Leverhume (William Hesketh Lever) (1991, p. 136)

Workout

1. If you were a client on the lookout for an agency, what qualities would you want to find in the agency of your choice? Why? Write your answer here:

   ____

   ____

   ____

   ____

   ____

   ____

   (about 100 words)

   If you were head of an agency, what sort of accounts would you pitch for—and why?

   ____

   ____

   ____

   ____

   ____

   ____

   (about 100 words)

   Date:

   If you are a copywriter looking for an agency, list your first five choices below and state the reasons why you would like to be employed in them.

   a. ____

   ____

   b. ____

   ____

   c. ____

   ____

   d. ____

   ____

   e. ____

   ____

   (By the time you have finished reading this book, flip back to this page and see if you still hold these views.)

2. a. Suggest 10 successful businesses that have dwindled.

   ____

   ____

   ____

   ____

   ____

   ____

   b. Suggest other uses for overstocked toothbrushes.

   ____

   ____

   ____

   ____

   ____

   ____

7

Agency Brief and Advertising Strategy

The *Agency Brief* contains all the raw material the agency needs to work out a sound *Advertising Strategy*. Both these documents are very important as they form the basis of the final creative work. In this chapter we will outline the elements that go into the Agency Brief, and how it is translated into Advertising Strategy. This translation task is generally done in close co-ordination with the client, who one assumes is more knowledgeable than the agency about the market and his marketing goals. It is in the light of the marketing goals and objectives that advertising goals and strategy are set. Different agencies have different names for this crucial planning exercise, following variously named disciplines like the T-Plan (HTA), Magic Lantern (O&M), or the X-Files (Xebec Communications). These terms may change over the years but the exercise remains the same.

The Agency Brief has to be converted into an Advertising Strategy in a manner that meets the client's approval and budget. The strategy may be short-term or long-term . . . covering a period of a few months, or the whole year. It is absolutely vital to get the client's signature on these documents, for reasons that will become clearer as we go on with our work of creating campaigns that sell.

The Advertising Strategy sets the guidelines for all the disciplines within the agency—creative, media, research and account planning. It ensures that every single person in these diverse departments is working harmoniously towards the same objectives. A diagram may help:

Agency Brief
(marketing objectives)

Advertising Strategy
(advertising objectives)

The Advertising Task
(multi-pronged)

1	2	3	4
Creative Brief and Strategy	Media Brief and Strategy	Account Planning	Research (IMRB or other is briefed)

In this book we shall only be concerned with No. 1—the Creative Brief and Strategy, though all four prongs are working simultaneously and in close co-ordination. Remember that advertising is *teamwork*. Information shared leads to sounder and stronger campaigns.

What can You Expect to Find in the Agency Brief?

1. Everything about the client's *company*
    - the history and background (chronology)
    - the company culture and philosophy
    - infrastructure
    - whether proprietor owned/professionally managed/public sector/private sector
    - structure/diversification, if any
    - production capacity
    - brands/product range
    - personnel/branch offices/factories
2. Everything about the client's *product*
    - its size, shape, colour, smell, price
    - how it is packaged
    - how it is manufactured
    - how it is distributed
    - how it is sold
3. Everything about the client's *marketing policy and objectives*
    - total market and brand's market share
    - overall marketing policy
    - current marketing strategy
    - intentions for the brand
4. Everything about the client's *sales policy and objectives*
    - sales force
    - dealers and retailers
    - incentives and below the line activities
    - annual sales of product by cash value, market share and quantity
    - advertising and sales promotion to date
    - sales projections/other goals
5. Everything about the client's *management policy*
    - organisational set-up
    - line of command
    - hierarchy
    - culture/philosophy/style of operation
    - type of managers employed
    - marketing set up
6. Everything about the client's *competition*
    - primary competition
    - secondary competition
    - unbranded competition, if any
    - market shares of competitive brands (in cash value and in volume of sales)
    - unorganised sector
7. Everything about the client's *current/prospective consumer*
    - demographics
    - psychographics
    - lifestyle
    - buying habits
    - attitudes towards the brand
    - any negative perceptions
8. Everything about the client's *future plans*
    - marketing
    - sales
    - organisational growth
    - cultural changes
    - in context of the government's current policies
    - global considerations
    - collaborations
    - diversification
    - research and development
    - attitude to technology
9. Everything about any *research* the client has undertaken
    - consumer research

- product research
- market research
- advertising research
- pricing research
- attitudinal research
- any other research

10. Everything the client thinks is unimportant and irrelevant but could be *important and relevant*
    - how he treats his wife
    - how he treats his secretary
    - where he goes on vacation (just kidding!)

Very often there are gaping holes in this document. Copywriters complain about the 'lack of information', and they are left to do some digging around themselves. So it is best to arm yourself with a list of questions to ask your elusive account executive. If the account executive (a very busy person) is not around, you might have to send for the *guardbooks* to look at past advertising of the client's products (assuming the account has been long enough with the agency). Otherwise you will just have to lie in wait for the account supervisor as he rushes out to yet another 'meeting'. Or buy the harried account executive a drink after hours to get the information you want. You will probably find the latter tactic works better . . . and as things get more relaxed and expansive, your account executive might even buy you a drink!

At encounters with your client servicing colleague, go armed with a battery of questions. This way it becomes easier for the provider of information to fill in the blanks, and precious time is saved. Ram Ray, who heads his own agency, Response India Limited, was an account supervisor, and later general manager of HTA's Madras office in the '70s. With just one remark, "June, you ask too few questions," he pointed out that I had not done my homework. A voracious reader, he taught by example. He introduced me to Stephen Baker's *Systematic Approach to Advertising Creativity*, which added greatly to my education. More recently, so have the books *Advertising Copywriting* and *Which Ad Pulled Best* by Philip Ward Burton.

Important *All the information in the Agency Brief is from the client's viewpoint. The agency's business is to look at the material from the consumer's point of view, and so lay the foundations for the Advertising Strategy as a whole.*

Setting the Advertising Strategy

Depending on the importance of the client, this exercise is undertaken by the senior managers of the agency. Creative, media and account planning, and if necessary, the research wing, sit down to develop the blueprint together. Once again, at the risk of repetition, it must be said that advertising is *teamwork.*

Different agencies use different terminology but the steps are common. For instance, the Advertising Strategy document could be called the:

Written Advertising Plan

- Statement of advertising objectives
- Written advertising strategy
- Product positioning statement
- List of reasons for buying
- Creative blueprint

(*Source:* Britt (1973, p. 935)

Basically, the Advertising Strategy lays down the blueprint for the various departments—media, creative, research, account planning—to implement their tasks according to a common brief and goal. Everyone must be very clear about where they are heading before they can take their own routes to arrive at the destination. The Advertising Strategy document studies the contents of the Agency Brief, *assesses the situation, defines the problems, and thinks of ways to overcome the obstacles* which stand between the client's current advertising status and what the advertising needs to achieve one year (or more) down the line.

Through all this, the agency has to make sure that the *advertising strategy is in line with the client's overall marketing goals and objectives.*

Advertising Strategy

- Decides *what* the advertising message is to be.
- Decides *how* it should be said: press, film, TV, radio.
- Decides to *whom* it is to be targeted.
- Analyses the *consumers' behaviour and attitudes* to the product.
- Thinks of the product as a future *brand.*

- Finds a *positioning* for the brand in the market.
- Thinks of ways to overcome or *eliminate competition's* advertising strategies.
- Lays the basis for *media strategy* .
- Decides on the *budget* and how to work within it.
- Considers what *research*, if any, should be undertaken, and in which areas.
- Works out a *time plan* for the advertising.

Roda Mehta, internationally known media person, formerly with HTA and O&M, now lives and works from her Pune home. She affirms how close coordination between creative and media strategies can spark off a great advertising idea.

The Creative-Media Spark

by Roda Mehta

When the client briefs the agency, it is not uncommon that client servicing passes the brief on to creative and media without making any changes. The client brief (Agency Brief) varies—advertising-savvy clients like Hindustan Lever, Proctor & Gamble and Colgate spell out specific objectives for the advertising and media to deliver during the campaign period. Most other clients just give their marketing objectives and strategy, and leave it to the agency to formulate the communication requirements.

Developing the Advertising Strategy is often a joint effort between client servicing and creative, because the nuances of what the advertising must achieve vis-à-vis the target consumer is intuitively better understood and articulated by creative.

On the other hand, the role of media is more closely linked to the client's marketing objectives and sales strategies. Media delivers the *absolute* target audience to be reached, the frequency with which they are exposed to the advertising, as compared to the competition, the markets in which the budget will be focussed, the months and time of day when the message will be delivered.

These are also linked with the client's distribution system, the product seasonality and competitive activity in the marketplace. Hence the value of media's direct interaction with the client in arriving at the necessary marketing support solutions.

What is more, the enormous media options now accessible to consumers across the country, what with language and editorial genre additions, have raised the demand on media to showcase the brand's message in an intrusive and memorable way.

The creative-media partnership is intensified in the current scenario. Creative must increasingly be exposed to the variety of media and their editorial/advertising environments: 60-odd television channels, new formats on radio broadcasting, newspaper editorial and advertising opportunities, growing magazine possibilities, outdoor moves, increasing rural media options. The latest icons, symbols, colloquialisms, styles and formats give rise to new ways to communicate, to stand out in the clutter, to prevent the remote from switching channels when the commercials appear!

In turn, media needs to understand the creative task, strategy and execution to find the best media match for the message. Media's recommendations are influenced by their judgement of how the creative message will be received by the target consumers.

Let me share an example of how creative-media co-ordination can spark outstanding brand delivery. In the mid-90s, the 1976 Indian blockbuster film *Sholay* was to be aired by Doordarshan for the first time on television. It was billed as a major event with large mass viewership, albeit at very high costs.

The media buyer on the Fevicol adhesive account saw in this an opportunity for his brand. He recommended the programme to client servicing. Given the low balance in the budget, this suggestion was rejected. However, seeing the excellent match between the likely viewers of this film and Fevicol's target audience, the media buyer approached his creative counterpart. Their subsequent brainstorming and joint viewing of the film led to the following ideas:

- identify how frequently the concept of *bonding* appears in the film, either visually or in the dialogue
- at that point, notice which actor/actress's voice comes over
- inject specially created five-second messages at these points, using the readily identifiable voice of the actor/actress to promote Fevicol's *lasting bond*!

The Big Idea was mooted to the client who bought it instantly. There were many ifs and buts in the execution of the idea, as it meant these messages would not appear in the regular commercial capsules as directed by Doordarshan—and the media buyer had to find a way out. He had to make the five-second *injections* appear without the commercial break swipe on either side of the message—so that it did not interrupt the flow of film to message and back to film. And he had to achieve all this without paying a premium!

When *Sholay* was telecast, it took everyone by surprise—Doordarshan, the sponsors, the viewers. Fevicol appeared just seven times during the course of the film, i.e., a total of 35 seconds. The sponsor of the film, Lux Toilet Soap, had taken a total of 1000 seconds spread across a number of Hindustan Lever brands. The day after the screening, viewer research fed back the highest recall for Fevicol, with the bonus perception that it was the 'sponsor' of this blockbuster event!

Story ending: The media buyer who thought of this idea was adjudged *Outstanding Young Media Person* by the Hindustan Times–Pearson joint TV venture and sent to the UK for a month's visit to media houses there.

In advertising there is a saying that if you can keep your head while all those around you are losing theirs—then you just don't understand the problem.

—Hugh Malcolm Beville Jr (1954),director of research at NBC, quoted in James B. Simpson (1964, p. 82)

Workout

1. You are the proprietor of a small company making excellent matchsticks (better than Wimco's *Ship*!). You have approached a medium-sized agency with a reputation for top-notch creative work to handle your account for the year. You have made very good profits in the previous 12 months and would like to spend X amount on advertising your product for the first time! Prepare an Agency Brief for your counterpart in the ad agency, which will warm the cockles of his heart.
2. You are the account supervisor who has been asked to deal with Mr Matchsticks. The budget is not large, but you like the fellow. After reading the Agency Brief, what Advertising Strategy would you propose to the client? (Be as inventive as you like, and file away your assignment to look at later.)

8

Creative Brief and Creative Strategy

Once the overall advertising strategy has been set, the account supervisor or account executive relays the *Creative Brief* to the copy/art team. This document contains the information needed for the team to come up with a good idea for a campaign. And no document creates as much trouble for those concerned as this one! The creatives are always complaining of information gaps and the servicing types are always replying, "Nonsense, it's all there in the Brief."

The trainee wonders if he should just stand by silently and watch, or whether to jump into the fray. Do not hesitate—jump, even at the risk of being caught in the crossfire. Sometimes an account executive wants to take a short cut with a sketchy verbal brief. This could mean trouble later on. To be on the safe side, always insist on a written

Creative Brief before you start work on a campaign. From this point on, every step taken in the agency has to be vetted at various levels.

The Creative Brief stands somewhere between the Agency Brief and the Creative Strategy. This document translates certain components of the Agency Brief into more user-friendly terms. You will see the difference if you compare what came under 'The Product' in the Agency Brief, and what comes under 'The Product' in the Creative Brief.

Note: At every stage in agency life we face the problem of 'communication'—the client sees things from his perspective, the agency from another, the consumer from a third. Remember the six blind men of Hindustan who touched the elephant? Everyone is right, and everyone is wrong—the paradox of advertising. Anyway, that is what makes it fun!

The Creative Brief

The Creative Brief tells you about a host of things that will help you prepare the ad campaign. It tells you about:

The Product

- what it looks like
- what it smells like
- what it is made of
- what it costs
- how it is packaged
- what it weighs
- what makes it different

The Competition

- primary
- secondary
- branded or unbranded
- substitutes
- what they are saying
- what positions they occupy
- their strategies/promotions
- their weaknesses and strengths
- their market shares

The Market

- how large the market is:
  - in terms of sales
  - in terms of money
  - distribution strengths/ weaknesses
- how the market is divided
  - in seasonal terms
  - in territorial terms

Consumer Profile

- demographics (age/income/territory)
- psychographics (culture/ mindset/attitudes)
- lifestyle
- other factors

Marketing Objective

- increase sales
- test market
- promote brand awareness
- change consumer attitudes
- launch new product
- widen usership base
- penetrate new market
- update the brand

Advertising Objective

- reach more people in towns
- change the brand image
- increase occasions for use
- introduce new packaging
- make current consumers use more
- introduce a new concept
- bring new users into the fold

Advertising Task

- use TV to make the brand visible
- show people how it is used
- devise a series of promotions
- make people aware of a new brand
- motivate them to use more of the product
- educate them about something
- explain a new concept

While the Creative Brief is being formulated, and this can take a great deal of 'toing and froing' between client servicing, creative and the client, it is worth doing some digging of your own. From the guardbooks, gather as much information as you can about your client's product, his previous advertising, competitive brands, competitive advertising. Talk to people about what they think and feel about your client's product (unless it is a new one and no one has heard of it). Then you can gather views on the product category, generic stuff.

Walk into shops and talk to dealers, retailers, showroom attendants and counter boys and girls. It is amazing how much you can learn just by listening to people.

The Internet, that information wonder, is a limitless source of hard facts and figures. But when you try to access soft facts and feelings you are up against a wall. There really is no substitute for people. The more people you talk to, and the more observant you are of human nature, the more likely you are to produce great campaigns. So keep interacting with all types of people. They are potential consumers. As David Ogilvy put it, '*The consumer is not a moron, she's your wife.*' (Some clients take this literally and will not approve a campaign unless their wives have seen and liked it!)

Rule: Never agree to start any creative work before digesting all the information about the client's product (in the Agency Brief) and studying the blueprint of how the advertising task should be tackled (in the Creative Strategy).

Setting the Creative Strategy

The Advertising Strategy, then, takes stock of the client's current position (in advertising terms) in the light of his future goals, both marketing and advertising. The obstacles that come in the way of achieving the goals have been listed, and ways and means discussed as to how to overcome them. For instance, consumer attitude to the product may be a problem. Or the entrance of a new brand could be eating into the share of our client's market. This assessment may be done by the client servicing folk, account planners and the creatives all working together. Even media could have a say in it.

Assessment is a crucial part of the hammering out of the *Creative Strategy*. Millions of little grey cells are at work thinking of ways to counter the obstacles to the final communication. When ultimately a course of possible action is arrived at, the Creative Strategy is born. This important document sets the creative guidelines for the advertising in *all* media: press/film/TV/outdoor. When the creative team goes to work, they will be working within tight parameters. Their campaign ideas will have to satisfy all the demands laid out in the Creative Brief and the Agency Brief. That is why it is vital to get the client's approval (his signature) on the Creative Strategy before you roll up your sleeves for the actual campaign.

RULE: Make sure the client's signature approval is on all important documents like the Creative Brief and the Creative Strategy.

The agency that tries to take a short cut in its haste to meet deadlines often ends up losing valuable time, because work has been produced to the wrong brief. Very frustrating.

The Creative Strategy

Based on the data contained in the Creative Brief, the creative team—often in collaboration with the account executive—goes to work to set the parameters of the advertising campaign they are to create. They will start by defining who the campaign should be addressed to, what it should say, and in what manner the message must be conveyed. The following parameters emerge:

- Target Audience
- Proposition/Brand Positioning
- Brand Image
- Tone of Voice
- Further recommendations, e.g., research

RULE: Cut through jargon to the commonsense under it.

Different agencies use varying terminology for the same thing. Do not worry unduly about all these. You concentrate on absorbing the basics, and then adapt according to which agency you join.

You will hear other terms used, such as Campaign Strategy, Brand Positioning Statement (or just plain Positioning), Brand Personality, and others which will need clarification.

RULE: When in doubt, ask for clarification.

These terms will be addressed as they come up, for the moment try not to get confused. Focus on the 'dry bones'. As you become more conversant with campaign creation, you will add to your vocabulary and understanding.

Imagine that you are in art school, learning to draw. You first learn about perspective and proportion and how to sketch before you learn to shade in the details. So hold your horses; there is no need to jump any fences till you are good and ready.

Warm-ups

1. Name three everyday items with potential for improvement. In each case suggest what specific improvement can be made.
2. What features in a home might be improved if they were curved instead of straight.
3. Complete the following:
   As happy as ... (100 examples).
   As sad as ... (100 examples).
   As angry as ... (100 examples).

Workout

1. Write an ad (about 60 words) for yourself in the matrimonial column of your daily newspaper. Give a short note on the type of reader of this newspaper. Would the kind of person you would like to marry be likely to read this paper? Choose your words carefully, making each word work hard for you. Remember, *you* are paying for this ad, not your father!
2. The following agencies are looking for trainee copywriters:
   Enterprise, Trikaya Grey, Lintas, O&M, McCann Erickson and Avenues. How would each of them advertise the post in the press? Assume the ads will appear in supplements devoted entirely to appointment ads.
3. Imagine you are a manufacturer of toilet preparations.
   You already have a talcum powder and a toilet soap doing well in the market. Now you want to launch a new product, a toothpaste called *Dentium*, which contains calcium. Select an agency and give reasons for your choice. Then work out an Agency Brief for Dentium toothpaste based on what you have read so far. Pack as much information as you can into it, being as inventive as you like.

Look at these assignments again after studying the parameters of the Creative Strategy.

To reiterate, these are:

- Target Audience
- Tone of Voice
- The Proposition
- Brand Image

9

Target Audience

All this time the user of your product has been referred to as the *consumer.* In the agency brief you were introduced to the *consumer profile.* You got to know the consumer's tastes, demographics, buying habits, psychographics, and you built up a mental picture of your customer. Knowing your customer or prospect is crucial in order to communicate your advertising message correctly. If your prospects speak only Hindi and have studied only up to Class X, it is no use talking to them as if they were residents of upper-crust Malabar Hill in Mumbai, educated at Oxford.

So what is all this about *Target Audience?*

Simple. Say that the consumers of your toothpaste are men, women, and children in the middle-income group, who reside in metros. They have been using your brand for years because it is good, and it is economical and their grandmothers used it. It is a toothpaste used by the whole family. Now the point is, in your advertising message, *who are you going to address?* The husband? The

wife? The kids? Who makes the decision as to which toothpaste the family should use? When you start asking yourself questions like this, you may make an educated decision that possibly the mother/housewife influences the family taste in toothpaste.

So, she is the Target Audience. Your advertising message is meant for her, and through her your toothpaste will get into the home and be used by the whole family.

Sometimes (say your toothpaste is peppermint flavoured) you may decide that the child should be the Target Audience. The taste will appeal to the kids who will then put pressure on their mothers to buy your product. These are considerations that the copywriter and art director have to deal with and make decisions on. The consumer is the *genus*, the Target Audience is the *species*.

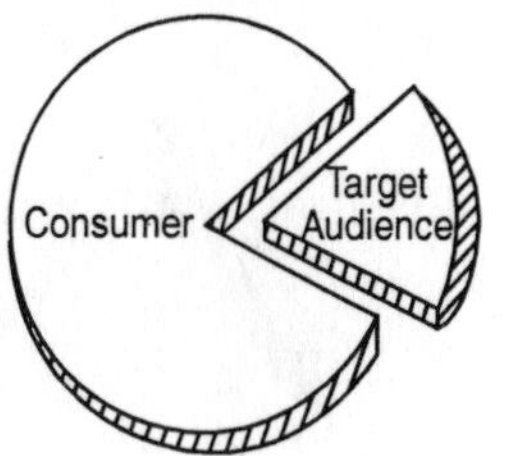

Once you get this clear, your large mass of consumers can be boiled down to a single individual. It is easier to speak candidly on a one-to-one basis than to a crowd. Flagging your Target Audience is like catching the eye of a single individual in an auditorium and speaking directly to that person. If you hold his attention, chances are you also have the attention of the rest.

One of the pointers to writing good copy is to imagine that your Target Audience is sitting across the desk from you. You know then, if it is a woman, how she is dressed, how many children she has, her age, her personality, her interests, her dreams and ambitions. With all this knowledge you can begin to think of your consumer as a person, and this will decide the manner in which you will go about selling the toothpaste to her. If she is already convinced about the quality of your brand, and has been a user for years, your task will be relatively easy. If she is someone who uses your brand, but also buys another brand for her children, you might have to give her good reasons why she should stop buying the other brand and encourage her children to use your brand.

There is no such thing as a Mass Mind. The Mass Audience is made up of individuals, and good advertising is written always from one person to another. When it is aimed at millions it rarely moves anyone.

—Fairfax Cone of Foote, Cone and Belding,
quoted in John O'Toole's (1981)

All this depends, as you can see, on what the client's marketing and advertising goals are. Everything outlined in the brief has to tie in. The client might want to increase the sales of toothpaste per family. Or he may be looking for new worlds to conquer and go after people who have not as yet tried his brand.

In this case, you may select as your Target Audience that section of toothpaste users who are currently users of another brand, and present them with a better alternative, *your* brand.

This will necessarily result in quite a different message from what you would have given a loyal user of your brand. However, whatever your message to the prospective users, you would also be addressing (indirectly) the current loyal users, and reinforcing their faith in your brand. It is not wise to alienate old customers in your efforts to win over new ones.

Here are two copy-based ads for *Foote, Cone & Belding* and *Leo Burnett*, two of America's best-known ad agencies. Read them carefully, and then write a paragraph describing who you think is their Target Audience. You will need to return to these two ads again and again in the course of your work.

(*Source:* Joyce, 1963, pp. 48, 49)

Headline: The Plain Short Story of Good Advertising

Text: There is a small group of advertising people in the United States who make advertising not only as a business but also for the sheer, continuing satisfaction of pushing good products past all competition.

This small group of men and women have no interest at all in either comfortable small businesses or questionable big ones.

Its members pride themselves on accomplishment but they have no truck with even the slightest exaggeration or deception.

They believe in the good judgment of the average adult American and they make advertising to excite this good judgment and to satisfy it.

The advertising these few exceptional people make follows four simple rules:

1. *It is always clear and complete (as to what the proposition is).*
2. *It is important (the proposition is worth caring about).*
3. *It is personal (it makes it easy for the prospect to identify with the proposition).*
4. *It demands that the reader or viewer do something about the proposition (it demands action).*

The reason why these simple rules are followed successfully only by a few exceptional agencies is because it is necessary to understand some things about these rules, and adhere to some principles in applying them, that are in themselves exceptional.

In the first place, advertising is something you do only when you cannot send a personal salesman.

When this is understood, you endeavour to make your advertising reflect nothing so much as the qualities and attributes of an exceptional personal salesman.

You will be pleasantly persistent but never offensive.

You will be imaginative, but you will never be misleading.

And finally, because of these qualities, you will be convincing.

◆ ◆ ◆

That is the story of good advertising.

And there you see why there is really so very little of it.

The rules are simple enough.

But failure to follow any one of the four, or to fail to reflect any one of the vital qualities, will be fatal.

And most people who make advertising *do* fail in some way or other.

We don't.

More than 30 products advertised by this agency stand in first place in their competitive sales position.

Baseline: Foote, Cone & Belding New York, Chicago, Los Angeles, San Francisco, Houston, London, Toronto, Frankfurt, Mexico, City

---

There are two kinds of readers: those who read to remember and those who read to forget.

—William Lyon Phelps

Advertising in its final analysis should be news . . . . In its proper use, the highest order of journalistic ability may be exercised, and through it a distinct public service may be performed.

Good advertising is of prime importance. It calls for the best talents—the same talents essential to the making of good editors, copy readers, headline artists, and all others engaged in gathering and presenting news, or expressing opinion.

—Adolph S. Ochs, publisher of *The New York Times*, 1896–1935

(*Source:* Joyce, 1963, pp. 94, 95)

Leo Burnett Company, Inc. Advertising

Headline: Born on August 5, 1935
Subhead: Reared on 12 principles
Caption: Only a bunch of optimists would have opened an ad agency on a day like that—and we still are

Text

1. Every message in print or over the air must have 'thought-force'—a central idea that offers an advantage to the reader or listener, in an interesting and plausible manner. We have no patience with double-talk or muddy thinking.
2. The reader or listener is presumably a human being and must be rewarded in some human manner for dwelling on your message.
   Much advertising, we felt, was as dull as dishwater. We decided, therefore, that we would try to make our advertising 'fun to look at' or listen to. Not funny—but fun in a broad, human sense. This involves what we call the 'overtones' of advertising, which are hard to describe but which make the difference between an ad that lives and one that is just so-so.
3. To plan the sale as you plan the ad—to build ads so strong in selling thought, and so attractive in appearance that they would find almost

automatic application at the point of sale. We have great respect for the instinctive judgment of a good salesman regarding the advertising of his firm. If he is not enthusiastic about it, there are two strikes on it going in.

4. To observe the fitness of things in terms of all-around good taste and to keep the advertising 'in character' with management thought and action.
5. To take the attitude that there is inherent drama in the product itself rather than leaning on tricks, devices, 'techniques' or borrowed interests. This also involves keeping the advertising *relevant*—shunning irrelevant approaches in headlines and illustrations, no matter how clever they are.
6. Wherever possible, to make important use of the advertiser's name and package rather than trying to *lure* people into reading your message.

   They know it's an ad and they like to look at good ads. Why try to fool them?
7. To keep it simple.
8. To know the rules but to be willing to break them. This involves a sense of good timing—an important factor in successful advertising.
9. To have the courage to go back to the client with a better idea whenever you can find one, even if he has already okayed the ad and is well satisfied with it. This involves a lot of wear and tear and is often expensive for the agency, but it usually pays off.
10. To keep our place free from prima donnas; to subordinate pride of authorship to a better overall result to which many different people may contribute.
11. To be human without being cute or smart alecky; to be sincere without being pompous.
12. To fight for what we believe in, regardless of contrary client opinion, providing our conviction is based on sound reasoning, accurate facts, and inspired thought; to be intellectually honest.

BASELINE: When you're reaching for the stars you won't always get one, but you don't come up with a handful of mud either.

Workout

Study the FCB and Leo Burnett ads carefully and give brief answers to the questions that follow *in the space provided.* This way, when you come to the end of this book, you can turn back to your answers and see if you still hold the same views.

1. Do you think the message in these ads is relevant today?
2. Who is the Target Audience?
3. Is there anything in the copy which you found difficult to understand?
4. What is your response to the ads?
5. Given the chance, which agency would you join and why?
6. Which statements (if any) in these ads do you strongly object to and why?
7. Re-do these ads by cutting the copy in half and replacing the cut copy with a visual element. Have you improved on the original?

10

Tone of Voice

You are sitting in the second class compartment of a local commuter train travelling from one of Mumbai's suburbs into the city centre. Close your eyes for a few minutes and use your ears. Instantly the scene comes alive. You will distinguish voices talking in many languages. You will know if the voice is that of a woman, child or man. You will even be able to judge the mood of the people by listening to their *Tone of Voice*. The soft crooning of a mother with a baby at her breast. The harassed ticket collector speaking in a sharp voice. A beggar whining for a coin. Two men arguing furiously about politics. Some teenage girls are giggling in the corner, they sound young and happy—you may assume they are discussing their boyfriends or how to spend the summer vacation.

Tone of Voice often communicates so much more than even the expression on your face. You are constantly engaged in changing your tone of voice as you speak. You admonish a naughty child in

one tone, and use another if the child is frightened and needs comforting. You can use Tone of Voice to allay fears, give orders, raise an alarm, evoke pity. In short, you use Tone of Voice to generate a mood, or to impel action.

So when you communicate through an ad, first decide what Tone of Voice you wish to use when talking to your target audience. What sort of feelings do you wish to inspire in the housewife's heart? Should you inspire confidence, or evoke fear? What sort of voice will make the reader of your ad eventually respond as you want him or her to respond? Tone of Voice is a crucial element in designing your communication message.

It is the copy that carries the Tone of Voice, but the visual must echo the same tone. It would be discordant to talk to the reader in a soft, gentle voice, while showing a picture of Hiroshima going up in smoke, unless of course you are aiming for a deliberate shock effect. (Techniques can sometimes be the Big Idea). As a general rule, both copy and visual should reflect the same Tone of Voice. You can break this rule as you become a master copywriter! But until such happy time, remember Tone of Voice is one of the foundation stones in brand building.

Cossy Rosario's example of how Tone of Voice can be used to impel action is branded in my memory. He said: "June, if I wanted to get you off your chair, I could do it in a number of ways. I order you to do so: *Stand up!*. Or I could request you: *Please try and get some exercise; you're putting on weight.* Or I could say: *Hey, there's some free beer being served in the next room!*"

Which Tone of Voice would you be most inclined to respond to?

Tone of Voice is closely tied up with the *appeals* we use in our campaign strategy. You will hear more about this in the next chapter on the Proposition. It also comes into play when you begin to actually think up ideas for your campaign. Ditto for the target audience to whom you are addressing your message. The thing to bear in mind is that all these *foundation stones* have to fit neatly into one another. As any good architect knows, the more aligned your stones are, the better and stronger the building. Ever wondered how they got those massive blocks of stone in the Pyramids of Egypt to fit so perfectly? They have lasted centuries.

As an exercise, think about this sentence:

I could murder you

What Tone of Voice would you use if you were talking to

- Your lover
- Your boss
- Your son
- Your grandmother

What do you imagine would be the circumstances in each case that would impel you to say these words?

As a second exercise, imagine you are the Queen of England.

She has just heard that the Third World War has broken out in Europe. How do you think she would convey the news to

- Prince Philip
- The British public
- Bill Clinton
- Her youngest grandchild

Tone of Voice sharpens the imagination and breeds ideas.

Here are two copy-based ads where Tone of Voice is the actual idea—thus eliminating the trite visuals that generally accompany tourism advertising. Ultimately, all beaches look the same, as do palm trees, blue seas and five-star poolsides. That is why these ads for Australian Tourism are among my favourites. The bonus is an element most writers never dream of using consciously—poetry in language.

Rhythm and Metre

In the two typographical ads that follow, for Australian Tourism, the body copy is truly brilliant. The text reflects the tone and flavour of the headline right through. You do not miss the visual element because *the writing shows it all*. The copy is worth studying. Note the differences in rhythm and metre in each case. The first one 'War Sigma Tilda' has a waltz beat to it. The 'Horse Rice' ad spurs you on at a gallop.

And to top it all, the body copy follows Aesop Glim's Six-Step structure (which you will learn about in Chapter 16), neatly finessing competition. Need I say more?

First Ad

HEADLINE: *War Sigma Tilda*

BODY COPY: You haven't heard it right until you hear "Waltzing Matilda" sung with an Australian accent. And there's no better way than in person in the Land Down Under.

"War Sigma Tilda."

Australia The Wonder Down Under

Say around a cozy campfire in the outback waiting for the billy tea to boil.

Or down on a farm during a stay with a family that'll make you feel like one of them.

Even around a piano at a luxury hotel in one of our cosmopolitan cities.

In the meantime, why not waltz through the helpful 120-page Australian Vacation Travel Guide that's yours free when you call 1-800-445-3000 and ask for Dept. GEO11.

Then come and share a song with us.

BASELINE: Australia. The Wonder Down Under

"Horse Rice."

Australia The Wonder Down Under

Second Ad

HEADLINE: *Horse Rice*

BODY COPY: Eh, rice for horses? No, Australian for horse race. Sports are a way of life for us. And horse racing is our biggest spectator sport.

Ever wonder who introduced the photo-finish camera? Or the pari-mutuel machine? We Aussies did.

And there's a whole continent of wonder down here. Just waiting for you to visit. So how about it, mate? Call toll-free 1-800-445-3000 and ask for Dept. GEO10 for your free 120-page Australian Vacation Travel Guide.

Then come and see our horses rice.

BASELINE: Australia. The Wonder Down Under

The Tone of Voice used is typically strine (a corruption of 'Australian') as those of you who have visited this country will immediately recognise. Aussies pronounce the word 'day' as 'die', 'mate' as 'mite'. They slur the language and it is not easy to understand English as it is spoken Down Under. The ads use the unmistakable Aussie accent charmingly, as a jumping-off idea. At the same time, they capture the casual, breezy approach to the Australian way of life.

Workout

1. Select at least 10 press or magazine ads which appeal to you.
2. Try and figure out who the ad is addressed to. Write a brief paragraph on the target audience in each case.
3. What Tone of Voice is used in each ad?
4. Do you think it is one that the target audience would respond to?
5. Do you think the Tone of Voice is one that you may expect to be used by the brand being advertised?

Put these ads in your Assignment File for future use.

11

Brand Image

Some time ago a young CEO of a newly accredited agency observed in the course of a workshop, "I wonder if there is a difference between Brand Image and Brand Personality." I replied there certainly was—and to answer the question turned to my dependable dictionary. Webster's revealed that the word *image* has various meanings, among the most relevant to our purpose being:

- IMPRESSION: a mental conception held in common by members of a group and symbolic of a basic attitude and orientation (e.g., a disorderly courtroom can seriously tarnish a community's image of justice . . . Herbert Brownell)
- IDEA, CONCEPT: a vivid or graphic representation or description
- FIGURE OF SPEECH: a popular conception (as of a person, institution or nation) projected especially through the mass media (as in projecting a corporate image of brotherly love and concern . . . R.C. Buck)

Under *personality*, Webster's offered the following:

- the complex of characteristics that distinguishes an individual or a nation or group
- the totality of an individual's behavioural and emotional tendencies
- the organisation of the individual's character traits, attitudes or habits

On reflection, the thought that floated up was, "I see, personality is what I am, and image is what other people think I am". It might be useful to apply this insight to the process of branding and brand building, which is crucial when it comes to understanding *Brand Image*.

Branding or brand naming a product is almost like christening a baby. Or like a naming ceremony. Give a child a name like Jane, and she will probably grow up plain and homely (unless of course she changes the spelling and becomes Jayne Mansfield!) On the other hand, Jane Austen is still the Victorian spinster who never moved out of her village but wrote with keen perception about human nature as observed in her immediate surroundings. Call your son Arjun or Deepak, and he probably will not grow up to be a Laloo or Mulayam! Would Marilyn Monroe have become the sex symbol of the century if she had retained her original name of Norma Jean Baker?

Brand Image is not built in a day. It is cultivated over years.

A woman of 40 has more poise than an average woman of 20. She has become familiar with herself; she knows what she wants, what looks good on her and what she is comfortable doing. She may have even acquired an image which dovetails with her personality—or not. Some very outwardly ice-cool maidens are sizzling volcanoes underneath! There was a time when every woman wore a bouffant hairdo, every young man sported an Elvis puff, whether it suited their personality or not. But the hairstyles did aid their image.

Hairstyles and similar fads promote short-lived images tried on for size. For a product to develop a durable Brand Image, it has to stay the course much longer in the market, be tested through consumer samples, and gain popular approval over a period of time. A product, too, has to be tried on for size by the Target Audience. Something like having to visit your tailor several times when you are being fitted for a dinner jacket/*sherwani*/tuxedo.

Brands are like children, and to some degree they may inherit the personality traits of their parents and their environment. Their *sex* too is predetermined in the research laboratory. Strangely enough, sometimes the *personality* may be male, but the *image* female. Once an agency was pitching for the Cadbury chocolates account. When the discussion turned to Brand Image, the agency felt that Cadbury (the company) was a sober gentleman in a grey suit, but Cadbury Gems (one in the range of its branded chocolates) was unisex, young and bright.

For the purpose of this writing we are only concerned with Brand Image. As you grow in stature and experience in the profession you will doubtless have occasion to discuss the nuances of brand terminology in finer detail in the boardroom. I have always felt that the higher rungs are more fraught with labels, jargon, split hairs and fog rather than rarefied atmosphere!

Get it clear that Brand Image is one of the main building blocks for a brand, if not actually the cornerstone. It is what the consumer perceives a brand to be. If you want to change the consumer's perceptions, you will have to modify your Brand Image.

Spend a little time thinking about Brand Image.

Just for fun, try this little exercise. Jot down in under 50 words how you would describe the following:

Taj Mahal Hotel, Mumbai	Gwalior Suiting
Oberoi Hotel, Mumbai	Raymonds Suiting
Le Meridien, New Delhi	OCM Suiting
Air-India	Reliance
British Airways	Mahindra & Mahindra
Singapore Airlines	ABB

Hypothetically you might write:

HOTEL X is an old dowager who wears discreet jewellery and is always clad in black bombazine skirts which trail the ground.

She has an air of faded elegance, very old money, and lavender water. She sometimes toys with the notion of having her face lifted, and she has grit enough to do what she is thinking of.

HOTEL Y is a flashy johnny-come-lately; dresses like a tart, her jewellery is flamboyant and her diamonds are paste. She is loud-mouthed, vulgar, extravagant and flaunts her new money. All the same, you cannot help admiring her effrontery.

HOTEL Z is a happy, casual teenager with a lithe figure who loves swimming and rock music. You will find her racing along a crowded beach in a bikini with a gaggle of other similarly-clad girls. How they enjoy the admiring glances and wolf whistles that follow them all the way to the barbecue!

Note that in speaking of Brand Image a certain target audience, with its own peculiar orientations and attitudes is being addressed. For instance, you may have observed the kind of clientele that haunts the Taj or the Oberoi five-star hotels in Mumbai. You may even have spoken to people about their perceptions of each hotel, and asked them why they patronise them.

People may visit these hotels for the same reasons (the service, the food, the location), but they will still carry different mental impressions of them. Why? Perhaps they have seen the advertising, or the decor has made a subtle impression, or the attitude of the hotel personnel, or even the type of people they see checking in. All this adds up to the Brand Image. A certain class or group of people feel comfortable in the Taj. Another type will not stay anywhere but at the Oberoi. Why?

The copywriter is always asking these questions.

The more curious you are about consumer behaviour, the more likely you are to create a campaign that works.

When you construct the Brand Image for a product, you base it on what you know of the people who are going to actually buy the product. You do not care what anyone else thinks. However, it is very important what your consumer thinks. That is why billions of rupees are spent on testing consumer reactions to a brand. Old brands will not change their packaging even a bit without first checking with the consumer. People are creatures of habit; and they do not care for unexpected changes in familiar brands.

If you look at the brands which have been around for ages, you will notice that there may be a difference in the advertising done in 1940 and that done in 1990. But the changes will have been so gradual and imperceptible that the consumer has hardly been aware of them.

So a brand grows and changes like a child grows and changes. You do not see the changes every day, but after a year or so you sit up and say, "Gosh, how he's grown, he looks just like his father, or mother or whoever." It is the same child: he is taller, or thinner, or fatter, or has grown a moustache.

But—it is still the same person!

Brand Image is also based on the very human response to first impressions. Although we are told never to judge a book by its cover, we do. (I cannot count the hours we spent deciding on the cover design of this one!)

Brand Image answers the question: What will people think? And also, what do we want people to think?

Brand Image has to evoke a desired response. We want people—our target consumer—to think well of us. To believe certain truths (or untruths!) about us. And so we cultivate our image. Alyque Padamsee once took me out to lunch at the Air-India cafeteria when I was a very junior writer. To pass what must have been a tedious hour he wove the conversation around a scheme: how to get me married.

First he talked about me, and my qualities (the product) and then about dressing nicely and wearing a little make-up (the packaging), and getting an older woman friend (he mentioned Mubi!) to escort me to parties and places where I would meet the right kind of guy (the media). There was a lot more, of course, but I remember the part about dressing up . . . and being seen in the right places. Then it would be obvious to the target audience that I was in the market for a husband! In this way he led me into a lesson in Brand Image. (I could not have learned it very well, as I am still on the shelf!)

So much goes into the creation of Brand Image. The name of the product, in the first place. Its quality and price. Its packaging most of all. And where the product is sold (grocery shops or supermarkets or boutiques), and what media is used to advertise the product. A brand is known by the company it keeps. The medium is the message. Everything adds up. So it is important to make a sort of mental picture of how you want your product to be perceived by the consumer, i.e., target audience.

In designing the advertising too, you have to be sure of what tone of voice you decide to use, what typeface reflects the tone of voice best, which models are best suited to the desired image and what they should wear, what colours ought to be selected to be associated with the brand. Everything adds up. You will find many books on the subject of Brand Image.

In this regard, you will be wise to consider the *Competition,* about which very little has been said so far. Imagine that your product, a toothpaste, is just one of many other toothpaste brands in the market. Each is selling itself on different copy platforms and speaking in various tones of voice to different target audiences. If you study the advertising done by competitve brands over several years, you will get a fair idea of their Brand Images.

Take the case of the Taj and the Oberoi hotels. They are competitive 'brands', and if you stop to think about it, you will agree that each of them is perceived quite differently by the consumer. Remember the little exercise (50-word descriptions) you did earlier in this chapter?

So also with almost every other product or service or company. It is important to bear this in mind while reading the chapters that follow.

This might be a good place to mention *generic* advertising. When a brand has been established for a long, long time, as the first and only, perhaps, then all succeeding competitive brands and even *non-brands* tend to be confused with the mother brand. For instance, the case of Dalda *vanaspati* (hydrogenated vegetable oil). Dalda became the generic household word for vanaspati, so even unbranded, spurious vanaspati sold loose at the grocer shop was referred to as Dalda—which did not make Hindustan Lever marketing men very happy!

To add to the confusion, many consumers and shopowners called Dalda . . . *ghee*—which is quite incorrect. Ghee (clarified butter) is made from milk, while Dalda is made from hydrogenated vegetable oils.

This reminds me of how Wipro's Sunflower vanaspati was launched—a tiny David bravely taking on the Goliath, Hindustan Lever's Dalda.

Wipro wanted to break into the Maharashtra market, then the stronghold of Dalda. Till the late-70s, Sunflower was a local brand in

Ahmedabad (Gujarat), Bhopal and Indore (Madhya Pradesh). HTA took up the challenge and created a campaign in English and Hindi that resulted in Sunflower making deep inroads into the Dalda market share. Having said so much, I leave you to think about what HTA's creative tactics were, and will reveal all in the chapter on Brand Positioning. (There, a clue!)

Workout

1. Try writing 50 words each on the Brand Image for well-known products, institutions and services.

   Do at least 10. Do not worry about being right or wrong.
2. Choose three products which belong to the same genre—example, three brands of soaps, three brands of lipsticks, three brands of computers, three brands of refrigerators, three brands of cars, and so on. Notice in what ways the Brand Image differs in the same product category. What elements, in your view, contribute to these differences?

   The wider your sample, the more you will learn that every brand has a different image, or should have. Where there is a sameness to the brands, we call it me-too advertising, which is often the case. Me-too advertising should be avoided because it can confuse your brand with someone else's and hence affect sales. For the moment, just concentrate on choosing products which have clearly defined messages and strong brand images.
3. How does the (Public) Image differ from the (Private) Personality of these well-known people?

   Mahatma Gandhi
   Bill Gates
   Imran Khan
   Tony Blair
   Elizabeth Taylor
   Rajiv Gandhi
   Nelson Mandela
   Sachin Tendulkar
   Amitabh Bachchan
   Khushwant Singh
   President Clinton
   Princess Diana
   Mother Teresa
   The Dalai Lama

12

The Proposition

Rosser Reeves, who wrote *Reality in Advertising* (circa 1970), coined the term Unique Selling Proposition (USP) which is still in use in various disguises. The *Proposition* is essentially the basic message which the advertiser wishes to communicate to his target audience. One of the hardest things in writing copy is to agree on what the advertiser wants to say, with all the nuances sounding right to everyone concerned. Alyque Padamsee made it simple for the copywriter. He came up with a definition of the Proposition which was so easy to remember it is unforgettable. It often saved my creative neck. I put it in the same league as Einstein's $e = mc^2$. This is how he put it:

Proposition = Consumer Benefit + Reason Why

In other words, every advertising message ought to contain

- a benefit to consumers
- a good reason for them to believe it is true

For instance, if you tell people Pears soap keeps your skin as soft and smooth as a baby's, you could believably justify the promise by saying *because it contains pure glycerine.* Of course, just exactly how much glycerine is a secret. But that is not the point; consumers want a reason, and a reason they will get. So,

Proposition = Consumer Benefit + Reason Why

Make it the basis of all your advertising communication. In other words, when attempting to develop the Proposition or message for your advertising (whether in press or in any other medium) you must give the target audience a *benefit* (what is in it for me) and then a *good reason* to believe you (substantiate your promise).

Take, for instance, a toilet soap like Lux. The slogan which is now synonymous with Lux advertising all over the world (and has been unchanged for decades) is the famous . . . "beauty soap of the film stars". What was the original Proposition mooted by the agency and the makers of Lux, the Unilever company? Perhaps it was so long ago that no one remembers. But you may try to *derive the proposition* by studying the combination of the headline/visual/baseline.

Stories Gita Siddarth's mirror could tell!
LUX
PINK
She uses almond oil for her skin.
Writes notes in lipstick for her husband.
Plaits her hair with strings of jasmine.
Uses nothing but LUX to keep her complexion beautiful.
"I keep my complexion soft and lovely with LUX," says Gita Siddarth.
Gita Siddharth
Pure, mild LUX-
beauty soap of the film stars
A quality product by Hindustan Lever Ltd.
HLL.5053

While looking at a Lux Toilet Soap ad, you usually see a close-up of a beautiful film star's face, her soft and creamy complexion, a picture of the soap, a headline that is usually in the form of a testimonial from the star, signed off with the baseline: *beauty soap of the film stars.* These are the elements that strike you immediately. The total advertisement is the creative expression of the basic (hidden) Proposition; and the creative expression is the sugar coating on the Proposition pill. So much so, the potential user is persuaded to believe that Lux soap will immediately produce a film-star complexion in even the plainest face!

Remember, there may be more than one creative expression of any given Proposition. There may be two or three or a hundred. But the creative expression will always reflect the original Proposition. (More about this later).

Coming back to the Lux ad. From the elements of visual, headline and baseline it is possible to derive the message intended to be conveyed. To do this, try to isolate

- The Consumer Benefit
- The Reason Why

The Consumer Benefit appears to be: a beautiful, soft complexion.

The Reason Why (basis for the promise) appears to be: a gentle soap specially formulated for tender facial skin.

Put together, you might derive the Proposition for Lux soap as being:

Gentle Lux toilet soap cares for your complexion beautifully.

The creative team has converted this proposition into what you see in the ad: a beautiful film star endorsing the gentle, caring properties of Lux toilet soap.

This creative expression is extremely believable to the target audience (women of all ages), as all over the world a film star is regarded as being beautiful and having lovely skin. And if a film star can endorse Lux, why, it must be good for your complexion. So, you get the makings of a campaign with universal, or at least global, appeal.

Why Lever Brothers decided to use the film star beauty concept for Lux toilet soap rather than any other creative expression is lost to history. But it may be safely assumed that it was not the only creative idea presented to the client by the agency.

Warm-ups

1. Imagine you are part of the original team asked to create a press advertisement for Lux toilet soap based on the Proposition derived above. The client, Hindustan Lever, has asked you to present at least *five different ways to express the proposition*. None of them, obviously, must use a film star.

   What would be your response ?
2. Keep a lookout for ads from your daily newspaper or favourite magazine that catch your eye.

   Derive the Proposition you think is the basis of their creative expression (i.e., from the headline/visual/baseline only). Do not bother with the body copy for the moment. (Generally 90% of selling the product is done in these three basic elements; the fine print does the rest when you have the reader's attention.) In each case, break down the Proposition according to the Padamsee formula.

This exercise is very important because it is the springboard for all sorts of advertising. Progress to the next chapter when you are sure you have mastered the art of writing a good Proposition for your product.

Some Famous Headlines

Each of the well-known headlines in this section has been based on a Proposition. You will soon notice that the Proposition has *many possible expressions*. That is to say, there are many ways of rendering the same thought. You can write half a dozen or more headlines on the same Proposition. The greater your imagination and copywriting skills, the more numerous your list of headline alternatives.

In the memorable list below, the advertiser had a basic message for the consumer, and the headlines ultimately selected are each the *best possible expression* of the Proposition, at least in the view of the advertiser and the agency concerned. These campaigns have become classics in their genre. We say that campaign ideas which last and last have *mileage*. One more thing, it is not always possible to derive the full proposition from the headline alone; the visual contributes to the complete message in varying degrees. Sometimes the Proposition is expressed 50:50 through copy and visual, sometimes 60:40, or 80:20, or even 20:80.

In the examples below, what do you think is the basic message or Proposition in each case? Use your imagination to supply the visual element.

Headline	*Proposition*
■ HOW TO WIN FRIENDS AND INFLUENCE PEOPLE (Dale Carnegie's famous book—this was first advertised in press and sold through mail order)	Dale Carnegie's book contains all the secrets of success and popularity.
■ FILL IT, SHUT IT, FORGET IT (Hero Honda)	
■ THE PAUSE THAT REFRESHES (Coca-Cola)	

- SOME COMPLEXIONS NEVER GROW UP
  (Pears soap)
- AT 60 MPH THE ONLY SOUND YOU'LL
  HEAR IN THE NEW ROLLS ROYCE IS
  THE TICKING OF THE CLOCK
- EARLY MORNING FRESHNESS AND FRAGRANCE
  THAT LASTS ALL DAY LONG
  (Ponds Dreamflower talc)
- LIVE LIFE KINGSIZE
  (Four Square cigarettes)
- WE ARE LIKE THAT ONLY
  (CHANNEL V)
- PUT A TIGER IN YOUR TANK!
  (Esso)
- WHITENING STRIKES WITH RIN!
  (detergent bar)

As part of this exercise, try to write alternative headlines expressing the Proposition you have derived from the original headline. Remember:

Proposition = Consumer Benefit plus the Reason Why

Techniques of art, layout, typography, radio and television production, and fine writing are important. Nevertheless, they are secondary to the basic selling Proposition around which the ad or commercial is built. It is not the purpose of the ad or commercial to make the reader or listener say "My, what a clever ad". It is the purpose of advertising to make the reader or listener say, "I believe I'll buy one when I'm shopping tomorrow," or "I wonder if Joe could get one for me wholesale?"

The place to start in advertising is the basic selling appeal. An appeal that fulfils some existing need in the prospect's mind, an appeal that can be readily understood and believed.

—Morris Hite (1988, p. 206)

Workout

Select 10 ads which appeal to you. Choose them for their clarity and punch. At this stage, ignore the body copy (set in small type). Make sure the brand name and product shot are clearly shown and the ad has a headline, a visual and a baseline.

Choose ads in the *fast-moving consumer goods* (fmcg) category, to start with. Do not pick a corporate ad or a financial ad. The brand should be something in everyday use—like talcum powder or a breakfast cereal. Now figure out what the advertiser is offering the consumer (benefit) and why he thinks the consumer will believe him (reason why). Do *you* believe him?

Points to consider in each ad:

- Try and understand the *message* of the advertiser. *What* is he trying to say?
- *Who* do you think is being addressed?
- What *tone of voice* is being used?
- What impression do you get of the *brand*?
- What particular *attribute* of the product is being promoted?
- What *consumer need* is being met?
- Why should the consumer *believe* the advertiser?
- What is the *competition* saying?

Blocking out the body copy, spend a few minutes on each advertisement, giving special attention to the visual. Try and derive the Proposition based on the information you get from just the headline/subhead/visual/baseline. Do *not* read the body copy or text. Write down what you think the Proposition is for each ad. Remember:

Proposition = Consumer Benefit + Reason Why

13

The Brand Positioning Statement

You must be asking yourself: proposition, expressions of the proposition, and now Positioning—what are all these words about? They can be quite confusing. Especially when sometimes the *Brand Positioning Statement* may also be the Proposition, but the Proposition may not always be the Positioning!

Let me try and explain what Positioning a brand is. One dark cloudless night when the power fails, go out and look at the sky. It will be filled with stars—and you can clearly see some important constellations, or note the *position* of Antares, or Castor and Pollux, or Orion's Belt. They are so accurately placed, navigators have been charting their course by them for thousands of years.

Just like the stars, brands have their place or position in the market, and more importantly, in the mind of the consumer. It is part of the advertising task to *position the brand* correctly and accurately. Take, for instance, the toothpaste market with a purely imaginary brand called *Dentium* as our product. The toothpaste market is our 'sky' or universe, and the various brands of toothpaste the 'stars'.

If we make a list of the various toothpaste brands and the positions they occupy we might come up with something like this:

COLGATE	fights bad breath and tooth decay
FORHANS	specially formulated for gums
PROMISE	the only toothpaste with clove oil
CLOSE-UP	clearly for young people who want fresh clean breath
DENTIUM	?????????

The question the creative team asks is, "Which position or slot can our brand Dentium possibly occupy?" Obviously, you want to position Dentium in a slot not already occupied by the others. So you start thinking of other slots or positions; perhaps you will have to *create a slot* for Dentium if an empty one does not exist.

When I applied for a job at Lintas, there were no vacancies. But after I was given two copy tests, mind you, two not one, the second being harder than the first, Alyque Padamsee decided to *create a vacancy* for me. This meant that he saw a possible use for me within the agency, a future need that might perhaps arise for a writer with a chaotic mind who was christened *a walking Thesaurus* by Cossy Rosario. The other trainee was a music buff who spent most of his time out of the office and in a recording studio (he was the dj for the Close-up Round-up sponsored radio programme), causing Alyque to call him *the mythical Jai Rao*!

In the case of Dentium, the job is quite easily done. The team discovers there is no other toothpaste in the market which contains calcium, besides delivering the 'goods' on whiteness and hygiene. A possible niche exists for a calcium-based toothpaste to maintain tooth enamel. (This is purely hypothetical, so take it with a pinch of . . . uh, calcium). So it might be conceivable to *create a vacancy* for Dentium in the consumer's mind, by drawing attention to the need for calcium to keep teeth strong.

You might end up with a Brand Positioning like:

New Dentium—India's first calcium-fortified toothpaste

If that sounds very much like a Proposition, you would be half right. In a chapter that follows, the example of Dentium is taken a step further, to derive a Proposition for this brand.

The Saga of Sunflower

Meanwhile, to complete the story of the Wipro company's Sunflower vanaspati (hydrogenated vegetable oil) versus Hindustan Lever's Dalda vanaspati. HTA's campaign for Sunflower was purely a successful exercise in Brand Positioning. Although as the copywriter on the account, I had arrived at the idea right from the start, I felt that doing some hands-on research in Bhopal and Indore—the heart of Sunflower country—would back up my hunch. (I am a great believer in research.)

So, accompanied by a lady executive from IMRB (Indian Market Research Bureau), who spoke Marathi and Gujarati, besides Hindi and English, I went off to spend three weeks in those Madhya Pradesh towns and surrounding areas. The client had already given us the Ahmedabad (Gujarat) research feedback. IMRB and I divided the areas we wanted to cover into sections and informally interviewed as many housewives and dealers as we could each day. The housewives were selected from all income groups and from all communities.

We made it a point to take a peek into the kitchens. Most of the ladies were only too glad to let us do so, to tell us about their families' food habits, and even to share a recipe. They answered questions about ghee versus vanaspati. The women we spoke to were mainly Sunflower users, and a few Dalda users. The common factor among both groups of women was their attitude to pure ghee (clarified butter), a vital ingredient in Indian cooking.

Pure ghee is expensive so we only use it for special occasions, like feasts, otherwise we use vanaspati.

Pure ghee is very healthy, very good, but eaten in excess gives you a tickle in the throat. So we use it sparingly.

All the women were convinced there was nothing to touch pure ghee as a cooking medium despite its drawbacks. It was obvious that here was *a position waiting to be filled*—one which the brand leader Dalda had not thought of occupying, because it was the first and probably a monopoly in the market. There was a possible slot for Sunflower—somewhere between pure ghee and Dalda!

And that is how HTA positioned Sunflower:

Next Best to Pure Ghee

The advertising (low budget!) was limited to one press ad—in Hindi and English, repeated several times. There were some hoardings and point of sale material. I cannot recall if there was a film. Anyway, Sunflower vanaspati was launched and eventually established itself even in the Dalda-dominated Mumbai market. A great example of how a strong Brand Positioning can help give a newcomer an identity.

Positioning a product simply means that you examine the product to determine just what it is you are offering, and to what kind of people, and how you want these people to think of the product. From these findings you begin to build your creative strategy.

To formulate the *Brand Positioning Statement*, you need to know as much as you can about the *three P's:*

1. **Product**
   - does it fill a definite need/desire?
   - are most users satisfied with it?
   - does it have any exclusive features?
   - is it of benefit to the user?
   - is it positioned correctly?
2. **Prospects**
   - men or women?
   - young, middle-aged, old?
   - rich, poor, average?
   - where do they live?
   - tastes in reading/tv/radio?
   - what do they know of the brand?

3. Purchases
- where do prospects buy the product?
- seasonal or special occasion?
- premeditated or impulsive?
- how does price compare with the competition?

The more you know, the more it shows, and the more accurate will be your Brand Positioning Statement. Astute planning, a simple selling proposition, and consistency in advertising have entrenched the following products firmly in today's marketplace. They are *well positioned* in the mind of the buying public.

Brand	*Positioned as*
CADILLAC	quality car
CHEVROLET	American car
VOLVO	rugged car
THE NEW YORK TIMES	thorough and authoritative newspaper
DAILY NEWS	people's newspaper
HOWARD JOHNSON	family eating place
MCDONALDS	the burger place
VIRGINIA SLIMS	cigarettes for women
CHIVAS REGAL	expensive Scotch whiskey
AMERICAN TOURISTER	sturdy luggage
AT&T	the telephone company
IBM	the computer company
XEROX	the copying company
STEINWAY	the piano company
POLAROID	instant photos
CREST	cavity-fighting toothpaste
MIDAS	the muffler-installing company

Advertising is criticised on the ground that it can manipulate consumers to follow the will of the advertiser. The weight of evidence denies this ability. Instead, evidence supports the position that advertising, to be successful, must understand or anticipate basic human needs and wants and interpret available goods and services in terms of their want-satisfying abilities. This is the very opposite of manipulation.

—Charles H. Sandage (1972)

Workout

1. Can you think of brands which have carved out a niche for themselves in the Indian marketplace? Briefly describe the Positioning of each.
2. Select three established brands and write Positioning statements for each of these categories:

fast foods/icecreams	steel
cold drinks	furnishings
cigarettes	travel agents
suitings	airlines
saris	hotels
household appliances	boarding schools
television sets	newspapers
department stores	shoes
pens	electronic equipment
computers	chocolates
tea	jewellery
coffee	fashion designers

For example:

Category	*Brand*	*Positioned as*
fast foods/ icecreams	McDonalds	
	Pizza Hut	
	Baskin Robbins	
	Vadilal	
	Kwality	
cold drinks	Thums Up	
	Coke	
	Pepsi	
	Mirinda	
	Canada Dry	
cigarettes	Marlboro	
	Four Square	
	Benson and Hedges	
	Wills	
	Charminar	
and so on.		

14

Brainstorming and the Big Idea

In his book *Ogilvy on Advertising* (1985, p. 16) David Ogilvy writes, "It takes a big idea to attract the attention of consumers and get them to buy your product. Unless your advertising contains a big idea, it will pass like a ship in the night. I doubt if more than one campaign in a hundred contains a big idea."

One way to arrive at a *Big Idea*—or any idea at all—is the time-hallowed one described here. At Lintas, a favourite pastime of bored or stuck copywriters was *Brainstorming*. This was always a nice occasion to share a cup of tea and let down one's hair and air a few gripes. Some senior creative people had no ego hassles about approaching one another in the privacy of their airconditioned cabins and saying, "Hey Noel (or Mubi or Joe or Shirley or Nina), I'm blocked.

Just can't seem to hit on the right idea. Help!" And it was always a pleasure to hear someone say, "Sure, anytime", and order that cup of tea. Thank you Joe, Noel, Nina, Shirley . . . if you are reading this. Mubi, God bless her, is making movies for the angels.

In other agencies, the practice of knocking ideas around with another creative person may be actually frowned upon. One agency head thinks it is a way of *wasting time.* Some copywriters just have to be alone, locked away in some tiny closet, (one used to hide in the loo!), to *ideate* and come up with the headline to end all headlines.

Once I shared a small cabin with a writer of the loo type. There was only one window in the room and I wondered if he would claim his right to a part of it. But no. He turned his desk to face a blank wall, stuffed his ears with cotton wool and got down to his work, his back to me. I realised that this was not a writer who would welcome a 'brainstorm'—though he was friendly enough at other times.

There are to my mind two kinds of brainstorming. The *disorganised* kind and the *disciplined* kind. The first can prove useful when you have been working on a campaign for a long time and need to unwind. Your mind seems to be going round in circles and you need the help of someone else to break the monotony. Of this sort of brainstorming one need only say it is a technique which should be used with discretion or it could just become a gossip session.

Disciplined brainstorming is more productive and effective, a useful tool. Here creativity is actually inspired and channelled. Usually a group of people take part in such a session, which is meant to achieve a particular purpose. The objective could be anything.

- The agency is pitching for a new account. The creative director calls in all the teams and briefs them. They toss ideas about until some definite approaches to the problem come to light. Then each team may be given an approach to work on. Time is of the essence.

The presentation is tomorrow. The agency is going to be up all night. Brainstorming at the initial stage is a shortcut to firming up on direction. *No waste of time here.*

- It could be an exercise in brand naming. An old client is about to launch a new product. He has the prototype ready—all the parameters are set, but nobody is satisfied with the name thought up by the marketing director's wife. Agency is called in and briefed. Then we are off and running. In the same time that it would take an individual writer to come up with say 50 acceptable brand names, a group of five or six persons could come up with several hundred. You get a wider choice for the client in a shorter period.

You could call a disciplined brainstorm for any number of reasons. But here again discretion is advised—or you could end up using the tool as a crutch.

How to Brainstorm

Usually there is a moderator in the group, someone senior who can keep order and also give direction in case the participants show signs of straying off course. Normally, the atmosphere is free and informal. No one is cramped. You are encouraged to say what you want without fear of criticism. Sometimes, even an asinine remark can spark off a great thought by some other writer. Silence is allowed, but rarely reigns at a brainstorm session. There ought to be a reliable individual present to take notes. Or better still, a hidden tape recorder; but a discerning individual is best. A lot of nonsense could take up tape time; it would be a tedious task to separate the wheat from the chaff.

Alex Osborn (of the American agency Batten, Barton, Durstine and Osborn) has written some great books on creativity. In *Your Creative Power* he has a couple of chapters that go as follows:

- Two heads are better than one, but not always
- How to organise a squad to create ideas

A quote from the latter:

"Group brainstorming needs a few simple ground rules, and the leader must make sure that these are understood by all present. So, in addition to outlining the problem, he should explain at the start:

- *Judicial judgment is ruled out:* Criticism of ideas will be withheld till the next day.
- *Wildness is welcomed:* The crazier the idea, the better; it's easier to tone down than to think up.
- *Quantity is wanted:* The more ideas we pile up, the more likelihood of winners.
- *Combination and improvement are sought:* In addition to contributing ideas of our own, let's suggest how another's idea can be turned into a better idea; or how two or more ideas can be joined into still another idea."

Osborn also speaks elsewhere of the *subject* for a brainstorm. He suggests that it is kept *simple and specific.* Giving people more than one topic or problem to think of simultaneously proves confusing and unproductive.

Creative brainstorming recharges fatigued imaginations even if there are disciplines. People should not feel cramped. They must feel as if they are playing a game and having some fun. The best ideas are generated when people feel encouraged and not under pressure to perform.

Of course, there are times when the pressure of a deadline also generates ideas, as when a presentation is due. Then the adrenalin starts flowing and all those stored-up ideas suddenly come flooding to the surface. My own method of 'unsticking' myself if I come up with a blank is to go home and sleep. This is when I know I am not getting anywhere because my brain is full of data about the product and has not had a chance to auto-sift it. This sifting process seems to get done while I sleep. I have learned to trust this method because it works for me. Some of my most inspired campaigns have been written after a good night's sleep!

Cossy Rosario called getting a great idea the *'aha factor!'* A Big Idea should tease and provoke the reader into amazing himself when he stumbles on the solution on his own. Alyque Padamsee described creativity in copywriting as taking two unrelated facts and putting them together to make something brand new (no pun intended). Like sticking a real-life automobile onto a hoarding with Araldite, and saying simply, *"It also sticks handles to teapots."* That's a Big Idea with a lot of understatement.

Ideas come from breaking down barriers and breaking new ground. As copywriters learn to rearrange the facts and display them in a new light, we get others saying "Aha—wish I had thought of that!" The trick is to arm yourself with as many facts as you can, so you can play around with permutations and combinations. In his wonderful book, *Systematic Approach to Advertising Creativity*, Stephen Baker has a limbering-up exercise: 201 ways to get an Idea. It is reproduced here with permission.

201 Ways to Get An Idea

There is time for strict mental discipline. But there is also time for uninhibited mind stretching. The two approaches to problem-solving are not inconsistent, any more than following a fixed training schedule is with boxing. So, go ahead and loosen up once in a while. Improvise. Free-associate. Try a variety of approaches:

1. Turn it upside down (whatever 'it' happens to represent, as layout, words, picture, package, product, advertising campaign, marketing strategy).
2. Stretch it.
3. Shrink it.
4. Change its colour.
5. Make it bigger.
6. Make it smaller.
7. Make it round.
8. Make it square.
9. Make it longer.
10. Make it shorter.
11. Make it visual.
12. Make the most out of a circumstance.
13. Put it into words.
14. Put it to music.
15. Combine words and music.
16. Combine words, music and picture.
17. Combine picture and music.
18. Eliminate the words.
19. Eliminate the picture.
20. Silence it.
21. Use repetition.
22. Make it three-dimensional.
23. Make it two-dimensional.
24. Change the shape.
25. Change a part.
26. Make it into a set.
27. Make it a collector's item.
28. Sell it by subscription.
29. Sell it by subscription only.
30. Animate it.
31. Mechanize it.
32. Electrify it.
33. Make it move.
34. Reverse it.
35. Make it look like something else.
36. Give it texture.
37. Make it romantic.
38. Add nostalgic appeal.
39. Make it look old-fashioned.
40. Make it look futuristic.
41. Make it a part of something else.
42. Make it stronger.
43. Make it more durable.
44. Use symbolism.
45. Be realistic.
46. Use a new art style.
47. Change to photography.
48. Change to illustration.
49. Change the typefaces.
50. Tell your story by a picture caption.

51. Make the ad look like an editorial.
52. Make the editorial look like an ad.
53. Use a new advertising medium.
54. Invent a new advertising medium.
55. Make it hotter.
56. Make it cooler.
57. Add scent.
58. Change the scent.
59. Deodorise it.
60. Make it appeal to children.
61. Make it appeal to women.
62. Make it appeal to men.
63. Lower the price.
64. Raise the price.
65. Change the ingredients.
66. Add new ingredients.
67. Twist it.
68. Make it transparent.
69. Make it opaque.
70. Use a different background.
71. Use a different environment.
72. Glamorise it.
73. Use optical effects.
74. Use another material.
75. Add human interest.
76. Change consistency.
77. Put it in a different container.
78. Change the package.
79. Make it compact.
80. Miniaturise.
81. Maximise.
82. Eliminate.
83. Make it portable.
84. Make it collapsible.
85. Go to the extremes.
86. Summerise it.
87. Winterise it.
88. Personalise it.
89. Make it darker.
90. Illuminate it.
91. Make it glow.
92. Make it flicker.
93. Make it sparkle.
94. Make it light up.
95. Make it fluorescent.
96. Make it heavier.
97. Make it lighter.
98. Tie it in with a promotion.
99. Run a contest.
100. Run a sweepstake.
101. Make it 'junior' size.
102. Make it grow.
103. Split it.
104. Understate.
105. Exaggerate.
106. Sell it as a substitute.
107. Find a new use for it.
108. Subtract.
109. Divide.
110. Combine.
111. Use the obvious.
112. Rearrange the elements.
113. Lower it.
114. Raise it.
115. Divide it.
116. Mix it.
117. Translate it.
118. Speed it up.
119. Slow it down.
120. Make it fly.
121. Make it float.
122. Make it roll.
123. Pulverise it.
124. Cut it into pieces.
125. Put sex appeal into it.
126. Condense it.
127. Bend it.
128. Match it.
129. Tilt it.
130. Suspend it.
131. Make it stand upright.
132. Turn it inside out.
133. Turn it sideways.
134. Weave it.
135. Mask it.
136. Make it symmetrical.
137. Make it asymmetrical.
138. Partition it.
139. Pit one against another.
140. Sharpen it.
141. Change the contour.
142. Encircle it.
143. Frame it.
144. Coil it.
145. Fill it up.
146. Empty it.
147. Open it.
148. Misspell it.
149. Nickname it.
150. Seal it.
151. Transfer it.
152. Pack it.
153. Concentrate on it.
154. Spread it out.
155. Alternate it.
156. Solidify it.
157. Liquefy it.

158. Jellify it.
159. Soften it.
160. Harden it.
161. Vaporize it.
162. Intonate.
163. Make it narrower.
164. Make it wider.
165. Make it funny.
166. Make it satirical.
167. Use short copy.
168. Use long copy.
169. Attach an instruction sheet.
170. Find a second use.
171. Prefabricate it.
172. Sell it as a kit.
173. Purify it.
174. Sanitise it.
175. Make it more nourishing.
176. Put it in a bottle.
177. Put it in a can.
178. Put it in a box.
179. Put it in a jar.
180. Put it in a pot.
181. Wrap it.
182. Fold it.
183. Unfold it.
184. Extend credit.
185. Offer it free.
186. Offer it at cost.
187. Make a special offer.
188. Add comfort.
189. Offer protection.
190. Use a different texture.
191. Sweeten it.
192. Sour it.
193. Moisten it.
194. Dry it.
195. Dehydrate it.
196. Freeze it.
197. Project it.
198. Make it blander.
199. Make it more pungent.
200. Simplify it.
201. Combine any of the above.

—Baker (1979)

Ideas Spring from Facts, and Sometimes from Desperation

Facts lead to information, which leads to ideas. Anywhere and anytime. Two occasions come readily to mind. The Boots Company (makers of drugs and pharmaceuticals) was celebrating its Silver Jubilee and wanted a five-minute audio-visual for the Big Day. They asked HTA to create a curtain-raiser to show their appreciation of the people who worked for the company. Looking for an idea, I paid a visit to the Boots factory (when I want to buy time I insist on visiting factories). I am completely enthralled by machinery of any type, probably because I am the least mechanical of people. Even a lighter designed for use by the Seventh Fleet in a tropical storm fell to pieces in my hands.

What I noticed at the Boots factory was a great many lines running all over the place. They were pipelines—red, blue, green, yellow—carrying chemicals and solutions to various departments of manufacture. It all looked very interesting, those parallel colours, forming a sort of network through the offices and buildings. They reminded me of the intricate circulatory system of arteries and veins in the human body. And eureka! the Big Idea flashed.

The whole Boots Company suddenly seemed to me a corporate body: R&D was the head, sales and distribution its arms and legs, the torso was management and manufacturing. But at the heart of the corporate body, pulsating with life and energy, were the people, working away with diligence and regularity to make the whole company function as a living, breathing entity. The client bought the idea at once, and the show was a great hit. Mr Ghosal, who was then the chief executive of HTA, said it was among the very best audio-visuals he had ever seen—a real compliment.

The second occasion which stands out in memory was the HTA creative directors' annual meeting at one of Mumbai's five-star beach resorts. The Bombay, Delhi, Calcutta, Bangalore and Madras offices would present their work and plans. Being slightly ignorant of such matters (I had rejoined the company after a long break and forgotten what these events were all about), I took a swimsuit and an evening dress as my sole luggage. Ivan Arthur—then creative vice president of HTA and the organiser of the conference—was aghast. He hastily thrust some felt pens and acetate sheets into my witless hands, urging me to *do something!*

"For goodness' sake, do you know what the others will be showing? Hi-fi computer pyrotechnics . . . the offices are very competitive."

That night I scurried off to my room, sadly forfeiting the dinner and merriment on the sands under the starry skies. Acetate sheets, forsooth! No one had used these since the dinosaur age. I wondered if there would be such a thing as an epidiascope (overhead projector) on the premises but decided to worry about that later. Now I had to get to work on a presentation for the next day. Madras was on first.

Bombay and Delhi offices had already made their fabulous presentations—very slick and heady. I sat staring at the dozen acetate sheets with something akin to despair.

The theme of the three-day conference was *Leadership,* and we had been served large dollops of wisdom by: C L Proudfoot of ACC, Jaitirth (Jerry) Rao of Citibank, Alfred D'Souza, the music conductor of the Bandra Stopgaps, a police commissioner and the Swamiji of an ashram—whose names escape me. What could a mere creative director add to what superior minds had already covered, while still managing to convey the future plans and performance of the Madras office?

It was 11 p.m. when my glazed eyes fell on the only book I had brought along—Robert Schuller's collection of daily meditations on Bible verses. It was the book I shared with the creative department at the Monday morning meetings in the office, which always began with a few minutes' silence and a reading from this book. Although it was Christian in character, it had universal appeal for the copy/art people who belonged mainly to the Hindu faith.

As I flicked through the pages of Schuller's book, a line from the scriptures caught my eye, and I idly wrote it down on an acetate sheet. Under it I wrote a few words pertaining to Leadership. In this way, I filled up all the sheets; each started with a Bible verse and led up to the facts and figures about the Madras office's creative work. My pen flew, the hours flew, suddenly it was 2 a.m. and I was through. I turned off the light and slept the sleep of the satisfied.

The next day, the Bombay office was awarded the prize for the Best Creative Work of the Year. The Madras creative director's presentation got a standing ovation . . . and a special on-the-spot award from Ivan Arthur and Mike Khanna, the CEO. The hastily-written, Bible-based, anachronistic acetate sheet presentation had brought tears to many eyes. The Big Idea: a moving juxtaposition of faith and filthy lucre!

(Details of this presentation are in the chapter "Presenting to the Big Dads" on pp. 252–56.)

The golden rule:

All Ideas Begin with Information

There are many excellent books written on ideation and creativity by Edward de Bono (Lateral Thinking, Po beyond Yes and No), Alex Osborn and others. Read them for fun and to learn to ideate.

The following excerpt is from Making the Creative Process Work by Walter Joyce.

The creative process is above all an act. It's an act in which a man encounters a problem and becomes intensely involved with every facet of it. The inductive or intuitive process takes over. He begins to imagine more than there is ground for, and finds relationships between things that nobody else ever saw before. Out of this he sees a new unity in his world—a unity that solves his problem.

It must be obvious to any marketing-advertising man today that the creative process is no good to anybody unless it can be made to work. Furthermore, it is pretty generally agreed today that there is more creative capacity locked up inside people than they ever bring to bear on a problem. So the more a man can consciously bring this process to bear on his problem, the more of his creative capacities will be used.

Although sophisticated advertising men often resent step-by-step procedures, there still is no better way of learning a process—and being aware of putting it to work—than an orderly, step-by-step procedure. Putting the creative process to work has been separated here into three phases.

The first phase is rather like a launching pad. A man who's tackling a problem, for example, would do well to examine his background: his education, his current reading and study, and what research he's done. Does his current reading, for example, include writings on social psychology, general semantics, economics? If he's specialising, is he learning everything that's possible to learn inside the field? Is he aware of what's going on outside his field so that he can continue to hold his union card of specialisation? This is an important phase. It should have begun, obviously, in high school and college. Too often an advertising man drops his reading the moment he leaves college.

Phase two is simply the recognition that man in a creative act usually functions even better when he's stimulated. Stimulation is achieved in many different ways—from such obvious methods as drinking coffee or tea to the inspiration one sometimes gets from beautiful music.

Phase three is getting the job done. Here is the suggested step-by-step procedure for putting the creative process to work:

1. *Define the problem.* Essentially, the creative process is problem-solving. A problem can't be solved unless it can be defined. And defining it is often part of the solution.
2. *Consciously question every accepted assumption about this problem.* Remember that almost all of us enter a new situation with preconceived assumptions. Too often we think these assumptions are beliefs that are true everywhere and for all time. And by having these assumptions, we often prevent ourselves from learning anything further. So question these assumptions that involve the problem. How did such assumptions emerge? Who made them? How valid are they? Unless this is done, the creative process is crushed before it gets started.
3. *Get involved with this problem.* The creative man in an act of creating can't be a dilettante. He must live and breathe his problem and develop an intense joy in getting involved with it. Research every facet of it.
4. *Begin to ask questions.* Asking questions at this point can always lead to new and productive answers.
5. *Consciously begin to adopt new assumptions, or try to renovate old ones.*
6. *Consciously let the inductive process start to work.* See if there is a relationship between things that nobody else has seen before. Let the imagination see more than there is ground for. Reach out for explanations that go beyond experience. Even if the facts don't seem to warrant it, speculate and guess at a new unity.
7. *Begin to form a judgment.* Dewey explored this process of judgment perhaps more thoroughly than anyone else. It is significant that his analysis of the creative and judgment functions accurately describes what goes on in the most creative agencies. Dewey described the exercise of judgment by the creative person as a conflict between inner vision (intuition) and outer vision. The non-creative administrator who must approve advertising can draw some solace from the fact that the intuition of the genuinely creative person does not run wild. Self-discipline and judgment are inherent in the creative process.
8. *Try to make a prediction.* At this point, try to see if there is a new unity in the world that surrounds your problem. Perhaps the solution can be seen only in pictures. Perhaps it will seem simple to you but too complex for others. This doesn't mean it is wrong. For example, Copernicus' theory in his day was not simple to others, because it demanded two rotations of the earth—a daily one and a yearly one—

in place of one rotation of the sun. What made his theory seem simple to Copernicus was an aesthetic sense of unity. The motion of all the planets around the sun was both simple and beautiful—almost as if he saw it in a picture.

9. *Now take action.* A man who has gone through the process of getting involved with his problem, and has achieved what he thinks is a new solution, must be willing to act and try it out.
10. *Develop the drive, the competence, to demonstrate the validity of the new theory.* Develop, in other words, the guts to survive the criticism of people who may oppose a new hypothesis until it's tried.
11. *Be ready, however, to question the new hypothesis—and start all over again if it doesn't solve the problem.* The creative process put to work can guide many more of us toward a more productive life in our jobs of communicating ideas and moving people to act.

(Reproduced from 'Making the Creative Process' by Walter Joyce in *Advertising Today/Yesterday/Tomorrow*, McGraw-Hill, 1963.)

Warm-ups

a. This is a feather.
   Write as many uses for it as you can think of in one minute.
b. This is a bicycle.
   How many ways can you think of to use it around the house?
c. Invent a new toy to amuse children under the age of 10.

Workout

1. Write the creative brief for a press ad to be released by the Co-ordination Committee for Vulnerable Children (CCVC) aimed at getting sponsors for earthquake victims (the objective is to get people to adopt an orphan).
2. Write the proposition
3. Write the ad

(Impel action. Give the reader a reason to shell out finances.
Tell him all the facts he needs to know about the CCVC.
Reassure him about its authenticity in the use of funds.
Tell him how his money is going to be spent.
Include a coupon/tel no./some way he can respond to you.
What response do you want from the target audience?)

Note: Save this ad in your work file to be compared with future ads you will write.

Another Workout?

Study the text of the ad for Lillian Eichler's famous *Book of Etiquette* (on p. 199). Featuring a girl who repeatedly ordered chicken salad when out on a dinner date, it ran in American newspapers in the early 1920s, and was written by Wilbur Ruthrauff, co-founder of Ruthrauff & Ryan.

Headline: ***Again She Orders—"A Chicken Salad, Please"***

What is the Product?
What is the Market?
Who is the Competition?
What is the Marketing Objective?
What is the Advertising Objective?
What is the Proposition?
What is the Tone of Voice?
What is the Brand Image?
What is the Impel?

Study the copy structure.
What do you notice?
Try and segment the structure. Are you being drawn into the sales argument?
How?

Try and pinpoint the sales argument used by the copywriter.
How many words are there in this advertisement?
Could you write it with fewer words?
Are there too many words?
Could you imagine this ad working in Hindi, Telugu, Oriya?

15

Marriage of Copy and Visual

When husbands and wives are compatible, it is assumed their marriage is a good one. Yet one partner may be stronger than the other without rocking the marital boat. Or there is a pleasant give and take where each is supportive of the other and gives the other space to show and grow. Likewise with a good press ad.

Sometimes the visual is the main attention-getter, sometimes the headline wins. Actually, you have only three ways of shouting *stop and read* to your potential user.

- Headline alone
- Visual alone
- Combination of both

The third way is generally the standard one and the most logical. Headlines fall into certain categories or types. Often the copy and visual are so closely linked that the creative team would find it hard to say where the thought originated. This is perfect compatibility—where the team as well as the advertising idea are concerned. A copywriter's relationship with the art person is crucial, and the stronger the understanding, the better the creative work produced.

The 'weightage' a team decides to give to the creative expression (headline and visual) depends on the *Advertising Idea* that springs to the mind. Some ideas for a campaign lend themselves more easily to the headline, some are most effectively executed visually, and some find the most suitable expression in an even balance. You will see this nicely demonstrated in the accompanying ads.

Where the Headline Does the Selling

- ALFA LAVAL (*Think Tank*)
  The neat blue square in which the headline is placed suggests water in a tank. The stark layout and sober typography is deliberately chosen: it is in tranquil surroundings that one can do one's

Think Tank.
Global technology is a battle-field where only the best can survive. Our philosophy is to act, rather than react: when it comes to advances in technology or breakthroughs in science we make the trail, rather than follow footsteps.
The world calls our team of professionals – "Innovators". We simply call them a "Think Tank".

Alfa Laval
Bringing technology to your doorstep
WE BELIEVE IN THE POWER OF PARTNERSHIP

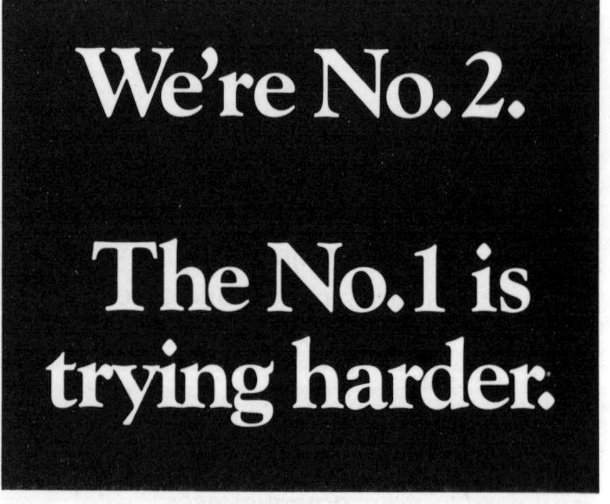
We're No. 2.
The No. 1 is trying harder.

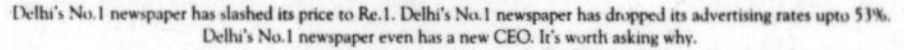
Delhi's No.1 newspaper has slashed its price to Re.1. Delhi's No.1 newspaper has dropped its advertising rates upto 53%.
Delhi's No.1 newspaper even has a new CEO. It's worth asking why.

THE TIMES OF INDIA
DELHI
Are you ready for the new No.1?

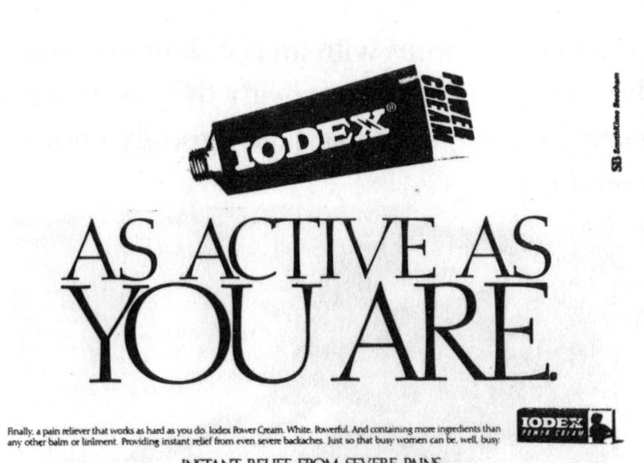

It isn't easy
being the backbone
of the family.

Wishing you a
Happy Mother's Day.

The trusted backache specialist.

most productive thinking. The advertiser's message is conveyed in just two words—but it needs the visual complement. Take away the blue square, and the ad falls flat, though the message is the same. Copy-strong ads do not negate the visual, they just depend more on the words to do the selling.

- Times of India (*We're No. 2*)
  Similarly, *The Times of India* ad, which omits a visual altogether, and states its message against a black background. Would this ad be improved by inclusion of a photograph or an illustration? Hardly likely. The copy says it all—effectively.
- Iodex (*As active as you are/It isn't easy being the backbone*)
  The Iodex headlines use puns relevantly and stylishly. They presume on the reader's familiarity with Iodex as a rub for body aches and pains. The visual of the reassuring, dependable pack/bottle is more than enough to clinch the headline.

Where the Visual is the Attention-getter

- Dr Scholls
  Ouch! Those visuals are powerful enough to make you want to rush out and buy a pair of comfortable Dr.Scholls shoes. Who has not experienced the horrors of unsuitable footwear? These ads brilliantly exploit a universal desire to pamper our feet—until we can get home and put them up.
- Pepsi
  The leaning tower of the Pepsi can is a delightful visual pun which conveys the spirit of the drink.

- HONGKONG BANK CARD

  The Hongkong Bank credit card comes with an accident insurance worth Rs 600,000. The picture of a helmet with the credit card superimposed immediately conveys the message strongly enough to make you want to read on.

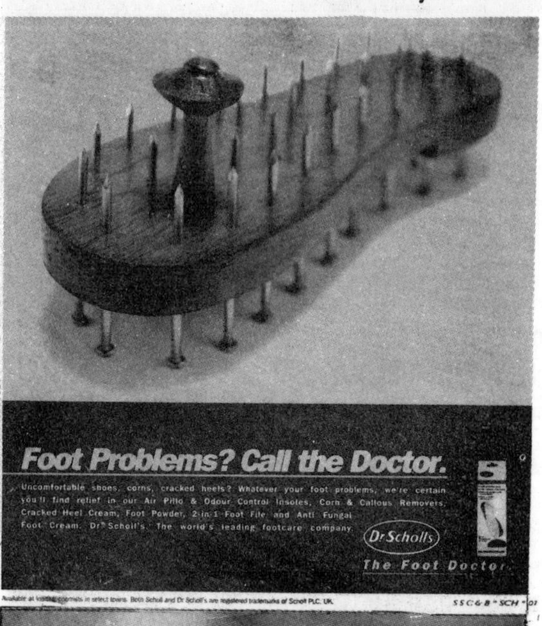

Foot Problems? Call the Doctor.
Uncomfortable shoes, corns, cracked heels? Whatever your foot problems, we're certain you'll find relief in our Air Pillo & Odour Control Insoles, Corn & Callous Removers, Cracked Heel Cream, Foot Powder, 2-in-1 Foot File and Anti Fungal Foot Cream. Dr Scholl's. The world's leading footcare company.
Dr Scholls
The Foot Doctor.

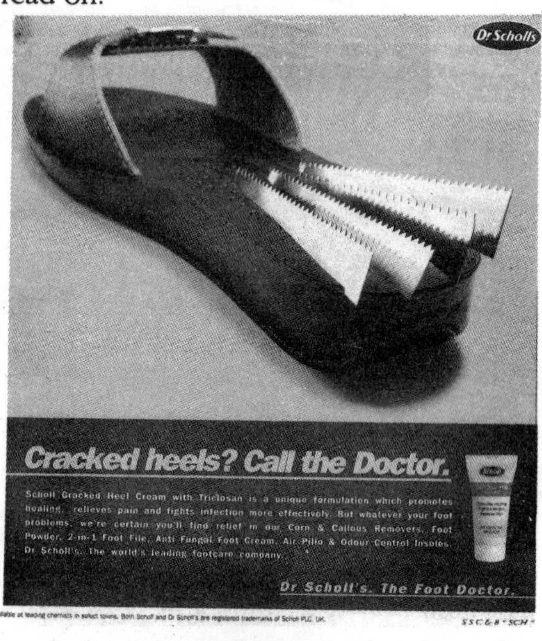

Dr Scholls
Cracked heels? Call the Doctor.
Scholl Cracked Heel Cream with Triclosan is a unique formulation which promotes healing, relieves pain and fights infection more effectively. But whatever your foot problems, we're certain you'll find relief in our Corn & Callous Removers, Foot Powder, 2-in-1 Foot File, Anti Fungal Foot Cream, Air Pillo & Odour Control Insoles. Dr Scholl's. The world's leading footcare company.
Dr Scholl's. The Foot Doctor.
wailable at leading chemists in select towns. Both Scholl and Dr Scholl's are registered trademarks of Scholl PLC. UK.

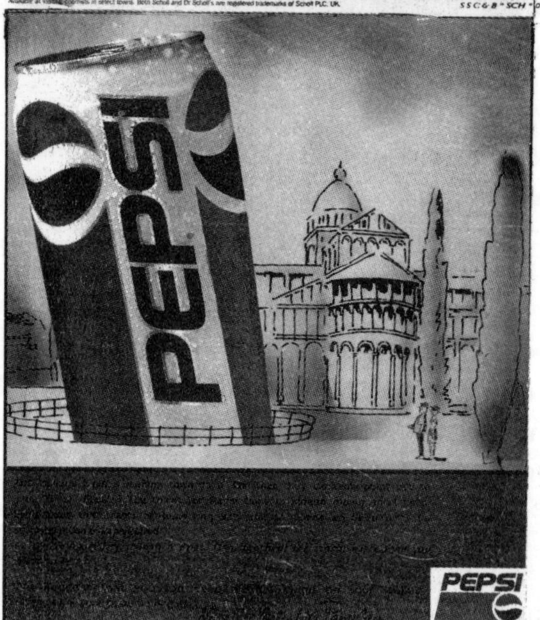

HongkongBank
VISA
How much accident insurance does your credit card offer you? The HongkongBank Credit Card offers free insurance against fatal accidents, of up to Rs. 6,00,000 for you and your add-on cardholders. That's considerably higher than what's offered by any other reputed credit card. To know more about the credit card that's brought to you by one of the world's largest financial services groups, call us today. The HongkongBank Credit Card. It's the best buy you'll get.
To apply call: 491 0001 (Mumbai), 373 0001 (Delhi), 220 8650 (Calcutta), 526 0001 (Chennai), 558 0001 (Bangalore), 56 6533 (Visakhapatnam).
HongkongBank
Your Future Is Our Future
Terms and conditions apply
Mudra HKB 6302

Where the Visuals do the Selling

A 50:50 Relationship Between Copy and Visual

- Wrigley's chewing gum
- Fedex
- Delta

In these ads there is a neat juxtaposition of visual and headline. The one needs the other. If you covered the visual element, the copy message would be incomplete—and vice versa. A perfect marriage!

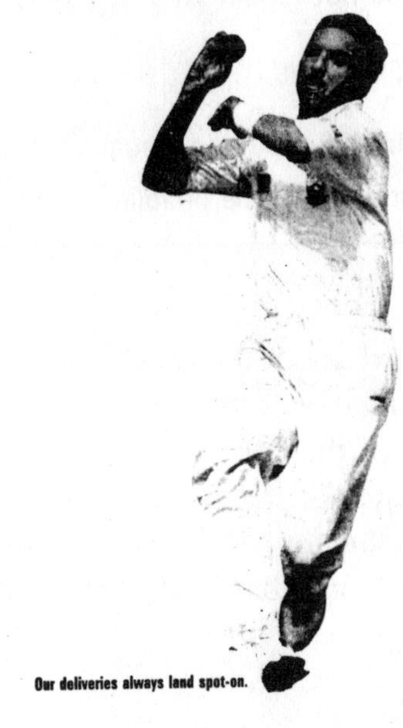

Our deliveries always land spot-on.
FedEx promises on-time deliveries in 210 countries, world-wide. Delivery, after consistent delivery. Such precision has become a part of life at FedEx over the last 25 years. You give us a spot on our network and we'll deliver. On the dot. Thanks to a line up of 625 aircraft, 42,500 ground vehicles and 1,45,000 people who believe in precision. Small wonder FedEx offers express delivery times. A feat achieved regularly without stepping over the line.
FedEx
Federal Express
The World On Time.
Call customer service at Mumbai 5708888 Delhi 6285911 Chennai 8237707 Bangalore* 5595633 or e-mail to track @ fedex.com
*FedEx services available with Blue Dart. Visit us at www.fedex.com

THE ONLY FLYERS WHO KNOW THE ATLANTIC BETTER THAN DELTA.
They're beautiful, they're graceful, and they know the wet bit between Europe and the States like the backs of their flippers. But they don't carry passengers. So we'd like to tell you about an airline that knows a thing or two about crossing the pond. Delta.
Delta have daily flights from Mumbai to Europe and onwards to 240 cities in the US. With over 350 transatlantic flights every week we can fly you from Mumbai to New York, Atlanta, Los Angeles, Cincinnati, Washington DC, Orlando and many other US destinations on the same day. We serve 28 European cities, and last year we flew 86 million people worldwide, more than any other airline.
There's no big secret to our success. We serve good food, in comfortable surroundings and lay on a fine movie to aid digestion. Any airline could do it, fortunately for us not too many do.
For further flight or ticket information, please call Delta in Mumbai on (022) 202 9020 or fax (022) 287 6167; or call us on any of the numbers given below.
Delta

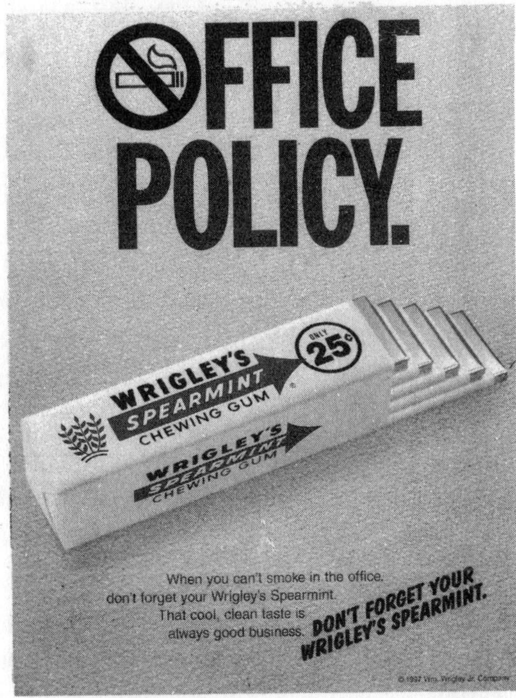

OFFICE POLICY.
WRIGLEY'S SPEARMINT CHEWING GUM
ONLY 25¢
When you can't smoke in the office, don't forget your Wrigley's Spearmint. That cool, clean taste is always good business.
DON'T FORGET YOUR WRIGLEY'S SPEARMINT.
©1997 Wm. Wrigley Jr. Company

Warm-ups

1. Study the 11 ads featured above.
2. Derive the proposition for each.
3. Now attempt to give a weightage to the *impact or arresting power* of the message. (Body copy must not be read at this stage). For instance, the weightage could be assigned as 40:60, i.e., 40 per cent power to the headline and 60 per cent to the visual.

4. Why have you apportioned these weightages? Ask yourself the following questions: is it a good marriage? Are the partners compatible? What are their weaknesses? Could they get along better? Ought they to file for a divorce? What life partner would *you* suggest for them if you think they are totally 'unmade' for each other?

Note: In order to do this assignment satisfactorily, it would help to cover the visual and read the headline/ baseline separately; then cover the headline and just look at the visual alone.

Some Tips on Writing an Ad

- Your headline sets a mood (tone of voice).
- This should be echoed in the first line of your body copy.
- Body copy reflects the mood but does not repeat what is already shown in the visual.
- The headline should evoke the visual.
- Creativity is a good marriage between the copy and visual.
- The visual should not be a mere illustration of the headline.

The Art Director, Your Partner

While on the subject of marriage, a word about the other person in the creative team, the visualiser or art director.

Headlines may be the prerogative of the copywriter, but either partner in the team may be the originator of the Big Idea. Here is what Bahadur Merwan, former creative director of HTA and of O&M, and veteran ad person and writer Frank Simoes have to say about the relationship between copy and art.

The Relationship between Copy and Art

by Bahadur Merwan

Marriages are made in heaven. So are the teams of copywriters and art directors. Beware, you may end up with a wierd partner, but if he or she has a creative spark, it will be an asset to you to create great campaigns and earn fame and fortune. Who knows, one day you may be considered the 'Cash Cow' of your agency! (YOU take the cream and leave the by-products for the rest of the agency workers!!).

Unfortunately in India, many small ad agencies have no proper structure, and hence, no proper creative team set-up. These agencies employ two copywriters for every half a dozen art people. So each copywriter has to work with more than one art director, with different styles of working, and this could be hard on the copywriter.

- Some art directors prefer to work in ivory towers.
- Some like to work just for art galleries and the annual Ad Club shows—for them copywriters are just word space fillers.
- Some are a combination of both art and copy, and so think that copywriters are redundant.

Let me tell you what happened to André Syson, creative director of JWT, London. When he was a copy trainee, he happened to work with one of the toughest art directors of his time. The man told Andre, "Listen boy, this is a scribble of my visual. I am giving you a two-inch square space for body copy and headline. Nothing more—because I don't want you to screw up my masterpiece!".

André wanted the job very badly, so he had to think up ways to win the art director over.

One way a copywriter can break the barrier of one-upmanship is to develop a good sense of layout and design. You should also be conversant with processing techniques. This will increase the art director's confidence in you, and lead to a fruitful marriage!

How to Design a Good Layout

Remember the first time you shot your first roll of film? You held your camera and struggled with the viewfinder to compose your picture. I'm sure you must have chopped off many heads and legs in the process! Then you must have practised hard to master the art of composing beautiful pictures. Likewise, art directors have their own theory of layout, which you can master quite easily.

This is the basic 'Grid Pattern' which helps you place the elements of an ad (visual/headline/subhead/text/logo/baseline) to look as good as any art director's layout.

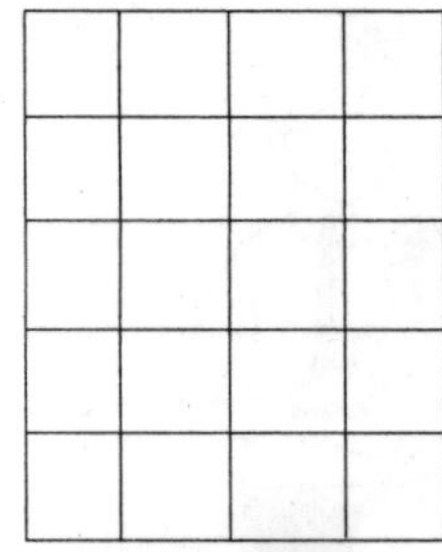

Step One Draw a square of 8" × 10" (the area of a single page/magazine)

Step Two Divide the square into 20 smaller squares or blocks of equal size.

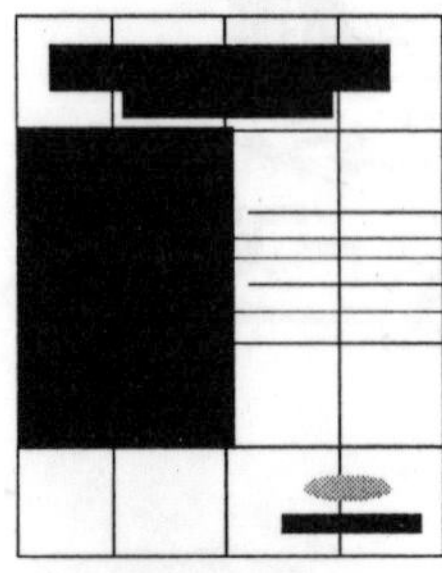

Step Three Now start placing each element (mentioned above) into these blocks. You may use any number of blocks to cover each element. (Black mass indicates the illustration or visual. Thick black lines are used for the headline and subhead. Fine rules are for the body copy. The grey oval shape is the logo, and the thick line below is for the baseline.)

Step Four Normally the reader's 'eye movement' starts from:

- headline/illustration (whichever is more striking)
- to the subhead
- then to the body copy
- to logo and baseline

The 'eye movement' is the only secret of a well-laid-out ad.

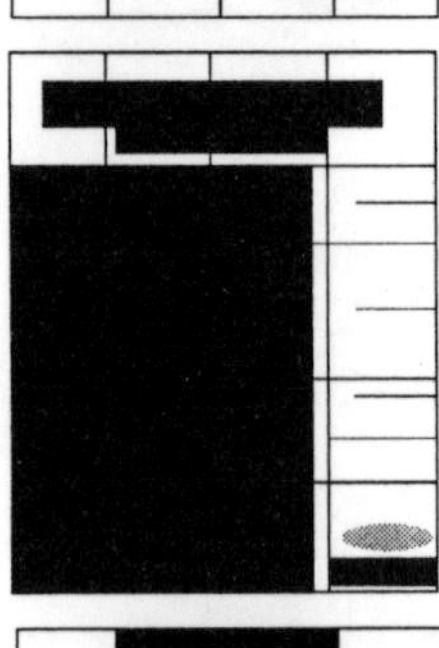

Step Five Now go ahead and have fun.

Two Heads are Better than One

Successful teams discuss the creative strategy together before presenting the campaign idea or TV commercial to their creative chief/account group. The teams also keep an open mind to any good suggestions and will not

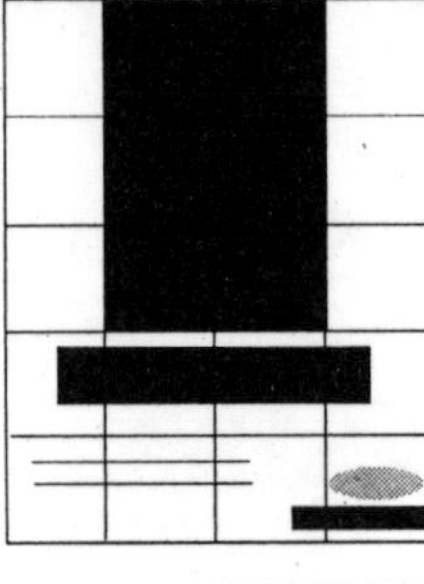

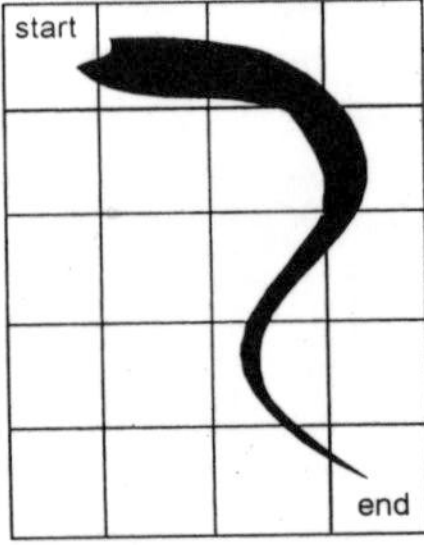

hesitate to incorporate them to improve the creative work. After all, it is in the team's own interest to produce award-winning campaigns which will earn them plaudits and fatter pay packets.

Copywriters should have an adequate knowledge of print production and film production.

Print	Film/TV
▪ Some knowledge of what type of papers and surfaces are needed for different types of printing (newspaper/magazine/packaging/outdoor)	▪ Visit editing studios to gain hands-on knowledge of how computer graphics can be used effectively
▪ Visit processing houses with your art director to see how computer effects can improve visual ideas	▪ Observe how editing and sound mixing is done
	▪ The rest comes with practice and experience

The Chicken and the Egg

by Frank Simoes

Which came first? A metaphorical conundrum never more in evidence than in the advertising business when I first began my career. A copy trainee, I sat at the smallest desk in a carefully segregated classroom (there is no other word for it) with a generous clutch of copywriters. At the other end of the office, as far from us as space allowed and similarly segregated, the visualisers sat en masse (three to every copywriter; the imbalance remains inexplicable till today). Under the benevolent and mutually exclusive tutelage of a Copy Chief and an Art Director, we were separated physically, conceptually and by a vague resentment at the perceived redundancy of each other's functions.

In terms of the end results of our endeavours—a specific advertisement, ad film, hoarding campaign—there were fiercely contested claims to the true origin of the creative effort. Copy sought first and last credit; art said, *"Rubbish!"* The controversy is best summed up in an exchange of slogans between Art Director and Copy Chief:

Art Director: "A picture is worth a thousand words."
Copy Chief: "It takes seven words to say that."

In hindsight I believe that, under the inexorable pressure of immutable media transformation, these oppositional definitions first blurred, then overlapped assuming new and kaliedoscopic patterns, and finally coalesced into a single entity: *the Creative,* at entry point a copywriter perhaps or a visualiser, but very soon, *a creator of communication concepts.* But it was a long, hard haul from early beginnings when copy was written and sent across to the art department with a visual suggestion (often longer than the copy!) which was angrily consigned to the waste paper basket, to today's intimate, osmotic relationship where wordsmith and visualiser sit together and roles are often inter-changed, headlines and visuals emerging from one or the other.

In short, the understanding has dawned that it takes both chicken and egg to make an omelette.

What caused this revolutionary breakthrough? I submit it was the ascendancy of commercial television which displaced print as the first medium of advertising communication. The process made the copywriter's typewriter and the visualiser's sketch pad virtually redundant. From a single creative dimension they were catapulted, willy nilly, into a three-dimensional world: sight, sound and movement. Words and pictures were no longer mutually exclusive, but mutually supportive, with sound getting into the act taking both into a fresh dimension. The whole became very much more potent than the sum of the parts. As the copywriter and visualiser were increasingly exposed to ever higher levels of television (news, entertainment, sports, documentaries), they, in turn, developed multi-dimensional responses in their roles as advertising communicators.

A self-fulfilling prophecy within a closed inter-active loop. And as the loop began to grow more intense in its complexity and ramifications—global satellite channels, 24-hour broadcasting, segmented programming—the pressure on the professional advertising communicator to perform successfully became increasingly severe. They could not compete in terms of time (30 seconds versus 30 minutes for a regular programme), budgets (tens of lakhs versus tens of crores), variety of content (one commercial versus 13 episodes). The only edge they possessed lay in the skills they had honed in the creation of concepts of communications: the brilliant idea which brought viewer's attention into sharp, memorable focus.

The idea could be biased in terms of words, or pictures, or sound, or situation. It had to be original, exciting, gripping, memorable and do justice to its primary role, to sell goods and services. No easy task, considering two factors: first, the irresistible rise and rise of television; second, the proliferation of media into uncharted territory. Direct marketing, tele-sales, mail order, sponsorships, event management, and latterly the Internet, more often than not, overlap in permutations and combinations, making Herculean demands on the advertising Creatives called upon to communicate within the new media parameters.

Less has become significantly more. A single consumer motivational insight, expensively and arduously realised, is more often than not the basis for an entire multi-media campaign. Simplified, pared-down form follows function, reflecting on the one hand the strictures of ever tighter advertising budgets, on the other the frenzied pitch and programming in the media, where the advertising message must stand forth with a greater measure of attraction, relevance, impact and conviction.

In this brave new world, "Last year's words belong to last year's language." Copywriter and visualiser have bowed out with good grace, feuds long forgotten, while doffing a nostalgic cap to a memorable past. *I daresay, "next year's words"–and pictures!–belong to the new Concept Creator.*

Workout

Choose at least six ads which appeal to you from popular newspapers or magazines. Study them in the light of what you have read so far. Pay special attention to the impact made by the headline and/or visual. Try and derive the proposition for each. Ask yourself who the target audience is, and what tone of voice is being used to address the consumer.

If it is an ad for a popular brand, think about what the positioning could be. Try and get the feel of the advertising message, and pinpoint the Big Idea (if any) in each case.

This is not an exam paper! Just a way to help you better understand the principles set down so far.

16

Getting Set to Create: The Press Ad

You have now looked at all the major ingredients which go into the campaign pot. The tone of voice, the brand image, the target audience, the proposition. When you cook these together, you get the brand positioning statement, more or less. You also know you are near the completion of your creative strategy blueprint. It is still a prototype, however, until you have tasted and tested what is cooking!

Brainstorming and ideation give you a glimpse into the working of a copywriter's mind . . . while wielding pen, pencil or keyboard. The art director is engaged in the same exercise with microtip pen or air brush. The next 10 chapters or so form the main meal of this book. You will find workouts at the end of each chapter, as right through. The more assignments you complete, the better for you. It is important to get an evaluation of your work at every stage. If you do not have a creative chief to guide you, you are welcome to send your efforts to me for appraisal—for a fee, naturally!

You have seen that a Press Ad is recognisable by most people, literate or illiterate, by its headline, visual, body copy and baseline. You know that a Press Ad can be of many types. It can stand on its own, or be part of a campaign. It can be supported by other media (film/TV/POP/hoardings) which reflect and strengthen the same message. Now drill a little deeper and enter the process of creation of this most important medium.

Great Campaigns are Based on Great Ideas

You may learn all the parameters of writing an ad, or a film script, or a hoarding, or whatever, but if you cannot come up with a really good idea where two plus two do not just add up to four but five, you will not have a memorable campaign. And you would be wasting your client's money. Copywriting is also about accountability. Good copywriters are well paid to think up good ideas.

The Big Idea

In this age of computer graphics and the Black Book . . . techniques have become the Idea . . . and since everyone has access to the techniques everyone has the same ideas . . . which means you are watching more of the same every day on the box and anywhere else. Some of the most memorable campaigns have been built upon a Single Big Idea.

- WILL'S MADE FOR EACH OTHER SLOGAN
- LIRIL'S WATERFALL FRESHNESS CONCEPT
- ONIDA TV (DEVIL)
- AIR-INDIA'S MAHARAJAH
- RIN'S WHITENING STRIKES
- THE SKYPAK MAN
- AMUL BUTTER'S SLOGAN AND GIRL

For the moment forget about brand positioning and all the ingredients. If these campaigns were dishes set on a table, you would be concerned with the taste of the dish, besides its appearance. If you are faced with a table on which were placed a steaming dish of

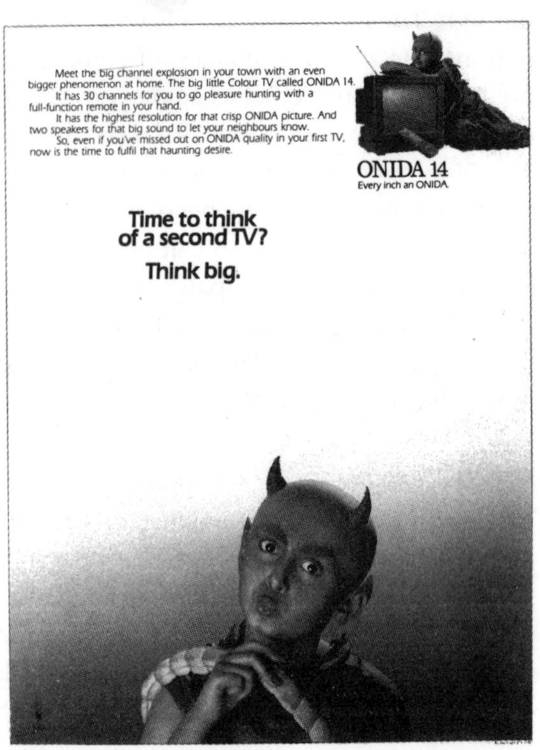

mutton biryani, a delectable soufflé, a titillating chicken curry, a fish mousse and a Russian salad . . . you would enjoy different sensations from savouring this varied fare.

When you compliment the hostess on her food, you are more likely to add, "What's the secret of your dish? When I make chicken curry—or fish mousse, or Russian salad—it doesn't taste like this at all!" And maybe your hostess will part with the secret. That secret, when it comes to creating a campaign, is the Big Idea. There are a lot of ways to cook the same chicken curry, but the master chef will produce a curry that beats the rest hollow—using the same ingredients. You are going to try to be like that chef.

A Good Press Ad

- Has a great idea
- Cuts through time barriers
- Appeals to all generations of the target audience
- Hits you where it hurts

- Uses simple words and expression
- Is ever fresh
- Is open to many renditions
- Has mileage
- Has strong identity with the brand/product
- Is relevant to the product
- Has visual sync

Warm-up

Think of some outstanding ads. What is the Big Idea in each of them? What makes them memorable? Jot down your answers here.

- Wills "Made for Each Other" (Mileage, visual sync, brevity, clarity, relevant to the product)

- ....
- ....
- ....
- ....
- ....

Aesop Glim

As cubs we learnt a great deal from Old Aesop Glim who came in a Dover paperback. Unfortunately very few writers have heard of him. He wrote a simple book called *How Advertising is Written and Why*. If you can lay your hands on it—try the roadside at Mumbai's Flora Fountain—grab it and devour it. Glim had a neat way of approaching headlines. He used nine basic appeals: the five senses and the four instincts.

Glim's Appeals

The five senses: sight, hearing, touch, smell, taste.
The four instincts: sex/love, anger/rage, fear/security, hunger.

Another Warm-up

Try your hand at writing headlines using all these appeals. Choose a common household product for this purpose—a cereal, a wristwatch, shoes, a telephone, crystalware.

Write at least three headlines using each appeal as a 'press button' to evoke consumer response

Here is an example, using any proposition that comes to mind. The idea is to get familiar with 'press buttons'.

Product: washing machine
Target audience: housewife

Sight

- "*Looks* so nice, wish I could keep it in the drawing room!"
- Choose from a range of 12 *pretty* pastels!
- Value for money, and the *beautiful finish* comes free!

Sound/Hearing

- Works without a *whisper.*
- While you *sing,* your machine *hums!*
- *Click, whirr, swish!* and your clothes are clean!

Touch

- "My cotton sheets come out feeling *like silk*"
- "Raju wants me to wash his *teddy bear*"
- It has *rounded edges*—no nasty corners!

Smell

- The *fresh aroma* of clean sheets!
- The end of *stinking* jeans.
- "Now I just sit back and enjoy my *fragrant* coffee."

Taste

- Gives you more time . . . to cook the family's *favourite dinners!*
- "My washing machine has brought back *elevenses!*"
- Looks good enough *to eat!*

Sex/Love

- Diapers *so soft* on baby's *tender* skin.
- "Darling, you're *glowing,* let's eat out tonight!"
- Have an *affair* . . . right in your home.

Anger/Rage

- "My husband wanted a *divorce* . . . then I got the washing machine!"
- "Curry stains used to *drive me crazy!*"
- "Finally, *we sacked* the dhobi."

Fear

- He *failed* the most important interview of his life . . . his collar was grubby.
- "I *never dared use* my Irish linen table cloth—till I got the washing machine."
- Who's *afraid* of turmeric stains?

Hunger

- Wash time has become *snack time!*
- "Mummy, these fritters are *yummy!*"
- "Every time Mrs Yadav hung out her husband's white shirts, *my mouth watered!*"

(Sometimes, you have to stretch an appeal to make a point!)

Get the idea? Now stretch your imagination and go to work.

If you think of Glim's appeals as buttons, you can decide which of your target audience's buttons you ought to press in order to get them to respond to your message and impel them to take action. This may sound terribly manipulative, but advertising techniques per se are neither right nor wrong; it is the use they are put to which may be judged as moral or immoral. The same buttons which can untie purse strings for famine victims, can also be used to induce young people to smoke cigarettes which carry the Surgeon General's warning. So, it is all part of the game!

Now, Back to the Proposition!

When you feel you are comfortable with headline writing, based on Old Aesop Glim's appeals, go a step further and base your headlines on *a specific message or Proposition.*

You would do well to use the simple Padamsee Formula here:

Proposition = Consumer Benefit + Reason Why

Working Out a Proposition

In order to arrive at a Proposition, it helps to mate the facts about a product (reason why) with the consumer needs which the facts can meet (benefits). For instance, take a product like a toothpaste. Make a simple grid as shown below, one column stating any consumer need you can think of, and the horizontal column setting down every conceivable attribute of the product that you know of. Remember to stick to facts where this is concerned, but use your imagination when it comes to thinking of consumer needs. You might think of a need which the consumer is currently unaware of!

Product Benefits* → **Consumer Needs** ↓	A	B	C	D	E	F	G	H	I
Whiteness	–	×	–	–	–	×	×	–	–
Kills germs	–	–	–	–	–	–	–	×	–
Fresh breath	–	–	×	–	–	–	–	×	–
Fights tartar	–	–	–	–	–	–	×	×	–
Lathers well	–	–	–	–	–	–	–	–	–
Strengthens gums	–	–	×	–	–	–	–	×	–
Maintains enamel	–	–	–	–	–	×	×	×	–
Tastes good	–	–	×	–	–	–	–	–	–
Trustworthy	×	–	–	–	–	×	×	×	×

*A. Made by the makers of Volgate toothpaste
B. White, non-foaming toothpaste
C. Pleasant flavour
D. Economically priced
E. Comes in plastic squeeze tube
F. Contains calcium
G. Has whitening agent
H. Has antiseptic agent
I. Free toothbrush offer

Let us assume our toothpaste is called *Dentium.* The client says it is different from any other toothpaste in the market because it contains calcium which strengthens tooth enamel. Mate the facts and the needs shown in the grid above. Put an X in each square where they mate and a—(negative sign) where they do not. Then tot up the Xes and see what you get.

Note that the 'antiseptic' properties coupled with 'trustworthiness' appear to win hands down. Yet, by looking around at the competition, you may decide that there is a brand positioning slot waiting to be filled . . . *Dentium is the only toothpaste in the market which contains calcium.*

But there are just three Xes in the F column—does that mean calcium should not be used as a benefit? No. Rather, the creative team may decide to create a need and offer the consumer a calcium-reinforced toothpaste, just as Promise toothpaste offered the benefit of clove oil. So you might end up with a proposition something like this:

a. **New Dentium is Calcium-enriched for Stronger Teeth.**
or b. **New Dentium with Calcium Builds Teeth While it Cleans.**

It is not unthinkable that a product may offer a double-pronged benefit with a primary and secondary emphasis. But for the sake of brand positioning, it is wiser to stay with the stronger or more unique claim. What do *you* think?

The time has come to express the propositions as headlines. Often you may base your campaign on two different/alternative propositions to see which comes out better. This is not unusual, specially when there is doubt; you leave it to the consumer to react to each in a test market situation. For instance you could test *Proposition A* expressed as a *concept ad* against *Proposition B*. Or you could develop different approaches or techniques for the same proposition and let the client decide.

This is all part of the creative process, chiselling away at the material until a well-honed campaign evolves. In this instance, a press campaign is being discussed, but the same proposition and/or campaign idea can be rendered in other media like TV and radio.

To work out an acceptable proposition takes time. And it will take some more time before you can churn out headlines which are on-proposition. Do not be discouraged, you are learning a craft. Good copywriters, no matter how brilliant they are, are made—not born. Listen to Shirley de Souza, who gave me my first copy test and who has made a very successful career of copywriting, share her experiences of this truth.

Copywriters are Made—Not Born

by Shirley de Souza

I literally stumbled into advertising when I joined Lintas in 1959. Actuallly, it was never meant to be, but God decided otherwise. So through several twists of fate and after two tests and as many interviews, I was selected to be secretary to the copy department. Gerson da Cunha told me later that I was the only one (among hundreds? thousands?) who spelt *Caesar* correctly.

At the time, Gerson da Cunha was the copy chief and Alyque Padamsee the films chief. The copy department comprised Shyam Benegal, Kersy Katrak, Uma Krupanidhi (da Cunha), Roque Pereira, the late Mubi Ismail (Pasricha) and Helen Anchan, the media legend who was doing a short stint in copy.

Before joining Lintas, the word *copywriting* meant a subject I had dreaded at school, having handwriting that was the despair of my teachers. However, the *stuff* was there, even at that stage. (Lintas would call it *spark*.) My English compositions are in the school archives—the English teacher was almost sure I would bag the English scholarship in the SSC—and my letters to our family, scattered around the world, were looked forward to, enjoyed and cherished. My creative outlet was writing limericks on my fellow-beings and providing lines for special occasion cards and posters for friends and family.

God certainly had special plans for me, because after marriage, three darling sons, and 11 very interesting years as secretary in the copy department, I switched to copywriting at the invitation of Alyque Padamsee and egged on by Mubi Ismail.

Since then, till my retirement in 1998, I have written for almost every category of product under the sun. From banks, foods, creams and cigarettes . . . to fabrics, airlines, detergents, public service and much, much more. I would like to share with you a few thoughts that have helped me.

- One opens a whole book of creative revelations by just watching and working with Alyque. But this is not about that. In Alyque's sprawling room at Lintas, one wall was covered with a panorama of choice ad clippings and pointers or tips. One of these, I think, summed up best what creative people should be aiming to do. It just said, *Surprise me.* Two little words—but when they come from *the god of big advertising ideas,* who had seen and experienced (almost) everything, it was certainly a challenge to us creatives. And did we work to achieve it!

- Copywriting is a craft that is a lot of hard work. What begins with a brief must be distilled to *bring into sharp focus the Proposition which is the consumer benefit with a reason why.* This is one of the basics I learnt from Cossy Rosario during my training. You couldn't find a better teacher of advertising creativity than him. He taught us *analysis, logic, relevance—some of the keys to selling.* Without them you have nothing. With these as the firm base—you are ready to take off.
- If Cossy provided the foundation, Mubi taught me to fly. Her advertising philosophy was: *stay away from cliches.* Her work was a brilliant testimony to this tenet; her ads films won award after award at the annual Advertising Club competitions.
- In 1971, a pretty young thing was called for a copy test, mainly on the strength of a single sentence in her application: *I have a lively sense of the ridiculous.* This caught Mubi's eye—and was one decision the advertising world has greatly benefited from. June Valladares had arrived. In later years, when asked to contribute a *memory* to our Lintas golden Jubilee souvenir, June came up with the delightful, "When I was in trouble, I used to breathe the prayer, ***L**ord, **I N**eed **T**hat **A**nswer **S**oon."*
- A great way of knowing if your advertising has made an impact; hear someone say, *"Wish I had done that!"* The nicest compliment—a dash of envy in the heady wine of success.
- I am happy to say that some of my contributions to advertising have been enduring. *Live Life Kingsize* for Four Square cigarettes started out as a caption for a competition . . . and stayed on as the campaign line. It *artfully combines lifestyle with brand feature* in three little words. It has outlived change of agencies for over two decades. I believe that *brand names have a very important job: to appeal to the consumer right from the shop shelf.* For instance, *Good Day* and *Park Avenue* became big sellers—both names attracting the target consumer. *An advertising idea goes a long way towards building a strong brand image.* Citibank's *The Un-Fixed Deposit* was one such idea which was an instant success.
- I'd like to include a couple of examples which made their impact strongly enough to be carried on the packaging. In the '70s, Glucose D was perceived as not being sweet enough. The trick was to *make the consumer*

actually feel and taste the experience even before opening the pack. The clients agreed that my line, "Glucose-D the sweet taste of energy" did just that and printed it on the pack. When Anikspray was lagging behind in sales, I thought a good way to sell it was to use its special packaging feature of looking like a milk bottle. The "No milk, no problem" *visual idea that was uniquely the brand's* was born. It showed an upside-down empty milk bottle next to the Anikspray pack. This idea too was carried on the packaging.

Today, copywriting comes naturally to me. I can barely analyse it. To write copy that sells, first of all, *experience the product.* Feel it, taste it, live it, breathe it. Then, very simply, put yourself in the shoes of the target consumer: *why on earth would he or she buy your product in preference to the competition? When you find that gold nugget—be it to offer the consumer a kingsize lifestyle . . . or a place on Park Avenue . . . or a bank deposit to delve into at any time . . . or just a good day—you've got it. Make the most of it.*

Workout

Choose 10 ads from the daily newspapers you read which you think are good. What is it about them that attracted your attention?

The headline?
The visual?
The message?
The tone of voice?
The layout?
The typography?
The position in the paper?
Because you are interested in the subject?

Another Workout?

Study the classified columns in *The Times of India,* e.g., matrimonial/for sale, etc.

1. Compose a Situation Vacant ad for yourself. Think of who you are writing to. Think about the response.
2. Write a 50-word ad to sell a house in the country.
3. Write a 30-word ad to sell a second-hand piano.

Important

While studying the classified ads, locate words or phrases that touched or moved you in any way. Why do you think they did? Make a list of these words in the space below.

Your Personal Note Pad

Pictorial Nouns	Active Verbs	Catch Phrases
____________	____________	____________
____________	____________	____________
____________	____________	____________
____________	____________	____________

17

From Propositions to Headlines

It takes a while to learn to write good *Headlines*. There is no need to be dismayed when account executives clutch their hair and complain to the copy chief, "All I get are lines, not ideas—and they're all off the Proposition!" If at first you do not succeed, try and try and try again. For every 100 headlines I wrote in the early days, about three got accepted. It was enough to drive anyone to suicide. The most galling experience is when you make a presentation to the client, he writes a headline worse than yours—and it gets used!

By the time you have soaked in all the information about your product, the target audience, the product, the advertising task, the marketing objectives—you could recite the creative brief backwards in your sleep. You have brainstormed, ideated, bitten your nails and had 10 cups of coffee. Now relax and let your subconscious take over.

On Headlines

- Avoid obscure words
- Be clear
- Headlines should complement the visual
- Be prolific in writing headlines
- Be imaginative
- Headline + Visual + Baseline reflect the Proposition
- 90 per cent of the sales job is done through HL/V/BL
- 10 per cent is done through body copy

  (Your customer/prospect is already largely persuaded by the headline and visual—he reads body copy for reassurance.)

Headline Techniques

A well-known adman used to freelance with HTA for a while. He churned out headlines like a one-man factory, much to the chagrin and amusement of the creative department. It was rumoured that he had a bank of typists working simultaneously for him, while he walked up and down dictating headlines to them for as many campaigns! When asked about this he would say airily, "Oh, there are just about nine or 10 types of headlines. So I just try them one by one and see what comes up." Would you agree with this adroit adman?

In an earlier chapter you learned that press ads fall into several recognisable categories or types: corporate, industrial, classified, public service, financial. Now you will see that headlines too may be of different types. Perhaps a better word would be *Techniques*. Experts in copywriting—David Ogilvy, John Caples, Philip Ward Burton—have given us their tested lists of Techniques. Each writer develops his own private list as he grows in his profession.

It might be a good idea to build up your personal list of Headline Techniques. Then if you are stuck for a headline, you could check it out. Another tip, *never throw away your old and rejected headlines*. File them away. Some headlines can be used at a later date for a product quite unlike the one you have thought them up for. Amazing, but true.

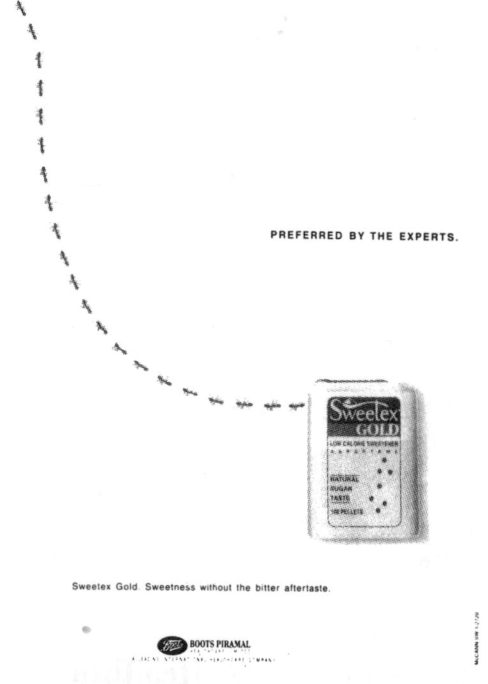

PREFERRED BY THE EXPERTS.
Sweetex
GOLD
Sweetex Gold. Sweetness without the bitter aftertaste.
BOOTS PIRAMAL

At 15* bucks
and 1 calorie
per can,
it's completely
inflation
proof.
Here it is. Diet Pepsi. The single-calorie, all guts, no-flab drink.
diet PEPSI
diet PEPSI Unleashed in India
*Special introductory price

Right? Then get set to look at some tried-and-true Headline Techniques gathered, like roses, along the way.

1. The Launch Headline

If your product or brand is new, or improved, or being tested in a new market, why not say it?

Announcing . . .
Introducing . . .
For the first time in India!
Never before . . .
Today's . . .
New!

This is probably the most time-worn of all techniques but it still works. People are as curious as ever. However, you will still have to keep their interest after you arrest their attention. It helps to use **bold** type in headlines like this.

2. The White Space Headline

This is where there is more 'no copy' than 'copy' in your ad. The visual is minuscule, or even absent. The point size is 6 or 8. The prospects' curiosity is aroused because they have to use a magnifying glass to read your message. Besides, white space shows up nicely against the density of news copy.

3. The Typographical Headline

This typographical ad takes the opposite route. The headline is made the hero. In fact, the way it is presented is almost pictorial. The fonts are carefully chosen to attract the eye. The personality of the brand, image, tone of voice, are all reflected in the type sizes. Many people find this sort of ad irresistible.

4. The News Headline

People always want to know what is going on. That is why they buy newspapers. So words like *New!* and *Have you heard?* and *Now you can . . .* are sure-fire attention-getters. Some copywriters go so far as to disguise their press ads as news items (with the word *advertisement* appearing in tiny print in the corner). It just can trick prospects into reading your message!

5. The Before-After Headline

It is also called the Problem-Solution technique. Present the problem, then offer the solution. Show what hair/teeth/clothes/furniture/anything looks like *before* the shampoo/toothpaste/washing powder/polish went to work . . . few people can skip this sort of ad. Headlines such as "I used to be a 90 lb. weakling" have gone down in history. Showing the prospect the magical way your product can

MESSY HAIR?

STYLE IT EVERYDAY WITH NUTRI-SHEEN.

ONLY NUTRI-SHEEN HAS NATURAL COCONUT PROTEIN

ITS COCONUT PROTEIN NOURISHES YOUR HAIR KEEPING IT HEALTHY AND BEAUTIFUL

Whatever your hair type, you can style it to look great with Nutri-Sheen. An Instant Hair Styling Liquid that's not at all oily and therefore perfect for everyday use. All you have to do is apply it on dry hair and comb for instant results. What's more, only Nutri-Sheen gives you coconut nourishment that keeps your hair healthy and styled all day long.

NUTRI-SHEEN
HAIR STYLING LIQUID
Everyday Styling. All day Nourishment.

100 %
NON OILY
Parachute
NUTRI-SHEEN

change his life, his body, his state of mind, his status, his lifestyle, in just one week (or less) is bound to attract his attention. Show a picture of a flat-chested girl, and three weeks later, hey presto, just by a few simple exercises, the girl has to throw away all her 32B cups and buy 36C . . . wow!

6. The Show-How Headline

Everyone wants to know *how to* do something or other, even if they never get down to doing it! That is human nature.

How to remove stains.
How to clean the gas ring yourself.
How to save five bucks on a detergent.
How to get your husband to get up early.
How to surprise your wife.

This never-fail technique is sure to pull in your prospect.

Try it—again and again and again.

7. Flag-the-Target Headline

Get your headline to reach out and grab your reader by the collar.

Free for *students!*
Housewives under 30 may be pleased to know ...
Senior citizens eligible for half-rate air fares!
Dog-owners your pet is going to love you more than ever!

Sometimes ads like these will even grab the attention of parents of students, husbands under 30, sons of senior citizens and cat-owners. So who is complaining?

8. The You-Too Headline

Amazing what people want to do, have, see, think . . . if someone else does, has, sees, thinks. The You-Too technique gets pulses racing. Try it and see.

You too can be a walking thesaurus.
You too can have a new bedroom — for under 30 dollars.
You too can give your daughter a wonderful wedding!
You too can have a wiggle like Marilyn Monroe!

Got it?

9. The Testimonial Headline

Close on the heels of the above follows what people say about your product—the testimonial. This hackneyed technique will never die. The Nawab of Pataudi will continue to endorse suitings, Cindy Crawford will keep using Omega watches forever, Karan Kapoor will advertise Bombay Dyeing, housewives will go gaga over extra lather, dentists and doctors will be believed if they speak out on behalf of a brand. Testimonials are the next best thing to word-of-mouth.

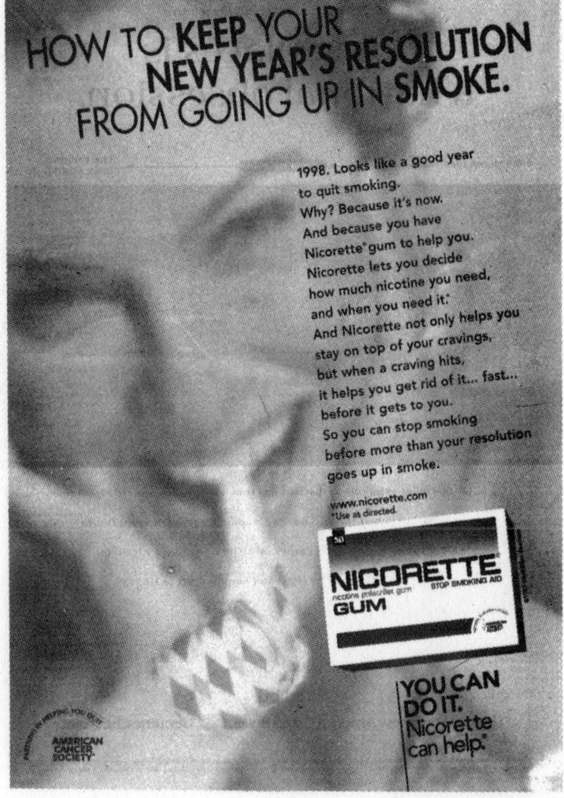

10. The Timely Headline

Sometimes a national holiday or some memorial/feast day prompts an idea for a headline. It is fairly easy to link up a product with any of the following

Mother's Day	Gandhi Jayanti (Oct 2)
Father's Day	Children's Day (Nov 14)
Valentine's Day (Feb 14)	New Year's Day (Jan 1)
Coconut Day	Easter Sunday
Onam	Holi
Dassera	Diwali
Christmas (Dec 25)	Bakr Id

You can build a special drive or contest around a holiday. Or you can just mention the holiday in addition to your current basic theme.

11. The Special Events Headline

In the same way, you can tie up your product with special occasions—man landing on Jupiter, the marriage of a king or queen, the fall of an unpopular government, a motor rally. If there is no special event round the corner, use your imagination and invent one!

12. The Seasonal Headline

Certain products are more likely to be bought in particular months of the year. Cough drops and vapour rubs in the monsoon, talcum powders in summer, antiseptic soothing creams for burns during Diwali, sweetmeat boxes and dried fruits at festival times. These seasons, like the national holidays, come around year after year—so keep a file of ideas ready. Whenever you have nothing much to do, stock up on headlines to suit these occasions, so you can just pull one out in two shakes of a duck's tail—and amaze your account executive!

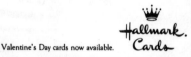

Love is forever. But it can do with the occasional reminder.

Valentine's Day cards now available.

Chaitra Leo Burnett B VCH 9021/99

13. The Teaser Headline

This was used a lot once upon a time. You take a series of ads in the same newspaper, revealing bits of the message till the final revelation. In this category would fall gimmicky use of magazines and newspapers. Like split ads. Or several pages of ads bunched together and bought up by the same client. Or the advertorial (the ad that looks like part of the editorial content). It would include, too, long thin ads, short fat ads, island placement ads, solus position ads. And even upside down ads! if it arrests attention . . . it might even sell the product. But gimmicky ads are generally an educated risk.

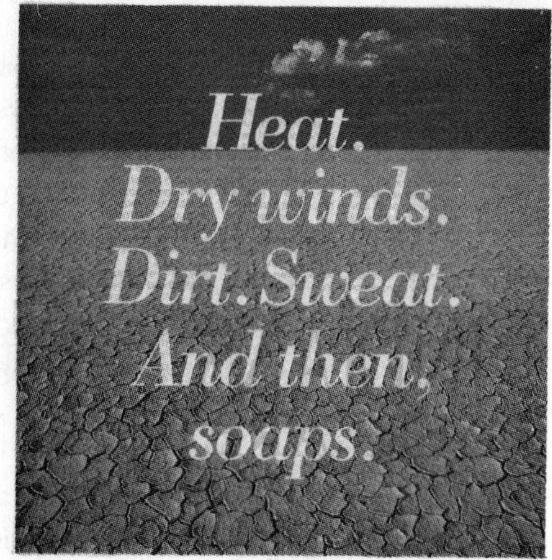

No wonder, your skin becomes dry and thirsts for care in summer.
Dove
In summer, for that squeaky clean feeling, you use soap. But, in the process, you disturb your skin's vital acid mantle and upset its moisture balance. Stop being harsh on your skin. Use Dove. It cleanses thoroughly, removing dirt from the deepest pore. And yet, after bathing with Dove, you are left with a feeling that's different from the one after using soap. It is proof that Dove is at work. Remember, Dove is not a soap. It is a mild, gentle blend of 1/4 moisturising cream and neutral cleansing ingredients. Try it for 7 days and discover the difference. Especially now that summer is here.
A quality product from Hindustan Lever.
Dove does not dry your skin like soap can.

14. The Lifestyle Headline

When there is no USP (unique selling proposition) for the product, you may well have tc invent one. You might build a reason-why into the target audience's lifestyle aspirations, e.g., Four Square cigarettes' "Live Life Kingsize" campaign. Or the Charms' "spirit of freedom". This technique is mostly used where (a) the market is saturated and (b) the product may be linked with status/snob appeal, as in cigarettes, textiles, liquor, cars and credit cards.

This list of Headline Techniques is by no means a comprehensive list. The sky is the limit to what you can think up to get your message across. As your mind gets accustomed to lateral thinking, you will be able to create your own techniques. Just remember to jot them down—in case memory fails at the crucial moment.

More Propositions and Headlines

As a copywriter you will doubtless give press ads more than a cursory glance as you browse through newspapers and magazines. Advertising and marketing professionals automatically glance at the key number in ads which they think are attention-getters.

You will soon be doing this too.

In the process, you will automatically register the headline thoughts and propositions that are the basis for these ads. All it takes is time and training. The following exercise will help you gain that trained eye.

Take another look at the press ads which illustrate the Headline Techniques listed above. Try and derive the propositions for each based on the headline/subhead/visual/baseline (never mind the body copy) information. Do not worry if you are not totally on target. Just get down to it.

When you have the propositions ready, think of at least five alternative ways to express each of them as a headline. By the way, you can do this exercise with any strong headline which catches your attention. Here's an example.

THE NEXT TIME YOU WANT TO RELAX,
TRY WRITING.
PARKER INTRODUCES FRONTIER
WITH SOFT TOUCH COMFORT GRIP.
The Parker Frontier, possesses the qualities you would expect of a fine writing instrument, yet is surprisingly well priced. With its wide diameter, soft touch grip it relaxes your fingers while writing for hours. Exceptional craftsmanship and lasting materials ensure lifetime performance (in fact, we guarantee it). And crowned with the solid good looks that are synonymous with Parker, it also comes in two exciting finishes of Two tone and Translucent.
PARKER
FRONTIER.
A PARKER IS IN THE DETAILS.
Available at all leading outlets across INDIA. For corporate enquiries: Delhi

Headline	**Proposition**	**Alternative headlines**
The next time you want to relax, try writing.	Parker introduces Frontier with soft touch comfort grip.	■ Parker Frontier pens don't write, they flow. ■ You'll never use e-mail again. ■ Silken writing . . . only with Parker Frontier. ■ Auto-writing is here. ■ Re-introducing the gracious art of letter writing . . . .

It's easy! It's fun!! Go to it!!!

Hard Sell and Soft Sell

Any of the headline techniques listed above may be used in a *Hard Sell* or *Soft Sell* manner. These terms are often confusing. To my mind, Hard Sell and Soft Sell are *descriptive of selling approaches.* They are not headline techniques but a manner of tackling the advertising. They have more to do with tone of voice and brand image than with the proposition or brand positioning. Think about this for a moment.

The impact of a Soft Sell ad can be as powerful as the impact of a Hard Sell ad.

When setting out to create an ad, you will have to decide which approach you want to use to get a desired response. In some cases like feminine products, or those involving babies, cosmetics, etc., you might prefer to use the Soft Sell. Products with a strong USP or well-defined product pluses usually impact better with Hard Sell.

But these are only general guidelines. A lot depends on the target audience and its perceptions about the product. You must be a bit of a psychologist when deciding on the approach. Shock treatment is fine, but you could make a fatal error by using a hammer to swat a fly.

"At 60 miles an hour the loudest noise in this new Rolls-Royce comes from the electric clock"

What makes Rolls-Royce the best car in the world? "There is really no magic about it—it is merely patient attention to detail," says an eminent Rolls-Royce engineer.

Special showing of the Rolls-Royce and Bentley at Salter Automotive Imports, Inc, 9009 Carnegie Ave., tomorrow through April 26.

Some Great Headlines that Use Soft Sell

At 60 miles an hour the loudest noise in this new Rolls Royce comes from the electric clock.

This was written in 1958 by David Ogilvy and its *impact* or *effect* has been such that it has become part of advertising history.

The visual showed a tranquil village grocer's shop in the background, with a shiny new Rolls Royce parked in front, by the kerb. A woman carrying a bag of groceries is walking towards the car.

The pause that refreshes
Drink
Coca-Cola
Delicious and Refreshing
The Coca-Cola Company, Atlanta, Ga.
EACH busy day tends down hill from that top-of-the-morning feeling with which you begin. Don't whip yourself as the day begins to wear. Pause and refresh yourself with an ice-cold Coca-Cola, and be off to a fresh start. The wholesome refreshment of Coca-Cola has made it the one great drink of the millions. A perfect blend of many flavors, it has a flavor all its own—delicious to taste and, more than that, with a cool after-sense of refreshment. It is ready, cold and tingling, at fountains and refreshment stands around the corner from anywhere.
THE BEST SERVED DRINK IN THE WORLD
A pure drink of natural flavors served ice-cold in its own bottle—the distinctive Coca-Cola bottle. Every bottle is sterilized, filled and sealed air-tight by automatic machines, without the touch of human hands—insuring purity and wholesomeness.
OVER 8 MILLION A DAY
IT HAD TO BE GOOD TO GET WHERE IT IS

Within the Curve of a Woman's arm
A frank discussion of a subject too often avoided

The illustration shows a man in evening dress dancing with a woman who has her right arm outstretched to rest on his shoulder.

The ad, written by James Webb Young of JWT in 1919, raised a storm of protest and 200 readers of the Ladies' Home Journal, where it appeared, cancelled their subscriptions. But the sales of the deodorant, Odorono, increased 112 per cent that year!

The pause that refreshes

These words have become synonymous with Coca-Cola. They first appeared in national magazines in America in 1929, featuring a working girl (typist) with a Coke in her hand and a smile on her face. The stock market crashed a month later, but Coca-Cola sales continued to soar. Soft Sell, great impact.

Some Great Headlines that Use Hard Sell

Reach for a Lucky instead of a sweet

This famous line for Lucky Strike cigarettes manufactured by The American Tobacco Company was coined by George W. Hill in the mid-1920s. The ad featured motion picture star Constance Talmadge saying "Light a Lucky and you'll never miss sweets that make you fat!" What a platform! Anyway, in 1925 the company's profits were $ 21 million. Thanks to this idea, profits rose to $ 46 million by 1931 . . . and to over $ 62 million in 1947. Plot that graph!

To men who want to
QUIT WORK some day

A simple illustration of a smiling old gent with a rod, reel and creel . . . has become symbolic of how it feels to get rid of money worries in retirement. This ad for the Phoenix Mutual Life Insurance Company, which appeared in 1929, was the brainchild of the agency Batten, Barton, Durstine & Osborn (BBDO). It resulted in a four times larger volume of sales than its 25 predecessors! Bruce Barton was the pioneer in the field of pre-testing display ads (with coupons, unthinkable for a dignified insurance firm in those days), and John Caples, the guru of direct mail and author of Tested Advertising Methods.

How to Win Friends and Influence People

Victor Schwab's all-copy ad promoting Dale Carnegie's book of this name sold over a million copies between December 1936 and November 1939. The sales to date are not so important as the fact that: an ad that brings in CASH for a million copies in three years solely via the coupon route, is a copywriting landmark.

HOW TO WIN FRIENDS AND INFLUENCE PEOPLE

JOHN D. ROCKEFELLER, Sr. once said: *"The ability to deal with people is as purchasable a commodity as sugar or coffee. And I will pay more for that ability than for any other under the sun."*

Wouldn't you suppose every college would conduct practical courses to develop this "highest priced ability under the sun"? To our knowledge, none has.

How to develop that ability is the subject of Dale Carnegie's amazing new book.

A few years ago Chicago University and the United Y.M.C.A. Schools made a survey to find out the prime interest of adults. The survey took two years, cost $25,000. It indicated that their first interest is health, and their second, how to understand and get along with *people*; how to make people like you; how to win others to your way of thinking.

Wouldn't you suppose that after the members of this survey committee had decided to give such a course, they could readily have found a practical textbook? They searched diligently, yet could find none suitable.

The book they were looking for was recently published, and overnight became a best seller. 36,000 copies were sold in three days of last week alone. More than 500,000 copies have been sold to date! IT IS OUT SELLING ANY OTHER BOOK IN AMERICA TODAY!

A New Book—and the Man Behind It

It is called *How to Win Friends and Influence People*, and is written by the one man who is perhaps better qualified to write it than anyone else.

Dale Carnegie is the man to whom the big men of business come for practical guidance on the subject of getting along with people, dealing with them successfully, winning others to their own way of thinking. During the last 25 years he has trained more than 17,000 business and professional men and women, among them some of the most famous in the country.

When he conducts his course on Public Speaking and How to Influence People in the ballroom of the Hotel Commodore or The Pennsylvania, or the Hotel Astor, the second largest hall in New York, the place is packed to capacity. Large organizations, such as The New York Telephone Co., Westinghouse Electric and Manufacturing Company, and many others listed elsewhere on this page, have had this training conducted by Mr. Carnegie in their own offices for their members and executives.

This new book, *How to Win Friends and Influence People*, grew and developed out of that vast laboratory of experience. As you can judge from the panel at the top of this advertisement, it is as practical as 24 years of actual successful experience with the problems of thousands of people in all walks of life can make it.

Consider the Case of Michael O'Neil

Michael O'Neil lives in New York City. He first got a job as a mechanic, then as a chauffeur.

When he got married he needed more money. So he tried to sell automobile trucks. But he was a terrible flop. He suffered from an inferiority complex that was eating his heart out.

On his way to see any prospect, he broke out into a cold sweat. Then, before he could get up enough courage to open the door, he often had to walk up and down in front of an office half a dozen times.

When he finally got in, he would invariably find himself antagonizing, arguing. Then he would get kicked out, never knowing quite why.

The Reader's Digest [illegible] voted 10 pages to this volume because, in their words, "From Mr. Carnegie's extensive reservoir of experience has come the wealth of anecdote and common sense lessons in human relations in which HOW TO WIN FRIENDS AND INFLUENCE PEOPLE abounds."

THIS IS A BIG BOOK OF THIRTY-SEVEN CHAPTERS, INCLUDING:

The Big Secret of Dealing with People
Six Ways to Make People Like You Instantly
An Easy Way to Become a Good Conversationalist
A Simple Way to Make a Good First Impression
How to Interest People
Twelve Ways to Win People to Your Way of Thinking
A Sure Way of Making Enemies—and How to Avoid It
The Safety Valve in Handling Complaints
How to Get Cooperation
A Formula That Will Work Wonders for You
The Movies Do It. Radio Does It. Why Don't You Do It?
Nine Ways to Change People Without Giving Offense or Arousing Resentment
How to Criticize—and Not Be Hated for It
How to Spur Men on to Success
Making People Glad to Do What You Want
Letters That Produced Miraculous Results
Seven Rules for Making Your Home Life Happier

He was such a failure he decided to go back to work in a machine shop. Then one day he received a letter inviting him to attend the opening session of a Dale Carnegie course.

"It may do you some good, Mike. God knows you need it!"

He didn't want to go; he was afraid that he would be out of place; that there would be a lot of college men. But his despairing wife made him, saying, "It *may* do you some good, Mike. God knows you need it."

He went to the meeting, and other meetings of the course. He lost his fear. He learned how to talk charmingly and convincingly, how to make people like him at once, how to win friends and influence others.

Today Michael O'Neil is a star salesman for one of the country's largest manufacturers of motor trucks. His income has mounted and skyrocketed. Last year at the Hotel Astor, he stood in front of 2500 people and told a rollicking story of his achievements. Few professional speakers could have equalled his confidence or his reception.

Michael O'Neil is a salesman, but his problem was exactly the same as that of thousands in other fields: the fundamental one of *getting along with people*. The way it was solved is just one example of what Dale Carnegie's help has meant to more than 17,000 people in all types of endeavor. *What Dale Carnegie has done for them he can do for you.* Look at the chapter headings. They indicate the amount of hard-hitting, priceless information Dale Carnegie's book contains. But the subject is so intensely important that we say, look at this book without obligation. Then decide whether or not you want to own it.

Only $1.96 if you decide to keep it

DALE CARNEGIE

Dale Carnegie is the man the men of business come to for practical instruction in getting along with people. During the last 25 years, he has trained more than 17,000 business and professional men—more than any other living man.

Large organizations such as:

Westinghouse Electric Manufacturing Co.
New York Telephone Co.
Bell Telephone Co. of Pennsylvania
American Institute of Electrical Engineers, New York
McGraw-Hill Publishing Company, New York
Brooklyn Chamber of Commerce
Philadelphia Chamber of Commerce
Philadelphia Electric Co.
Philadelphia Gas Works Co.
Carrier Engineering Corporation
Philadelphia Association of Life Underwriters

have had this training conducted in their own offices for their members and executives.

This new book is a direct result of Dale Carnegie's experience, the *only* working manual of its kind ever written to help people solve their daily problems in human relationships.

SEND NO MONEY

Try Dealing THIS WAY With People—for just FIVE Days!

This book has been published for only a short time. Yet it is now outselling any *other book*—fiction or non-fiction—in America! The presses are now running continuously to turn out 5,000 copies daily.

When you get your copy simply *read it*; there are no "exercises" to be practiced. Then try for five days Dale Carnegie's simple method of dealing with people. Judge for yourself, in your daily social or business life, how easily what ever you do, say, or write can win the friendship and the hearty cooperation of others instead of arousing resentment, friction, and either a negative response or no action at all.

It is not necessary to send any money now. You may pay for "*How to Win Friends and Influence People*" when it is delivered—with the definite understanding that its price of only $1.96 will be refunded to you if you wish it. If this book does what we claim, it will mean more to you than *ANY* book you *have ever read*. If it doesn't we do not want you to keep it. Mail this coupon at once.

SIMON and SCHUSTER, Dept. C-628, 386 Fourth Ave., New York

SIMON and SCHUSTER, *Publishers*
Dept. C-628, 386 Fourth Ave., N. Y. C.

Please send me *How to Win Friends and Influence People*. I will pay postman only $1.96 plus few cents postage charges. It is understood that I may read it for 5 days and return it for refund if I then feel that it does not in every way live up to the claims made for it.

Name
Address
City *State*

Check here if you prefer to enclose $1.96 plus 4¢ New York Sales Tax WITH this coupon, in that case WE will pay the postage charges. The same refund privilege applies of course.

Warm-up

Choose five each of Soft Sell and Hard Sell ads.

Show them to several people (not from your office!) who could be possible target audience.

Make a note of their comments.

Were the Soft Sell ads more appealing?

To men or to women?

Did the Hard Sell ads get their message across?

Which ads were more persuasive?

Which impelled people to act?

What about them caused this?

Which products—consumer durables, fmcgs, industrial—benefited most by which technique?

Now try writing headlines for these products using a Hard Sell approach where the current approach is soft, and Soft Sell where it is hard. Do your efforts work better? Test them out with the same people as before. Note their comments!

With our industry being watched so carefully by governmental agencies, with the FTC ready to pounce on every claim we make, what we *can* say in our ads is forever narrowing and the sharpest tool left for us is *how* we say it.

— William Bernbach (1989)

The New Media Creativity

Sometimes the proposition for a press ad may be translated into an advertising idea that lends itself to an unusual or never-used-before medium. Here the medium itself becomes the technique. Today more than ever before, creative people are looking for unconventional media to hang their propositions from. The medium is practically the message. Media can be high-brow or low, and be invested with a brand image of their own. You might scrawl your message about bras and matches on a wall, but you would hardly be happy to sell Master Card or Visa on a public latrine wall. Over the decades, finding innovative media is becoming like hunt-the-thimble. One sees all sorts of advertising messages on

Kiosks
Trains
Buses
Car windows
Car fenders
Bridges
Lamp posts
Walls
Umbrellas
Gift items
Desk sets
T-shirts
Peak caps
Mountains
Balloons
Skywriting
Banners
Matchboxes
Bus tickets
Theatre tickets
Pens
Wall clocks
Calendars
Tunnels
Shop windows
Anywhere
Everywhere

Workout

Re-read Chapter 16 paying special attention to the section on Glim's appeals. It must be noted that *appeals* differ from headline techniques, advertisiing approaches and press ad categories! (Goodness, who told you copywriting is *easy*!)

Just in case you have forgotten all about this dear reader, here are nine carefully selected press ads, each based on a Glim appeal.(You should know them by heart now!) Study each carefully and then describe the Headline Techniques used in each.

Appeal	*Press Ad*	*Headline Technique*
Hunger	La Mallorquina	
Sex/Love	Calida Jocks	
Anger	Ad Banning Dog Waste on Boston Streets	
Fear	Listerine	
Taste	Maggi Tonite's Special	
Smell	Superwrap	
Touch	Nivea	
Sight	Sil Jam	
Hearing	Post Breakfast Cereal	

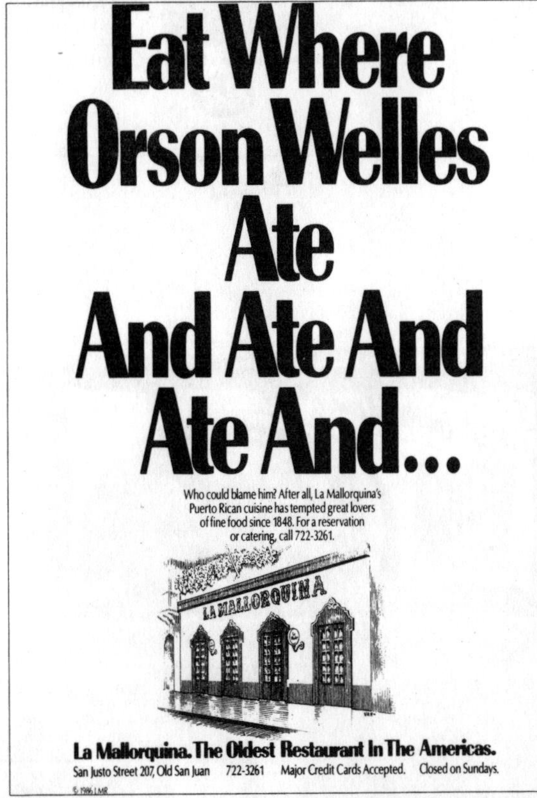

Hunger

Sex/Love

PARKE-DAVIS
How to succeed at work: Watch your mouth.

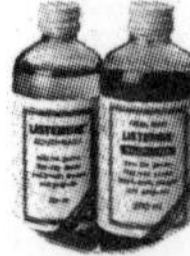

Even flattery won't get you that promotion if your breath is bad. Instead, rinse with Listerine twice daily after brushing. Because it's a mouthwash that kills 92% of the germs causing bad breath. Just what you need to get rid of the competition.
LISTERINE
MOUTHWASH
SAY GOODBYE TO BAD BREATH
To make sure your boss stays on talking terms with you, write to us for a free booklet on oral hygiene at: Listerine Cell, Parke Davis (I) Ltd., Pavilion House, Prabhadevi, Mumbai 400 025.

Fear

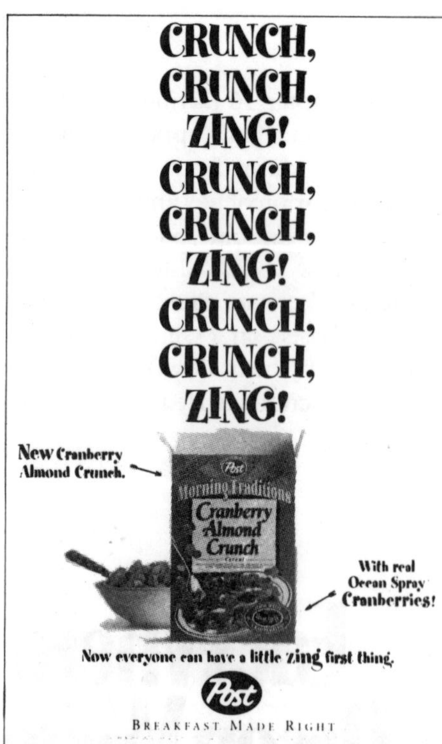

New Cranberry Almond Crunch.

Cranberry Almond Crunch
With real Ocean Spray Cranberries!
Now everyone can have a little zing first thing.

BREAKFAST MADE RIGHT

Hearing

PUBLIC
ENEMY
NO.2

WHAT DOGS DO IN BOSTON
CAN BE A CRIME.

Anger

Pizza tonite, Mom?
ITALIAN PIZZA
The 'let's eat-out' taste.
At home. In minutes.
NEW
MAGGI
Tonite Special
READY-TO-COOK GRAVY
PERFECT. EVERYTIME YOU MAKE IT.

Taste

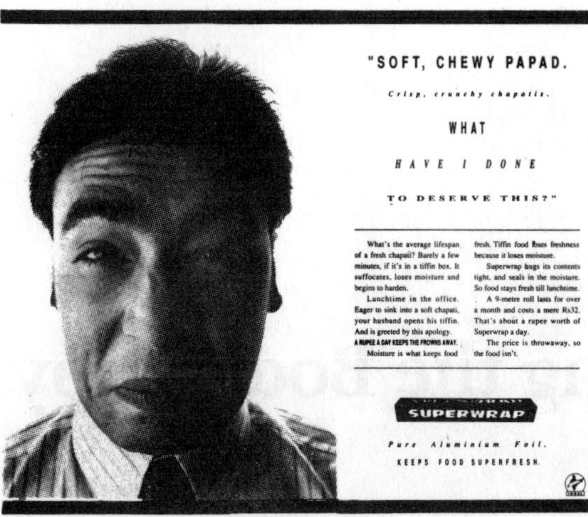

Smell

Sight

Touch

18

Building the Body Copy

There is a school of writers that pooh-poohs *Body Copy*. (That is the fine print text you have been asked not to bother about so far.) Visuals are the thing, they aver, a picture speaks a thousand words.

People do not read long copy, says another. David Ogilvy would disagree. He is a great believer in long, long, long copy. Better a long headline that sells, he is supposed to have said, than a short headline that says nothing.

Who is right? Who is wrong? You be the judge.

Body Copy has its place in a copywriter's life. Much depends on the constraints of the job, e.g. pre-set size of the ad (what can you fit into 100 column cms which may have to be reduced by 50% to adapt to another magazine?). Body Copy must follow a set of rules which you break at your peril, and at the cost of wasting the client's money. They are not a bunch of words slapped together to fill in a space where the art director got lazy.

Some ads warrant a few, succinct words of Body Copy; others are more demanding. The main point is that *every word of Body Copy must be made to work as hard as possible*.

You have just so much space to sell your product, so pack a punch. Some writers think this means placing full stops after every few words. Like this. No verbs. Sheer folly. Irritating. Get the point?

When in doubt, never cut copy. Rewrite it . . . .

It took me a while to learn to write Body Copy. Gerson da Cunha once said wryly when presenting the annual campaigns to Pond's, "June writes the headlines; I write the body copy." Truly, you do not begin to be a professional copywriter until you have learned to write the best Body Copy in the world. Writing Body Copy will probably take up more than 50 per cent of your working life. So you may as well learn to write it, and write it well. When you do, the satisfaction is enormous.

Just for starters, here are some types of copy you will be expected to churn out in double quick time.

- body copy for print ads
- for direct mailers
- direct response ads
- classified ads
- appointment ads
- for technical leaflets
- house journals
- mail order copy
- use of coupons
- for contests (rules and regulations!)
- minutes of meetings

- for pharmaceutical literature
- for press releases
- one-time occasional ads
- for souvenir ads
- for client's birthday/wedding/ anniversary cards
- promotional literature
- synopsis of what the creative director said
- the chairman's speech
- the managing director's speech
- the account executive's speech
- the janitor's speech
- anything and everything that needs to get written!

You are a writer. So write.

The Challenge of Body Copy

I learned a lot from Old Aesop Glim as he likes to call himself. So might you. Glim talked in terms of *copy policy.* Not to be confused with the Creative Brief, please. Copy policy outlines the steps to take to write the copy (headline/text/baseline) for a particular ad. For the sake of example, let us return to the hypothetical toothpaste, Dentium.

You know the facts about Dentium.
You have even arrived at a proposition for it.
You know who the consumer is.
You have decided on the target audience for our message.
You have set down a few tentative headlines based on the proposition.
Now what?

It helps to get back to what Stephen Baker calls the Big Picture. This means visualising the problem, the marketing objective, the advertising goal, and the advertising task ahead. It means reading the creative brief again, assimilating all the facts about the product, the consumer, the company, the competition. This is just revision. If your brand is Dentium, work out a creative brief (invent one) according to the guidelines set down in previous chapters (tone of voice/brand image/positioning statement). Get it fixed in your mind that your ad has a task to do—to get the advertiser's message across to the potential consumer.

Keep telling yourself you are not paid to be Danielle Steele or John le Carré . . . you are paid to write words that *sell the product.*

Remember the famous quote by Adlai Stevenson while introducing a candidate for the Presidency who succeeded where he failed, in Los Angeles, in 1960. ". . . in classical times when Cicero had finished speaking, the people said, How well he spoke—but when Demosthenes had finished speaking, the people said, Let us march against Philip . . . ."?

You are in this business to sell, to impel action, to make people stop, read and then buy your product. You are working within many parameters and constraints. They are the foundation stones of your campaign. You have to be aware of all of them when you get set to build your copy structure.

Aesop Glim's copy policy gives *Six Simple Steps* to work out your selling sequence. Here they are.

Step One: Arresting Power

Get the immediate attention of your target audience. You do this in your headline—whether provocative, Soft Sell, Hard Sell, long or short. Your headline must stop the prospects in their tracks.

With Dentium as example, you might come up with a powerful launch headline like

From the makers of Volgate
NEW DENTIUM TOOTHPASTE WITH CALCIUM—
builds teeth while it cleans

That is a stopper, that is. Okay, so it is not the most 'creative' headline in the world. But people are going to say—Volgate? New? Calcium? Strong teeth? Must try it. Then if they are interested, they will get down to the fine print. You have hooked them into reading, now you have to sustain their interest so they will not turn the page.

Step Two: Substantiation

At once get down to justify, to prove the claim you have made in the headline. You might say as your opening line of the text:

Lab tests prove that small doses of calcium ingested through the gums strengthen tooth enamel. Calcium not only builds bones in children, it helps maintain and fortify bones in adults. Pregnant women, and those over 40, need calcium daily to keep brittle bones at bay.

There, that ought to satisfy them. Of course, I am stretching the truth a bit to accommodate the hypothetical product.

Step Three: Transition

Get into your subject while you still hold the readers' interest. What is in it for them?

> Protect tooth enamel. Give your teeth
> a daily dose of calcium—
> while you brush. With NEW DENTIUM.

Now you have made a neat transition and introduced your brand.

Step Four: Competition

This step is frequently omitted—but if you can sidestep your rivals, nothing like it. You might say:

> No other toothpaste guarantees
> stronger teeth while it cleans.

That takes care of the lot of them! Glim advises you to ignore your competition—by and large—if your product has the virtues you claim it has, and is rightly priced. If your copy is soundly constructed, you will get your share of the market.

Step Five: Your Product

Speak openly about the good qualities of your brand. If your prospects have read this far, they are ready to believe you.

> ONLY NEW DENTIUM is reinforced with high-density
> calcium to slow down wear and tear on your teeth.
> Its germ-reducing properties make it the trusted
> toothpaste . . . from the makers of Volgate.

Now you have given them both rational and emotional justifications for using New Dentium. The proven toothpaste company Volgate seems to clinch the argument.

Step Six: Business Ending

Impel action; tell your readers what they should do about your product. Do not just leave them gawping. You could end up . . .

Get yourself a lifetime guarantee
against dentures. Start brushing with
NEW DENTIUM—TODAY!
(Available with your chemist.)

Then sign off with a good baseline or slogan—

It's the calcium in Dentium that does it!

To make the points the Body Copy has been slightly exaggerated. Try for crispness and clarity. Make one word do the job of three. But never sacrifice important facts about the product just to keep your copy brief. On the other hand, resist the temptation to use material which obscures your sales argument.

After you have written your body copy according to the Six-Step formula, read through it again. Check logic and structure, work in rhythm, and tighten up with metaphor.

Warm-ups

1. Select ads for consumer goods. Examine their copy structure. Do they follow Glim's copy policy? How would you redo the text to make it more persuasive?
2. Write the Body Copy for New Dentium using Aesop Glim's Six-Step formula. Base your copy on this headline:

The Lifetime Guarantee
Against Wearing Dentures
New Dentium from Volgate is here!

On Writing Body Copy

- Long opening sentences in the first paragraph are no-no
- Too many *ands* and *buts* are also no-no
- Work towards easy reading
- Avoid using all CAPS in headlines/subheads
- Use active verbs and pictorial nouns
- Be simple, crisp, clear
- Go slow with adverbs and adjectives
- Remember to work in rhythm and metre
- Never talk down to your prospects (the customer is not a moron, she is your wife!)
- Stick by the right selling sequence
- Use the word 'you' often
- Mention the brand names often

The more books you read about the craft of writing copy, the more rules and regulations you will come across. The point to remember is *you are paid to sell the client's product.* Accountability is everything: whether in a press ad, film, or TV commercial. Too much money is wasted on verbiage, clutter and technical sleight-of-hand that wows them in the gallery but leaves the brand name forgettable.

Craft, craft, craft your copy. Never be satisfied with the first draft. Cut unnecessary words. Replace 10 words with three. It can be done. Show your efforts to someone in authority, like your copy chief, from time to time. The final test comes on the job itself . . . bad copy will get rejected, good copy immediately recognised.

More on How to Structure Body Copy

1. Follow Glim's Six-Step formula.
2. Use language your target audience understands.
3. Write as if your prospect was sitting across the desk from you.
4. Maintain the flow—no jerky sentences.
5. Pick a leitmotif (a theme associated with a person or a thought, recurring when the person appears on the stage or the thought becomes prominent in the action) and follow through.
6. Use similes and metaphors sparingly.
7. Use short sentences.
8. Keep the tone of voice consistent.

9. Use pictorial nouns.
10. Use active verbs.
11. Avoid hackneyed phrases.
12. Be idiomatic, but give a fresh twist to words.
13. Avoid puns.
14. Respect your prospect.
15. Do not waste his time.
16. Respect your client and his product.
17. Do not waste his money.

Warm-up

Watch out for ads that seem to waste the client's money. Re-do the ads, bearing in mind the principles discussed till now.

Indian English

More and more Indian language words are creeping into headlines and slogans. This is a sign of the times and a reflection of how English is evolving and adapting to Indian culture and thought.

This is no excuse, however, for poor grammar or wrong use of English in Body Copy. While 'Hinglish' or 'Hindish' has become acceptable, phrases like "cope up", "waiting on the bus stop", "a dozen of mangoes" are NOT! I say this advisedly, or you may end up writing a headline like the one presented proudly by a five-star hotel in the tranquil town where I live: COME AND STAY AT HOTEL XYZ . . . FOR GREAT MOMENTS OF MONOTONY!

We multilingual Indians tend to translate from one language into another instead of thinking in a particular language. That is why you hear phrases like "What you are doing?" and "I am going to go" and "You are eating my head" and "Don't do kit-kit, man" and "Rain is coming". This is where we could use good old Fowler's!

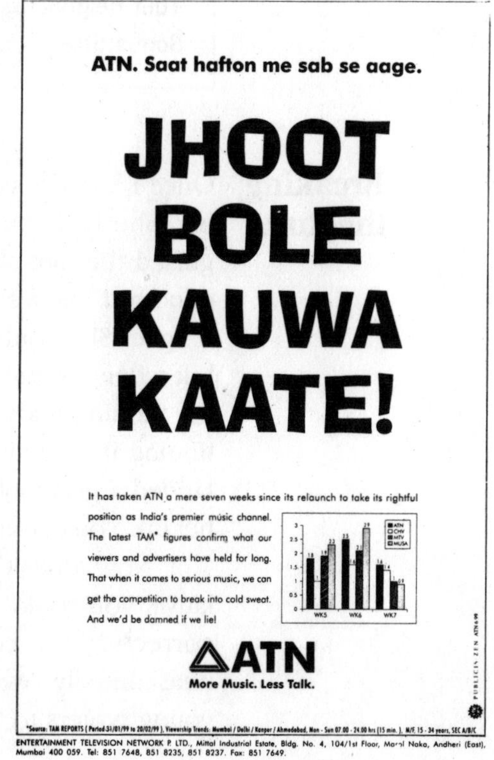

ATN. Saat hafton me sab se aage.
JHOOT BOLE KAUWA KAATE!
It has taken ATN a mere seven weeks since its relaunch to take its rightful position as India's premier music channel. The latest TAM* figures confirm what our viewers and advertisers have held for long. That when it comes to serious music, we can get the competition to break into cold sweat. And we'd be damned if we lie!
ATN
CHV
MTV
MUSA
WK5
WK6
WK7
ATN
More Music. Less Talk.
PUBLICIS ZEN ATN6-99
*Source: TAM REPORTS (Period 31/01/99 to 20/02/99), Viewership Trends: Mumbai / Delhi / Kanpur / Ahmedabad, Mon - Sun 07.00 - 24.00 hrs (15 min.), M/F, 15 - 34 years, SEC A/B/C
ENTERTAINMENT TELEVISION NETWORK P. LTD., Mittal Industrial Estate, Bldg. No. 4, 104/1st Floor, Marol Naka, Andheri (East), Mumbai 400 059. Tel: 851 7648, 851 8235, 851 8237. Fax: 851 7649.

Tried and True Words to Use

How to	While stocks last
New!	HURRY!
For the first time in India	Last day for ...
Introducing, presenting	YOU TOO CAN
The ONLY soap/tea/clothes	Join the hundreds (thousands/millions . . .)
Now YOU can have/be/do	You can trust (the company) which gave you . . .
NEVER BEFORE	SAVE . . . per cent
Value-for-money	Good news!
A bargain!	For those who . . .
Economical	For women who . . .
Two for the price of one	For men who . . .
Goes a longer way	Girls! Boys! Executives! Housewives! (flagging the target)
It's easy! It's fun! (contests)	Extra! with this pack
No sweat, no strain	Free! with this carton
FREE!	New, improved!
Your neighbours will envy you	
Bonus offer	

Breaking the Rules

Once I had occasion to select a bright young person for copy training. She had spunk, spark and imagination—but her portfolio disguised the fact she did not know English! She had been 'convent-educated' as we say in India, and considered English her mother tongue. She could dash off short two-word headlines with flair . . . but when it came to writing Body Copy . . . ! Fortunately, the girl quit the training midway, so I was spared the embarrassment of discontinuing it. A year later, she phoned me, bubbling with joy. She had landed a good job with a leading agency! They had simply snapped her up. You could have knocked me down with the proverbial feather.

Now, does that cheer you up? If your 'ideation' skills are superlative, you could end up being creative director, while someone else corrects your copy! One CEO, who was also creative chief, unashamedly owned up to atrocious spelling. He kept a stable of young writers to 'brush up' his work!

A certain TV campaign featuring a devil and a smashed screen would never have passed muster with me. Yet it went on to capture the public imagination and make unprecedented sales. The world is a strange place. Full of rules to be broken!

A Master Speaks

When David Ogilvy came to India in 1982 for the Advertising Congress in Delhi, it was a signal honour. He hated to travel by air. He made a gaffe on opening day by referring to the West as the 'hare' and India as the 'tortoise' in the advertising race. He later apologised, saying he had not read the speech before delivering it! He knew very little about India, it was obvious, but made up for this by seeing parts of the country—by train! He was also very careful to say something positive about advertising in India after that.

If a Master is prepared to learn, how much more ought mere mortals be prepared to listen to him. You will benefit from reading the section 'How to write potent copy' in Ogilvy's famous book *Confessions of an Advertising Man* (1963).

After reading it carefully, return to the ads featured in Chapter 17. From Propositions to Headlines. Look at them in the light of Ogilvy's guidelines. How many of his principles, if any, apply to them? In what way? If Glim and Ogilvy were to meet, would they be friends? Or just friendly rivals?

The Body Beautiful

by Anita Sarkar

Larry Grant wrote body copy standing on his head (still does, I'm told). Nina Verma wrote it mainly in her head (while filing her nails). Kewlian Sio squiggled and scratched, filling pad after pad, none of which he could bear to discard. Baruna Dutta found writing it just a tad more difficult than the *London Times* crossword she breezed through every morning. Balaji would pat his pocket and say, "It's all there." What was there was a neatly folded sheet of paper—blank. But yes, it was all there—in his head. Alyque Padamsee wrote it (in an emergency, when lesser mortals couldn't come up to scratch) in the lift, in the car and even in the client's office, minutes before the presentation. Gerson da Cunha wrote it in his neat round handwriting, every comma and colon in place—the right words, the right length, saying it all without saying everything. Frank Simoes wrote it brilliantly, seductively, daring you to say, "Who reads body copy!"

Names. They were part of my world, fellow 'craftsmen', if you like, many of whom have moved on to other (I won't say, 'better') things.

I've spoken about how some people I know wrote copy. What about me? I often write it in my sleep! This isn't being arrogant or blasé. I think about it, wake up excitedly, jot down an 'inspired' line, which more often than not sounds positively strange in the cold light of day. It's all part of the process, I guess. In the BC (Before Computer) days, I would start with a fresh page on a fresh pad, and soon the waste basket would be full of crumpled sheets and crushed non-starters. Now the computer screen is my blank page. I write—delete—write—delete—delete. But I'm in good company. No less a writer than V.S. Naipaul once produced only the word 'The' carefully caligraphed through one whole day. Ernest Hemingway recommends that you get up from the table before your thoughts have dried up. (Is that why you find so few writers at their desks?)

There's an old song that goes, "Baby, if I'm the bottom, you're the top." Which exactly sums up the body copy-headline relationship. BC takes over where HL leaves off. And that's the challenge. How do you get that stranger whose eye you've caught to linger on? Well, let him (I refuse not to be gender-biased here) feast on The Body Beautiful. The body copy that you've caressed, shaped and trimmed (very important) and made exciting, so he (okay, or she) just can't take his (if you must, her) eyes off it.

There's no great secret to this. Just talk their language. Talking babies to mums? Talk lullabies, like Nandita Challam did for Johnson & Johnson. Talking bargains to housewives? Talk value like I did with Lalitaji for Surf. Talking engineering to engineers? Don't talk 'engineering'. "Engineers are human beings," said Frank Simoes, which resulted in a memorable, non-engineering engineering campaign for Siemens. Talking to housebound women? Talk 'escape'. The insight that perhaps the only private space housewives have is the bathroom led to the bath in the waterfall concept for Liril. I try to get to know my target audience intimately and share the excitement that is in the product. This often means shameless eavesdropping, snooping and pestering but it's all worth it for the glorious quest, the impossible dream, of getting that fine print—that thing called 'body copy'—read, believed and acted upon.

I once wrote an ad for Diners Club (before it became Citibank Diners) and was delighted that the busy client service director had actually read it.

"I loved the ad," he said. I looked again at the finished product. A smart executive, briefcase in hand, walking towards an aircraft. The visual had taken all the space. So the visualiser cut—what else?—all the body copy, merely leaving the headline in: "It's all a matter of belonging to the right club." Turned out for the best.

Here's a litle doggerel about the lowly body copy:

It's what the headline hasn't said
What the client insists must be said
For some visualisers it has no place
Except to fill that empty space
But written from the heart, it can't fail
To make that all-important sale

Workout

Here are a clutch of ads used in *The Age of Communication* by William Lutz (1974). Each is accompanied by a set of topics to get your grey cells whirring!

1. Study the Body Copy and see if it follows Glim's Six-Step formula. If it does not, ask yourself why. Were the rules broken deliberately?
2. Have a go at the topics for discussion. Save any insights you may glean in your work file.
3. Rework the ads using Indian equivalents—for the product, the models, the situations. For instance, instead of Dewar's Profiles, you could have McDowell's Profiles, and instead of Bill Drake you could feature a popular Star Plus or MTV DJ or VJ. Follow the same selling logic in your body copy as the original ad.

Dewar's White Label Scotch

Headline:

Dewar's Profiles
(pronounced Do-ers White Label)

Body Copy:

Bill Drake

Home: Bel Air, California
Age: 33
Profession: Designs the format for pop music programmes on radio stations around the country.
Hobbies: Pool, monitoring his radio stations.
Last Book Read: The Godfather.
Last Accomplishment: Created *Solid Gold Rock and Roll* and *Hit Parade 71*, two of the most successful musical formats on radio today.
Quote: "You can't dismiss the rock groups as 'far out'. The fact that their music succeeds, suggests that their ideas are widely circulated and probably accepted by a lot of people. I think more attention should be paid to them. Listening might give everybody a better idea about what's on young people's minds."
Profile: Intuitive. Shrewd. Disarmingly casual. His sometimes abrasive manner has helped make him the most powerful force in broadcast rock.
Scotch: Dewar's White Label.

Caption to Product/Log in Fine Print:

Authentic. There are more than a thousand ways to blend whiskies in Scotland, but few are authentic enough for Dewar's 'White

DEWAR'S PROFILES

(Pronounced Do-ers "White Label")

BILL DRAKE

HOME: Bel Air, California

AGE: 33

PROFESSION: Designs the format for pop music programs on radio stations around the country.

HOBBIES: Pool. Monitoring his radio stations.

LAST BOOK READ: "The Godfather."

LAST ACCOMPLISHMENT: Created "Solid Gold Rock and Roll" and "Hit Parade 71," two of the most successful musical formats on radio today.

QUOTE: "You can't dismiss the rock groups as 'far-out'. The fact that their music succeeds, suggests that their ideas are widely circulated and probably accepted by a lot of people. I think more attention should be paid to them. Listening might give everybody a better idea about what's on young people's minds."

PROFILE: Intuitive. Shrewd. Disarmingly casual. His sometimes abrasive manner has helped make him the most powerful force in broadcast rock.

SCOTCH: Dewar's "White Label"

Authentic. There are more than a thousand ways to blend whiskies in Scotland, but few are authentic enough for Dewar's "White Label." The quality standards we set down in 1846 have never varied. Into each drop goes only the finest whiskies from the Highlands, the Lowlands, the Hebrides. ***Dewar's never varies.***

Advertisement for *Dewar's* Scotch Profile, from *Playboy*, September 1971, reprinted by permission.

Label'. The quality standards we set down in 1846 have never varied. Into each drop goes only the finest whiskies from the Highlands, the Lowlands, the Hebrides. DEWAR'S NEVER VARIES.

Discuss

- Advertisers often have famous people endorse their products. Is this such an ad?
- Why is the text presented in formal outline? What is the effect of this format?
- What is the ad's appeal?

Rhetorical

- What information are you given about the man endorsing DEWAR's? How pertinent is this information?
- The copy states "there are more than a thousand ways to blend whiskies" but Dewar's is authentic. What is the fallacy here? How do you know Dewar's is authentic? What does authentic mean?

New England Life Insurance Company

Headline:

"My insurance company? New England Life, of course. Why?"

Very fine print—almost invisible—at the top of ad:

1971 NEW ENGLAND MUTUAL LIFE INSURANCE COMPANY, BOSTON SUBSIDIARY NEL EQUITY SERVICES CORPN; AFFILIATE: LOOMIS, SAYLES & CO. INVESTMENT COUNSELORS.

Discuss

- What product is advertised? Where is the product mentioned—and why is it so understated?
- How does the cartoon help sell insurance? Is the cartoon humorous—or morbid?
- Is life insurance concerned with life or death? Why is it called life insurance and not death insurance?
- Is this an effective ad? Why?

Rhetorical

- Study the arrangement of the elements in the ad. Why is there so much white space? How does the arrangement lend emphasis to the point the ad is making?
- The caption is an answer to a question not stated in the ad. How does the cartoon make clear who has asked the question and who is answering? How does the cartoon make clear what the unstated question is?

Crest Toothpaste

Headline:

Teeth don't die a natural death.
You kill them.

Body Copy:

Chances are, when you lose a tooth, it's because you killed it with neglect. By not eating the right foods, or seeing the dentist often enough, or brushing properly.

Such neglect can lead to cavities, and cavities can lead to tooth loss. In fact, the average person loses 6 to 9 teeth in a lifetime just due to cavities.

Crest with fluoride fights cavities. So, besides seeing your dentist and watching treats, make sure you brush with Crest.

Because the more you fight cavities, the less your teeth have to fight for their lives.

Teeth don't die a natural death. You kill them.
Chances are, when you lose a tooth, it's because you killed it with neglect. By not eating the right foods, or seeing the dentist often enough, or brushing properly.
Such neglect can lead to cavities, and cavities can lead to tooth loss. In fact, the average person loses 6 to 9 teeth in a lifetime *simply* due to cavities.
Crest with fluoride fights cavities. So, besides seeing your dentist and watching treats, make sure you brush with Crest.
Because the more you fight cavities, the less your teeth have to fight for their lives.
Crest
Fighting cavities is the whole idea behind Crest.

Advertisement for *Crest* toothpaste from Life, July 7, 1972 reprinted by permission.

Logo/Baseline: Fighting cavities is the whole idea behind Crest.

Discuss

- What do you notice first—the tooth or the headline?
- Why isn't 'Crest' mentioned in the headline?
- How does the tooth in the ad differ from others?
- What is the basis of the appeal? How does this ad differ from other toothpaste ads?

Rhetorical

- Three words in the headline refer to death. What effect does this have?
- Does the text at the bottom have a paragraph structure?
- The second sentence in the text is a fragment. How does this fragment function in context?
- What tone of voice is being used in this ad?
- What is more noticeable about the headline—what it says or how large the type is? Why is it so large?

AT&T/Bell Company

Headline:

The phone company wants more installers like Alana MacFarlane.

Body Copy:

Alana MacFarlane is a 20-year-old from San Rafael, California. She's one of our first women telephone installers. She won't be the last.

We also have several hundred male telephone operators. And a policy that there are no all-male or all-female jobs at the phone company.

We want the men and women of the telephone company to do what they want to do, and do best.

For example. Alana likes working outdoors,"I don't go for office routine," she said, "But as an installer I get plenty of variety and a chance to move around."

Some people like to work with their hands, or, like Alana, get a kick out of working 20 feet up in the air.

Others like to drive trucks. Some we're helping to develop into good managers.

Today, when openings exist, local Bell Companies are offering applicants and present employees some jobs they may never have thought about before. We want to help all advance to the best of their abilities.

AT&T and your local Bell Company are equal opportunity employers.

AT&T/Bell

Headline:

The phone company wants more operators like Rick Wehmhoefer.

Body Copy:

Rick Wehmhoefer of Denver, Colorado, is one of several hundred male telephone operators in the Bell System.

Currently Rick is a directory assistance operator. "So far, my job has been pleasant and worthwhile," he says, "I enjoy assisting people."

We have men like Rick in a lot of different telephone jobs. Both men and women work as Bell System mechanics, truck drivers, installers and engineers.

We want the men and women of the telephone company to do what they want to do, and do best.

Today, when openings exist, local Bell Companies are offering applicants and present

.dvertisements for A.T.&T. from *Glamour*, July 1972 and *Playboy*, August 1972. Reprinted by permission of A.T. & T.

employees some jobs they may never have thought of before. We want to help all advance to the best of their abilities.

AT&T and your local Bell Company are equal opportunity employers.

Discuss

- What is the purpose of these two ads?
- What is the target audience in each case?
- How important is the visual? Would the texts be as effective without the pictures?
- Alana MacFarlane is pictured by herself, but Rick Wehmhoefer has someone next to him. Reason?
- How many similarities are there in these two ads?
- Why is Alana called an 'installer' and not a 'lineman'?
- Why does the headline refer to 'the phone company' and not to AT&T?

Rhetorical

- Why do the ads refer to 'male telephone operator' and 'women telephone installer'? Why is it necessary to emphasise the sex of each job holder?
- Compare the text in each ad—what similarities are there?
- Each ad has a quotation by the person featured. Why?
- The ad refers to AT&T as 'we' and 'our'. What effect does this achieve?

Nice'n Easy

Headline:

It lets me be me.

Body Copy:

Color that becomes part of you (not the other way around!)—that's what you get with Nice'n Easy from Clairol. Whether you want to color or conceal, to change a little or a lot, choose Nice'n Easy, for beautiful coverage, healthy-looking hair and honest-to-you color.

Baseline/logo:

Nice'n Easy haircolor
It sells the most

Discuss

- What is your first reaction to this ad? Do you find this ad sexy? Why?
- To whom would it appeal more, men or women?
- Does this ad demean women, as some allege? If so, give your reasons.
- Why is the text not included in the picture but set off by itself at the bottom of the page?
- This is an ad for hair coloring or hair dye. What relation does this picture have to the product?

Rhetorical

- What does "it lets me be me" mean? To what does 'it' refer? To whom does 'me' refer?
- "In hair color, as in make-up, clothes, love, work . . . a woman wants to be herself." What is the significance of the order of items in this sentence? Why use three dots in the middle of this sentence and not another punctuation mark?
- The caption of the ad refers to 'me', while the text of the ad refers to 'you'. Why is there a shift in person?

19

A Classic is Forever

Someone wise said God creates, man rearranges. But some geniuses are reflections of God in this respect. Theirs is the beauty and discipline that is handed down the centuries, that break time and culture barriers. Whether it is a Beethoven sonata, a Picasso blue period, the Taj Mahal, or Dante's Inferno.

These works are awesome. They bring a song to the heart and the hope that you too might produce a press ad or commercial that will earn you a place in the Advertising Hall of Fame. (Who knows, one day there might be a room in the Louvre or the Tate Gallery for copywriters!) In New York, the Museum of Modern Art is already heading in this direction, with exhibitions of Andy Warhol and Escher, as well as contemporary design in furniture and other functional items, such as chairs and computers. Today's surprise could be tomorrow's classic. But the same criterion prevails. Will it stand the test of time?

Advertising Age has compiled a list of the Top 10 Slogans of the twentieth century. Tomorrow's classics?

1. Diamonds are forever (DeBeers)
2. Just do it (Nike)
3. Thirst knows no season (Coca-Cola)
4. Tastes great, less filling (Miller Lite)
5. We try harder (Avis)
6. Good to the last drop (Maxwell House)
7. Breakfast of Champions (Wheaties)
8. Does she . . . or doesn't she? (Clairol)
9. When it rains it pours (Morton Salt)
10. Where's the beef? (Wendy's)

Honourable mentions went to:

- Look Ma, no cavities! (Crest toothpaste)
- Let your fingers do the walking (Yellow Pages)
- Loose lips sink ships (public service)
- M&Ms melt in your mouth, not in your hand (M&M candies)
- We bring good things to life (General Electric)

Though mores change, standards vary, the basic elements of a classic, in any field, are worth examining. Take a look.

1. His Master's Voice
   The terrier Nipper, that became world famous. Catch that 'listening' look—RCA Victor Gramophone Company.

Classic Element	*Examples*
Use of mnemonic relevant to the product or service.	1. Air-India Maharajah 2. Gattu of Asian Paints 3. MRF Muscle Man

2. Uneeda Bakers

   Introduced packaged biscuits for the first time in grocer's shops.

   —National Biscuit Company 'Uneeda Bakers'

   Agency: N.W. Ayer & Son

Classic Element	*Examples*
New concept in retail advertising	1. Paan Parag 2. Frooti in tetrapaks 3. Reuseable PET jars

STEINWAY

The Instrument of the Immortals

There has been but one supreme piano in the history of music. In the days of Liszt and Wagner, of Rubinstein and Berlioz, the preeminence of the Steinway was as unquestioned as it is today. It stood then, as it stands now, the chosen instrument of the masters—the inevitable preference wherever great music is understood and esteemed.

STEINWAY & SONS, Steinway Hall, 107-109 E. 14th Street, New York

Subway Express Stations at the Door

3. Steinway Piano

   The Instrument of the Immortals. Author Raymond Rubicam did his homework and found that the piano had been used by maestros and composers since Wagner and Liszt.

Classic Element	*Examples*
Association of product with prominent persons who really use it (not mere endorsements!).	1. Taj Tea/Zakir Hussain 2. Reebok/Azharuddin 3. Samsung/Kapil Dev 4. Pepsi/Shahrukh Khan

4. Woodbury Soap

"The skin you love to touch" has become one of advertising's unforgettable lines. First published in the *Ladies' Home Journal* in May 1911!

Classic Element	*Examples*
Basic appeal to the deepest human need. Sensory perception and instinct are a tight fit.	1. Johnson's baby products 2. Vadilal icecream 3. Onida/neighbour's envy

5. US School of Music

"They laughed when I sat down at the piano . . ." Written by John Caples in 1925 when he was still a copy cub. Worth studying as a masterpiece in direct mail and couponing.

For the full text of this ad, see p. 201.

Classic Element

Deprecatory headline with a twist in its tale . . . turns the tables on the scoffers to achieve the "aha" effect.

Examples

1. Maggi Sauce/It's different
2. Tata Press Yellow Pages
3. The Benetton (United Colors) series

6. Chesterfield

"Blow some my way" would never be acceptable in the America of the 90s! FOR THE FIRST TIME a woman was shown in cigarette advertising (1926)
Agency: Newell-Emmett

Classic Element
Breaking attitudinal barriers. Taking a risk. And setting a trend.

Examples
1. Kama Sutra condoms
2. Ariel/man washing clothes

7. Rubber keeps a Motor Bus Singing in the Rain

For 15 years this campaign for B.F. Goodrich (first in rubber) appeared every few weeks with the same layout, the same type faces, and the same kind of copy. That's a record.

Classic Element
Long-running campaign. Sticks to product performance story, while being consistently competent. An ad that will not win awards for creativity, just for being a good work horse.

Examples
1. Colgate toothpaste (bad breath/tooth decay)
2. Surf (washes whitest)
3. Philips (let's make things better)

8. HAMILTON WATCHES

To Peggy—for marrying me in the first place . . .

Author: Carl Spier, copy director of BBD&O. The watch company has received hundreds of letters in response to this ad which is released each year at Christmas with NO COPY CHANGE. Only the art and the watch are updated.

Classic Element	*Examples*
Honest, emotional copy with broad appeal that never dates.	1. Raymond's (The complete man) 2. DeBeers (Diamonds are forever)

9. MERRILL LYNCH, PIERCE, FENNER & BEANE CO.

6000 words of copy that were read—again and again and again. First appeared in the *New York Times*. Though the ad was not designed to pull enquiries, two varied writein offers were made. One month later, over 5000 rerequests for 20,000 copies of either or both of the items offered had been received—4000 in the first week alone.

Classic Element	*Examples*
Important information gets read.	1. Mauritius tourism. 2. Beauty without cruelty.

10. HATHAWAY SHIRTS

Who does not know of the famous eye-patch worn by the man in the Hathaway shirt? Written in 1950 or so by David Ogilvy. Remembered by millions. The eyepatch has been widely copied the world over, and even inspired a school of advertising—a school which Mr Ogilvy deplored!

Classic Element	*Example*
Gimmicks work when the product is good. The consumer often reacts surprisingly!	The Onida Devil

What everybody ought to know . . .
About This Stock And Bond Business

Some plain talk about a simple business that often sounds complicated.

WHY WE ARE PUBLISHING THIS INFORMATION

A little while ago we were talking with the editor of a big national magazine, a well-informed man. He said that he had never done business with a broker because he was afraid he wouldn't understand the "lingo they talk."

Since we are brokers, you can imagine that was something of a shock . . . made us think.

The financial business *does* use a lot of specialized words, but there really isn't anything complicated or mysterious about what those words *mean*. Because we've used them so long and so frequently, we've just assumed that everybody understood them.

That has been our mistake. And a big mistake. For if people don't understand what stocks and bonds are, they aren't likely to invest their money in them.

"So what?" you ask. Well, here's "what".

If people do not invest their funds in securities, American business and American government will not have the capital they need for growth—for new products, new plants, new jobs. That capital can come from just one place: People. Not just a few people with great fortunes—there aren't many of them any more—but from millions of people.

Or look at it from the social point of view. People who don't understand investments are easy prey for a wide variety of "get-rich-quick" artists.

Or look at it from the purely personal point of view. A lot of people might like to invest their surplus savings where they could earn a fair return on them. But if they are unfamiliar with securities, they aren't likely to invest their *money* in them.

For all these reasons, it is important that people should know as much as they can about this stock and bond business.

But where do you start?

Well, it would seem that a good place to start would be with the "lingo" that our friend the editor complained about. And we might as well go back to the most common words in the business. You may find a lot of this explanation pretty elementary. But the next fellow *may not* be wholly clear about the exact difference between a stock and a bond. So we'll start right there, in the belief that you'll be obliging enough to skip what you already know.

MERRILL LYNCH,
PIERCE, FENNER & BEANE

What Are Stocks?

The stock of a company represents the ownership of that company. If you own a share of stock in a company—let's call it the Typical Manufacturing Company—you own a piece of that company—a part of its plant, its production, a part of everything in that company. If the Typical Company has 1,000 shares of stock and you own 10 shares, you own one hundredth of the company, or 1% of it.

Some companies have only a few shares of stock and a few owners, while others—the big corporations like U. S. Steel and General Motors—have millions of shares of stock and hundreds of thousands of stockholders or owners.

Why Should Anybody Buy Stocks?

For the same reason that he might go into any other business for himself. To make money.

If you own 1% of the Typical Company, you own 1% of whatever it earns. Normally, some of those earnings or profits will be paid out to you and the other stockholders as dividends—so much on each share. The rest of the earnings will be put back into the business to do more work, make more earnings, more dividends.

How Big Are Dividends?

That depends on the company and how much it earns. Some companies pay out a substantial portion of their earnings as dividends. Other companies, particularly those that are expanding, may plow a greater proportion of earnings back into the business. Some companies pay no dividends. Of all the companies whose stocks are bought and sold on the New York Stock Exchange, about 90% are paying dividends. (That was the record last year.) The average dividend paid by these companies is a little better than 5% of what the stocks are selling at. Thus, if you bought one share of stock in each you could figure on making 5% on your money in a year. Some pay more. Some pay less.

Most companies try to pay dividends regularly. (The Pennsylvania Railroad has paid a dividend every year for more than a century.)

A company's board of directors decides what dividends will be paid and when. These directors are your representatives. You and the other stockholders elect them, each for a definite term. Ordinarily, you get one vote for every share of stock you own. The directors are the real heads of a company. The president and other officers are responsible to the directors for their management of the company.

What Do Stocks Cost?

The price of a stock, like the price of food or clothing, depends on how much other buyers are willing to pay for it, how cheaply those who own it are willing to sell. When a company first offers or "floats" its stock so that it can raise the money it needs to begin business, a specific price is set on that stock. But once the stock is traded in the market, its price is *not fixed or pegged by anybody or any agency*. It is determined by free and open bidding—by supply and demand.

That's why stock prices rise and fall constantly—sometimes rapidly. Some people who buy Typical Company stock do so not because they want to get the dividends that are paid on it but because they think the price of Typical stock will rise and that they will be able to sell it later at a profit. This is risky business for anyone who cannot afford to lose money, because the price of Typical stock may drop. Nobody ever knows for sure what's going to happen to the price of *any* stock.

What Are Preferred Stocks?

In addition to its common stock, some companies also have preferred stock, usually offered at $100 a share. This stock generally bears a set dividend rate, say of $4. Holders of preferred stock get those dividends before common stockholders get anything—that's one reason why it is called "preferred"—but if the company has a good year, preferred stockholders don't, as a rule, get anything *more* than the specified $4 dividend per share.

The stock is also called "preferred" because if the company is liquidated, holders of such stock get a first claim on whatever assets may be left after creditors' claims are satisfied. (Assets are property, such as plants or goods, that can be converted into money.)

Although preferred stocks differ widely in the *exact* terms of the preferred treatment which they provide owners, they always offer *some* preferences. Hence, the prices of preferred stock usually do not fluctuate as much as the prices of common stock over a given period.

Although preferred stockholders, like common stockholders, are part owners of the company, they often have no voice in management, no vote in electing directors.

What Are Bonds?

Bonds are a kind of promissory note. People who buy a company's bonds lend their money to that company, and the company agrees to pay them back at a set date, known as the maturity date. For the use of the money, the company generally agrees to pay a set rate of interest of, say, 5% per year. Bonds are usually backed by a mortgage on the company's property or by the general credit of the company.

Unlike stockholders, bondholders are *not* part owners of the company. They are *creditors* of the company.

Of course, as creditors their claims must be satisfied if the company goes broke, before stockholders—the owners—can divide so much as a dime's worth of the company's assets—*if any*.

Because bonds have this prior claim, they are regarded as the safest kind of security. That's why they appeal to conservative investors—widows, retired people, anyone who is willing to take a smaller return on his money, provided it's a safer one.

In times of economic uncertainty, bonds are always comparatively more attractive than stocks. Their prices do not fluctuate as much as stock prices, because they bear a fixed rate of interest and the element of risk is not as immediate a factor in the price.

Of course, the price of any bond is apt to be depressed, especially if there is any suspicion that the company is having a hard time.

In addition to corporate bonds, there are state, city, and government bonds. On state and city bonds, the revenue from taxes is frequently pledged as security for repayment. Back of U. S. Government bonds—the highest-grade investment there is—lies the integrity of the nation. Just that and nothing more, because nothing else is needed and nothing could add greater security. The integrity of the country is the standard of investment values.

State and city bonds are attractive to many investors, because the federal government does not tax the income from these bonds, as it does the income from company stocks and bonds or most U. S. Government bonds.

Bonds are usually issued in $1,000 units (sometimes $500), but as a matter of tradition they are usually quoted as though the price were a percentage of the face value. Thus, if a corporate bond is said to sell at 98½, it actually sells at $985.

Government bonds are quoted in 1/32nds. Thus a quote of 100.16 means 100 16/32 or in actual dollars, $1,005.

What Are Common Stocks Worth?

That depends on what people are willing to pay for them. And what they are willing to pay for a particular stock is largely determined by one factor—earnings. That includes what the company *has* earned (its past record), what it *is* earning (its present state of health), and what it *might* earn (its prospects for the future).

So you see it's not just a matter of figures. It's a matter of facts . . . knowledge . . . judgment. How aggressive is the company? How good is its management? How popular are its products? What part of earnings will have to be paid out as preferred stock dividends or bond interest? After all, these must be paid first, and what is available for common stockholders depends on how much is left.

Then you have to look outside the company and consider the whole industry in which it operates. Is its future bright? (The buggy industry once offered many good investments.) And what about competitors? Are they in better shape than your company? Might they take the market away from Typical Manufacturing?

Finally, you have to consider general business factors. For instance, will rising costs of labor and raw materials pinch your company?

These are just some of the questions to which the intelligent investor wants answers so that he can form a reliable opinion of what his stock is likely to be worth—*tomorrow*.

Investment values constantly change. That's why this firm has always urged stockholders to "Investigate—then Invest", and to keep on investigating afterwards.

Why Do Stock Prices Change?

At any given time, you may not agree with the price at which a particular stock is selling. You may think it is too high or too low.

There is a simple reason for that: What a stock is "worth" is a matter of personal opinion. But what it actually sells at is the sum total of a lot of individual judgments about it. The *price* of a security is nothing more than the collective expression of all the opinions of all the people who are buying or selling it.

If a number of people conclude at about the same time that a particular stock is overpriced, they may decide to sell it, and the price will probably fall. Or they may think it is selling at bargain prices and decide to buy it. Their combined orders may cause the price to rise.

That's why stock prices sometimes fluctuate sharply. Instead of changing by an eighth or a quarter of a point—which means an eighth or a quarter of a dollar—the price may change by several dollars, either up or down, in a short time.

Whenever there is a sharp price movement in either direction, it may pick up momentum and continue for a little while. That's because such a price movement is likely to attract other buyers or sellers.

For instance, if the price of Typical Manufacturing were suddenly to advance from $25 to $27 a share, others might notice the advance and quickly conclude that it was a good buy. So they might decide to buy it too, and that would lift the price still higher, perhaps to $28 or $29. At that point, some of those who originally bought Typical stock at, say, $25 might decide to take their profit of $3 or $4 a share and sell out. Then the price might start down again.

What Are Bull and Bear Markets?

Sometimes a great many people will decide more or less at the same time, perhaps just on the basis of the general business outlook, that it is a good idea to buy stocks—all kinds of stocks. Such general buying action raises the average price of all stocks. If the price rise is big enough and lasts long enough, we have what is called a bull market.

A bear market is just the opposite. The average price of all stocks drops because of widespread selling. To be bullish or bearish simply means to believe that stocks are going up or down.

Incidentally, it is a simple business to keep track of whether the market as a whole is moving up or down, because almost every major newspaper in the country publishes daily the average price of some group of key stocks and reports whether that average is moving up or down. The Dow Jones Averages are the best known of these indexes.

When Should You Buy or Sell Stocks?

Deciding when to buy or sell is often just as important as deciding what to buy or sell. This matter of timing is particularly important to the speculator.

But first, what is a speculator? And what useful purpose does he serve?

A speculator is a man who buys securities, expecting the price to rise so that he will make a profit on his purchase, usually in a short period of time. Or he may sell securities expecting the price to drop. The important point is that he doesn't buy securities as investments—for the sake of the dividends that they pay.

The speculator performs a valuable service in the stock market because he is willing to take risks—and risk, the risk of a sudden price change, is an inevitable part of any free market, whether it be a market for securities or foodstuffs or any other commodity.

Suppose you own stock in Typical Manufacturing, and suppose you want to sell that stock because you think the earnings outlook is bad. You might not be able to sell at anything like a fair price if it were not for a speculator and his willingness to assume the risk that you want to dispose of.

But no one should speculate unless he can afford to take risks. We've said that repeatedly in public advertisements and in counseling our customers. Nevertheless we are realistic enough to recognize the fact that there's enough desire for gain in even the most conservative investor so that he naturally wants to buy as low as he can and sell as high as he can. He doesn't want to lose an unnecessary dollar by an ill-timed purchase or sale. That's why we are always urging stockholders to make close and continuous study of the markets, for it is only through such study that one can reduce the risks in deciding *when* to buy or sell.

That point is especially important with respect to the *sale* of stock. If you own a stock which has risen to such a high price that you wouldn't consider buying it, it is only good sense that you at least consider selling it.

Too *many* people make the *mistake* of buying stocks, then putting them away and forgetting about them. That's bad business. If you want to invest successfully, you've got to pay attention to your securities and be always alert to new investment opportunities. What may have been a good buy last year or even last month may not be a good buy next year or next month.

Like everything else in this world, "securities are perishable."

How Are Stocks Traded?

There are thousands of different stocks and bonds—they are both called securities—but the ones that are bought and sold *most* frequently are those that are traded on the floor of the New York Stock Exchange. The securities of more than 1,100 major companies are "listed" on that Exchange, which means that they have been accepted for trading there.

All buying and selling on the Exchange is done between the hours of 10 A.M. and 3 P.M., New York time, Monday through Friday, and 10 A.M. to noon on Saturdays except in the summer.

What is the New York Stock Exchange? Physically, it is a large area, about two-thirds the size of a football field, in the Stock Exchange building at the corner of Wall and Broad Streets in New York City. Functionally, it is an organization consisting of 1,375 members who have bought memberships (commonly called "seats") on the Exchange.

Many of these members represent brokerage firms whose primary business is carrying out the orders of other people, the public generally, for the purchase or sale of securities. They are paid commissions for executing these orders for their customers. To provide service for investors throughout the country, these firms maintain many branch offices. All told, there are 609 member firms of the Stock Exchange that operate 936 branch offices in 370 cities. *This firm* alone has 98 offices in 96 cities.

What Is the Stock Exchange?

The Exchange is a voluntary association, as it has been since it was established 157 years ago, and it functions as an open auction market.

Before the Exchange agrees to list the securities of any company, it *must* be assured that the company is a substantial concern, that its securities are legally issued, that those securities are widely owned, and that the company agrees to issue regularly adequate public statements of its financial health.

Only member brokers can execute orders to buy or sell listed securities on the Exchange. If you give an order to someone who is not part of a New York Stock Exchange broker's organization, he turns that order over to a member broker. In such circumstance, you may be charged a small commission or service fee over and above the commission to the member broker.

What About Unlisted Stocks?

The New York Stock Exchange or "Big Board" is the biggest formal market for stocks and bonds, but there are thousands of security issues which aren't traded on that Exchange. Many are traded on the 24 other exchanges, such as the New York Curb Exchange, the Chicago Stock Exchange, or the Los Angeles Stock Exchange.

Still other stocks and bonds aren't listed on any exchange. These securities are called unlisted or off board securities; they are traded in what is popularly called the over-the-counter market. Government and municipal bonds are mainly traded in that market. So are the stocks of most banks and insurance companies, as well as the securities of many big corporations such as Time, Inc., Texas Eastern Transmission Corp., and the Weyerhaeuser Timber Co. By and large, however, unlisted securities are those of small companies that are apt to be better known locally than nationally.

They are bought and sold not only by many brokers who are members of the New York Stock Exchange but also by thousands of local security dealers.

Suppose a man in New York owns some stock in an Ohio machinery company and he wants to sell it. He doesn't know what it's worth because there is no regular market for that stock, and its price may not be published in the newspaper, as New York Stock Exchange prices are in many papers.

He goes to his broker, and the broker may ask for a price quotation by phone or wire from other brokers or security dealers who trade entirely in unlisted securities. He may find that the best bid for the stock is $23, while the lowest that anybody else is willing to sell it for is $25. If the stock is traded very frequently, the difference between bid and offer prices may be less. If it is almost unknown, the broker may have a hard time finding a market at any price. In this transaction, the broker acts as an agent and is paid a commission. However, in many over-the-counter transactions, the broker or dealer will buy the security himself, or he will sell such a security out of the supply of such stocks that he owns. In such trades, the dealer acts as a principal instead of as an agent, and the customer and the dealer agree on what is a *fair net price*, which includes a return to the dealer in place of a commission. In the end, the dealer may gain or lose on such transactions.

Merrill Lynch handles over-the-counter transactions either as a principal or an agent *as the customer chooses*. If a transaction is handled on a *commission* basis, it is the policy of this firm to charge commission rates that are even lower than those that now prevail on New York Stock Exchange transactions. If we handle such transactions on a *net* basis, we believe our price will be as low (if you're buying) or as high (if you're selling) as any you are likely to find. Further, we will trade only those stocks on a *net price* basis whose quality has been approved by our Research Division.

Who May Buy Stocks and Bonds?

Anybody—or perhaps we should say any honest and responsible citizen. For their own protection, brokers have to be sure about the responsibility of their customers because they accept oral orders to buy or sell. You'll find it a relatively simple matter to establish your reliability with a broker and to open an account.

Many potential investors haven't bought stocks and bonds simply because they don't know how to go about it. *Some* may have hesitated simply because they don't know a broker. They may even have thought of him as a somewhat unapproachable individual. He isn't. You can walk into any brokerage office in America without fear.

Finally, a lot of people probably have the idea that brokers only do business with people who invest thousands or tens of thousands of dollars at a time. Well, in our 98 offices we're proud to do business with people who talk in hundreds of dollars as well as people who deal in four and five figures. Last year, we found that 41% of our customers had incomes of less than $5,000 a year. At the other end of the scale were some who counted their income in hundreds of thousands. So you see, regardless of how big a customer you are, you'll always be welcome in any Merrill Lynch office.

But not everybody should buy stocks and bonds. We have consistently said that nobody should invest in the stock market unless he has savings sufficient to meet an emergency. And he should have insurance to protect his family. Then if he has surplus funds, he can probably invest them in stocks or bonds to his advantage.

You can tell your broker just as little or as much as you want to about your money problems, but whatever you tell him will be held in strict confidence.

Frankly, we hope you will want to tell us enough so that we can help you work out an investment program that will best fit your needs.

Does that mean that we will tell you how to invest your money? This is a point we want to make absolutely clear, for it involves a fundamental Merrill Lynch principle. Certainly, we'll try to help you if you want us to—if you *ask* for our advice and counsel. But we will not give you *unasked* advice; we will not foist our opinions or our recommendations upon you. What you buy or sell is your own business. We don't want to be accused of trying to make up your mind for you.

This firm spends about a *million* dollars a year in preparing and distributing to investors factual information about securities.

We'll give you all the facts and figures *we* have on any stock or bond you are interested in. There'll be no charge for them. We *want* you to have them—before you buy and *after* you buy. If you ask us, we'll even tell you how we think those facts and figures add up in terms of your own investment needs.

But in the end, the *decision is yours*. That's what we mean when we say

"Investigate . . . then Invest."

How to Buy and Sell Securities

How Do You Do Business with a Broker?

Here is what actually happens when a customer—let's call him Kenneth Smith—comes into our office, at 70 Pine Street to place an order for a hundred shares of Typical Manufacturing Company.

Mr. Smith goes directly to the desk of the man who regularly handles his business. (We'll call him John Ross.) Ross is registered with the New York Stock Exchange, which means that he is qualified as a man of good character and has passed an examination on the operation of the securities business. He is an employee of ours, with the title in our firm of "account executive." He's a man who thoroughly knows his business.

Smith might ask Ross for information about Typical Manufacturing from our Securities Research Division, and discuss the findings with him. But in this instance Smith has already checked on the company and knows that he wants to buy 100 shares of common stock. So he gets right down to business.

"What's Typical selling at now?" he asks.

If Typical Manufacturing were one of the major companies, Smith wouldn't have to ask, for he could look at the big electric quotation board which automatically shows the price at which the last previous sale was made. It also shows the high and low prices for the day and the closing price on the preceding day. The quote board in our 70 Pine Street office provides that information on 209 leading stocks, but Typical isn't among them.

"Sorry, I don't know the quote", says Ross, "but I'll let you know in a minute". Ross knows he can get that quote by a quick phone call, and the account executives in any of our 96 out-of-town offices can give equally good service by using the leased teletype wires that connect direct to our New York headquarters.

While Smith waits, he looks at the Trans Lux screen on which the ticker tape is projected to see if any sales of Typical are being reported right then. When a stock is sold on the Exchange floor, that transaction is reported on the tape. The price is shown and the number of shares involved in the sale. Because there are so many transactions, it is necessary to use a kind of shorthand, and the various stocks are referred to by initials or combinations of letters, such as C for Chrysler Corporation, CP for Canadian Pacific, and CGW for Chicago Great Western.

"Typical is quoted at 25 bid, 25¼ asked", says Ross in a minute or so. By that he means that $25 a share is the highest price that anyone is then willing to pay for it and that $25.25 is the lowest at which anyone is willing to sell it.

"Shall I place your order at the market?" he asks. *A market order* is one for immediate execution at the best price that prevails when the order reaches the floor of the Exchange, regardless of how the price may have changed—up or down a fraction of a point, sometimes more—in the interval between the time the order is placed and the time it can be filled.

Smith agrees. His order is immediately phoned over to one of our booths on the floor of the Exchange. There one of our floor brokers goes to the trading post at which Typical is bought or sold. There are 18 such posts on the floor of the Exchange, and at each of them a certain number of stocks are regularly traded.

At the trading post, our broker asks what the market is. Other brokers with orders to buy or sell Typical Manufacturing make their bids or offers in an audible voice. Secret transactions are not permitted on the Exchange floor.

Our broker immediately fills Smith's order at the lowest price at which the stock is offered, and Ross is advised by phone that the order has been filled.

The whole operation may have taken only two or three minutes. Smith may still be in the office. If he is, Ross will tell him that the purchase has been completed. If he is gone, Ross will telephone him.

As a matter of fact, most of our customers are apt to place their orders and handle all their business on the phone. Others do it wholly by mail. *It isn't necessary for a customer to come into the office at all to place an order.*

A customer can, if he wants, set the price that he is willing to pay. This is called a *limit order*. Smith might tell us, for instance, to buy Typical only if it could be bought at 24½. Further, he might say that any such order is good for a day, a week, a month, or indefinitely. Then if Typical is offered at 24½ within the time that Smith has set, his order to buy is executed, unless there are other similar orders on file that have precedence. Of course, the price of Typical might move right on up to 26 or 27. In such case, Smith would have lost his chance to buy at 25 or thereabouts. That's why any decision to buy that turns exclusively on the probable gain of a fraction of a point is apt not to be a good decision for most investors.

Limit orders can also be used in reverse—in selling stock. Thus, if Smith *owned* Typical, he might tell us to sell his stock for him, if we could, at 26.

How Big Does an Order Have to Be?

One hundred shares—a "round lot"—is the usual unit of trading on the New York Stock Exchange. But that doesn't mean that a customer can only buy or sell a hundred shares at a time. Many people want to buy only 5 or 10 or 25 shares at a time. These are called odd lots.

Suppose Smith wanted to buy only 10 shares of Typical. When we get that order we would fill it through an odd-lot dealer whose business it is to buy or sell in less than 100-share units. Such odd-lot dealers do business only with other brokers on the Stock Exchange floor, not with the public.

For rendering their service they charge one-eighth of a point or 12½¢ for every share of stock that they buy or sell to fill odd-lot orders for the customers of other brokers.

Apart from that extra eighth, odd-lot dealers don't charge any more for the stock that they sell than the price prevailing in the *general market*. On a 10-share order for Typical, Smith would pay that price which prevailed on the *next round-lot sale* after our broker gives Smith's order to the odd-lot dealer. Suppose the next sale was at 25. Smith would pay 25 per share, plus ⅛ for the odd-lot dealer, or 25⅛. If Smith were selling the stock, he would sell at 25, less ⅛ for the odd-lot dealer, or 24⅞.

What Does It Cost to Buy or Sell Stocks?

All transactions on the Stock Exchange are handled by member firms at reasonable commissions. The rates vary with the size of the order, being a little less proportionally on big orders than on small ones. At the present time, however, commissions on stock transactions average only 0.85 of 1%. On bonds the average commission is even less.

New York State and the federal government also levy transfer taxes on security sales or transfers, but these involve only a few pennies a share.

When Smith gets our bill the next day, it will state exactly what he bought, what price was paid, what commission is due, what postage or a tax, if any, is incurred, and what total amount is due. We do not make any charge for special services, such as research or information or carrying an inactive account or safe-keeping of securities, etc.

After Smith pays his bill—probably by check—he can obtain his stock certificate which shows that so many shares of Typical Manufacturing Co. have been registered in his name and that he is entitled to all rights, privileges, and dividends due stockholders in that company. But Smith, like an increasing number of our customers, may find it more convenient to leave the certificate in safe-keeping with us. That way he has protection against losing the certificate, and it is right here whenever the time comes that he wants to sell the stock. He will thus be relieved of the responsibility of personally delivering it at such time.

"WHAT'S THIS? . . . WHAT'S THAT?"

This isn't the *complete* story of how to buy stocks and bonds, of course. That would take volumes.

All we have tried to do here is set down answers to some of the most common questions that are asked us. And we have excluded a lot of things many people are curious about but that bear little relation to a program of prudent investment for *most* people.

For instance, there's "short selling", which simply means reversing the normal procedure—selling a stock first in the belief that it is overpriced, then buying it back at what you hope is a lower price.

Or maybe you'd like to know about buying "on margin", which means buying partly on credit.

In the main, these procedures are not important to the investor. But we'll be glad to tell you anything more you want to know.

Other market terms such as "rights", "ex-dividend", "stock splits", "debentures", "noncumulative preferred", "stop orders", and dozens of others we've had to omit simply for lack of space, but an understanding of them isn't likely to be important to most investors, except in occasional cases.

Again, for lack of space, we have not defined a whole host of financial terms that you are likely to encounter when you begin investigating various companies.

These terms are defined in a booklet, "How to Invest", which we have just published. A basic guidebook for all security owners, this new publication develops in greater detail the story of how this stock and bond business works. It reviews the basic principles of sound investing, such as the analysis of market trends, the diversification of holdings, and the management of a portfolio. We will be glad to send you a copy.

Copies of this advertisement in pamphlet form are available on request. No charge, no obligation. Just write or phone . . .

MERRILL LYNCH, PIERCE, FENNER & BEANE

Underwriters and Distributors of Investment Securities
Brokers in Securities and Commodities

10 Post Office Square
BOSTON 9

Telephone: HUbbard 2-5700

11. The Marlboro Man
    This campaign, which has run for more than half a century, with few changes, was created for a "cigarette designed for men that women like". A perfect bridge for the macho man to step across to smoking filter cigarettes without sacrificing flavour.
    Originator: Leo Burnett Company, Inc.

Classic Element	*Examples*
Perfect marriage of copy and visual tells sales story simply and strongly.	1. Wills—Made for Each Other 2. Liril Soap—waterfall freshness

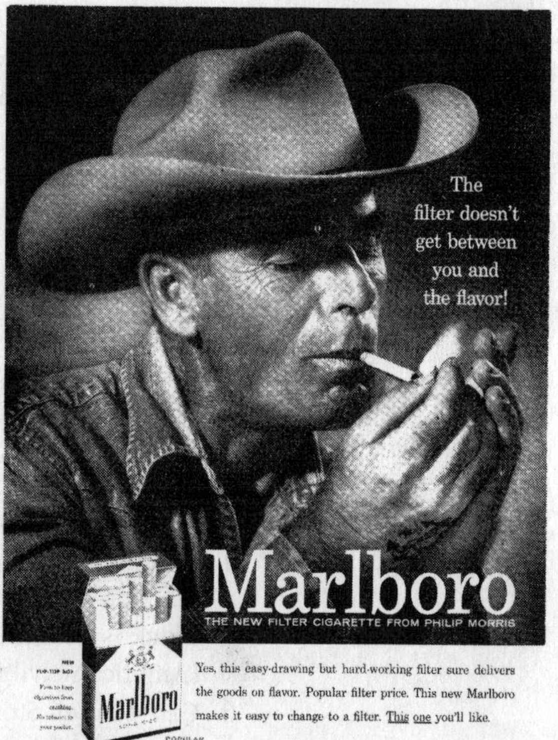

The filter doesn't get between you and the flavor!
Marlboro
THE NEW FILTER CIGARETTE FROM PHILIP MORRIS
Marlboro
POPULAR FILTER PRICE
Yes, this easy-drawing but hard-working filter sure delivers the goods on flavor. Popular filter price. This new Marlboro makes it easy to change to a filter. This one you'll like.
(MADE IN RICHMOND, VIRGINIA, FROM A NEW PHILIP MORRIS RECIPE)

How Long is Long?

As a copywriter you will be exposed to hundreds and hundreds of ads in The One Show, the Art Directors Annual, Graphis Annuals and other tomes. You will view Clio Award showreels and the winning commercials at Cannes. Each will be more brilliant than the last. So much so your head will spin in an effort to remember all the fantastic stuff you have seen and read. You will attend the Ad Club awards ceremony every year to view what your peers are doing. Perhaps your work too will come in for acclaim. All this is heady stuff indeed.

But only a few campaigns will stick in your mind. Those with the truly big ideas that form the basis of a classic. It could be the headline (Blow some my way), it could be the visual (the Man in the Hathaway shirt wearing an eyepatch), or a mix of both (Marlboro man).

Ultimately, the classic campaign catches the consumer's imagination and stays there for a long long time. Many clients and agency folk are easily bored with a long-running campaign and want to change. It is a fact that by the time you and the client get to this stage of ad fatigue, your consumer is just about beginning to notice your campaign. So do not be in a hurry to throw the baby out with the bathwater.

You may not be aware of how much of English idiomatic speech is drawn from classical literature like Shakespeare and the Bible.

In the same way, classic advertising slogans tend to get absorbed in the living expression of language. Sooner or later they become an intrinsic part of our everyday thought. How many of the following have you heard or used?

Some Deathless Lines

1. ACCESS—your flexible friend
   (Credit card advertisement 1981 onwards)
2. All the way with LBJ.
   (in the *Washington Post,* 4 June 1960)
3. American Express? That'll do nicely, sir.
   (F. Jenkins' *Advertising,* Chapter 1, 1985.)
4. Ban the bomb.
   (US anti-nuclear slogan, 1953)
5. Black is beautiful.
   (American civil rights campaign slogan, mid-60s)
6. Can you tell Stork from butter?
   (British ad for margarine, 1956)
7. Careless talk costs lives.
   (World War II security slogan)
8. Don't ask a man to drink and drive.
   (UK Road Safety slogan, from 1964)
9. Even your closest friends won't tell you.
   (Listerine mouthwash advertising slogan, 1923)
10. Full of Eastern promise.
    (Fry's Turkish Delight, 1950 onwards)
11. Go to work on an egg.
    (The British Egg Marketing Board 1957—written by either Fay Weldon or Mary Gowing)
12. The hands that do dishes can be soft as your face, with mild green Fairy Liquid.
    (ad for Procter & Gamble washing-up liquid)
13. If you want to get ahead, get a hat.
    (Hat Council, UK, 1965)
14. Just when you thought it was safe to go back in the water.
    (Ad for Jaws 2, 1978 film)

15. Kentucky Fried Chicken . . . "It's finger lickin' good."
    (*American Restaurant Magazine*—June 1958)
16. Labour isn't working.
    (British Conservative Party slogan on a poster outside an unemployment office)
17. Let the train take the strain.
    (British Rail ad, 1970 onwards)
18. Let your fingers do the walking.
    (Bell Systems telephone directory Yellow Pages, c 1960)
19. Make love not war.
    (Student slogan, 1960)
20. Power to the people.
    (The Black Panther movement slogan, 1968 onwards)
21. Snap! Crackle! Pop!
    (for Kellogg's Rice Krispies, 1928 onwards)
22. To err is human but to really foul things up requires a computer.
    (*Farmers' Almanac,* 1978)
23. We're number two. We try harder.
    (Avis car rental slogan)
24. You'll wonder where the yellow went
    when you brush your teeth with Pepsodent.
25. Thirst has no season.
    (Coca-Cola)

(Source: *Oxford Dictionary of Quotations,* Fourth Edition)

In the last 25 or 30 years some wholly Indian advertising campaigns have taken their place in the sun. How many of these do you think have the makings of a classic?

■ Made for Each Other	Wills cigarettes
■ Live Life Kingsize	Four Square cigarettes
■ Neighbour's Envy, Owner's Pride	Onida TV
■ Whitening Strikes	Rin detergent bar
■ Elle Colour Cosmetics	Hindustan Lever/Lakme

Warm-up

Use this space to continue the list. Do you believe they will be remembered 50 years from now, even if the brand fades out? Why?

Your Choice	*Your Reason*
■	
■	
■	
■	
■	

(NOTE: For *The Top 100 Advertising Campaigns* of the century, see the *Advertising Age* list at the end of the book.)

Workout

1. Imagine you are an art dealer of sorts. It is your business to keep an eye open for new talent that will mature into a Hussain or an Ara or a Laxma Gaud. What qualities would you look for in the paintings submitted by new artists?
2. Keep a lookout for memorable campaigns that could be tomorrow's classics. Note them in your file. Later, look up your list to see how right—or wrong—you are.
3. Tell yourself that every year of your working life you are going to create at least *one campaign that will go down in history*. Then live up to your promise!

20

Crafting Copy for Direct Mail

Writing copy for press ads is like standing in the market-place and shouting your wares over the calls and cries of other vendors. Or like putting up a stall which is more colourful, more attractive and more interesting to the people who have come to look and buy, than others. Sometimes it is like being at Calcutta's Howrah Station at peak hours trying to hail a cab in a thunderstorm when you are late for a client meeting. But all of the time it is like going up to a perfect stranger, tugging at his shirtsleeve and asking to borrow a hundred bucks. The joys of copywriting!

I like afternoon naps. After lunch is when a delicious languor sets in and the shaded bedroom beckons. Just as I snuggle into the pillows, the doorbell rings. Being a child of the times, I leap out of

bed and rush to the door. There is a man standing on the steps with a big black bag stuffed with . . . . My instincts tell me if I open the door, he is going to put his foot in it.

I open the door—and I am done for. Half an hour later I am the new owner of nine kitchen knives, roller skates for the gas cylinder, six cotton bras with pointy tips and two dozen plastic jars at 20 per cent discount. The man has vanished, and so has my zzzzz.

Direct mail is something like getting your foot in the door. Not all your prospects will succumb easily. Some of them will slam the door in your face before or after giving you a punch in the face. The only comfort you as the writer have is that you are not actually out there on the doorstep to hear it slam. But you still have a job to do: to get the housewife/prospect/consumer to read your mailer, and then *act* on it.

The *Reader's Digest* does some super work in this area. Incredible how they find out your name and address, send you affectionate letters, wheedle you into sticking a stamp here, saying yes and no in boxes, sending for their diaries at no extra cost, before they get you signing up for a six-year subscription for your arthritic old aunt in Darjeeling and one for yourself. Till now, you had been reading the dog-eared copy in the local library. The guy who coined the phrase *salesmanship in print* must have been talking of direct mail.

John Caples is known as the master of direct response copy. He has written *Tested Advertising Methods, Making Ads Pay, Advertising for Immediate Sales*, and *Advertising Ideas*—all Dover Paperbacks. Learn his books by heart!

Reproduced below is the full text of some great ads designed to gain a direct response from the reader. Julian Watkins included them in his collection of The 100 Greatest Ads Ever Written. *They could easily, with minor modifications, be used as direct mailers today. Here goes:*

1. Again She Orders—
"A Chicken Salad, Please"

This ad to sell a *Book of Etiquette* brought out by Nelson Doubleday was written by a smart young copywriter—Lillian Eichler. Study the structure of the text, and follow the sales argument to the end. Take one paragraph at a time, and figure out the point it makes. Yes, there are a great many paragraphs, but be patient! Your effort will be worth it.

Text

For him she is wearing her new frock. For him she is trying to look her prettiest. If only she can impress him—make him like her—just a little.

Across the table he smiles at her, proud of her prettiness, glad to notice that others admire her. And she smiles back, a bit timidly, a bit self-consciously.

What wonderful poise he has! What complete self-possession! If only SHE could be so thoroughly at ease.

She pats the folds of her new frock nervously, hoping he will not notice how embarrassed she is, how uncomfortable. He doesn't—until the waiter comes to their table and stands, with pencil poised, to take the order.

Again She Orders—
"A Chicken Salad, Please"

FOR him she is wearing her new frock. For him she is trying to look her prettiest. If only she can impress him—make him like her—just a little.

Across the table he smiles at her, proud of her prettiness, glad to notice that others admire. And she smiles back, a bit timidly, a bit self-consciously.

What wonderful poise he has! What complete self-possession! If only *she* could be so thoroughly at ease.

She pats the folds of her new frock nervously, hoping that he will not notice how embarrassed she is, how uncomfortable. He doesn't—until the waiter comes to their table and stands, with pencil poised, to take the order.

"A chicken salad, please." She hears herself give the order as in a daze. She hears him repeat the order to the waiter, in a rather surprised tone. Why *had* she ordered that again! This was the third time she had ordered chicken salad while dining with him.

He would think she didn't know how to order a dinner. Well, did she? No. She didn't know how to pronounce those French words on the menu. And she didn't know how to use the table appointment as gracefully as she would have liked; found that she couldn't create conversation—and was actually tongue-tied; was conscious of little crudities which she just knew he must be noticing. She wasn't sure of herself, she didn't *know*. And she discovered, as we all do, that there is only one way to have complete poise and ease of manner, and that is to know definitely what to do and say on every occasion.

Are You Conscious of Your Crudities?

It is not, perhaps, so serious a fault to be unable to order a correct dinner. But it is just such little things as these that betray us—that reveal our crudities to others.

Are you sure of yourself? Do you know precisely what to do and say wherever you happen to be? Or are you always hesitant and ill at ease, never quite sure that you haven't blundered?

Every day in our contact with men and women we meet little unexpected problems of conduct. Unless we are prepared to meet them, it is inevitable that we suffer embarrassment and keen humiliation.

Etiquette is the armor that protects us from these embarrassments. It makes us aware instantly of the little crudities that are robbing us of our poise and ease. It tells us how to smooth away these crudities and achieve a manner of confidence and self-possession. It eliminates doubt and uncertainty, tells us exactly what we want to know.

There is an old proverb which says "Good manners make good mixers." We all know how true this is. No one likes to associate with a person who is self-conscious and embarrassed; whose crudities are obvious to all.

Do You Make Friends Easily?

By telling you exactly what is expected of you on all occasions, by giving you a wonderful new ease and dignity of manner, the Book of Etiquette will help make you more popular—a "better mixer." This famous two-volume set of books is the recognized social authority—is a silent social secretary in half a million homes.

Let us pretend that you have received an invitation. Would you know exactly how to acknowledge it? Would you know what sort of gift to send, what to write on the card that accompanies it? Perhaps it is an invitation to a formal wedding. Would you know what to wear? Would you know what to say to the host and hostess upon arrival?

If a Dinner Follows the Wedding

Would you know exactly how to proceed to the dining room, when to seat yourself, how to create conversation, how to conduct yourself with ease and dignity?

Would you use a fork for your fruit salad, or a spoon? Would you cut your roll with a knife, or break it with your fingers? Would you take olives with a fork? How would you take celery—asparagus—radishes? Unless you are absolutely sure of yourself, you will be embarrassed. And embarrassment *cannot be concealed*.

Book of Etiquette Gives Lifelong Advice

Hundreds of thousands of men and women know and use the Book of Etiquette and find it increasingly helpful. Every time an occasion of importance arises—every time expert help, advice and suggestion is required—they find what they seek in the Book of Etiquette. It solves all problems, answers all questions, tells you exactly what to do, say, write and wear on every occasion.

If you want always to be sure of yourself, to have ease and poise, to avoid embarrassment and humiliation, send for the Book of Etiquette at once. Take advantage of the special bargain offer explained in the panel. Let the Book of Etiquette give you complete self-possession; let it banish the crudities that are perhaps making you self-conscious and uncomfortable when you should be thoroughly at ease.

Mail this coupon now while you are thinking of it. The Book of Etiquette will be sent to you in a plain carton with no identifying marks. Be among those who will take advantage of the special offer. Nelson Doubleday, Inc., Dept. 3911, Garden City, New York.

A Social Secretary for Life!

The Famous Book of Etiquette
Nearly 500,000 Sold for $3.50

NOW ONLY $1.98

Nelson Doubleday, Inc., Dept. 3911
Garden City, New York

Name........................

Address........................

"A chicken salad, please." She hears herself give the order in a daze. She hears him repeat the order to the waiter in a rather surprised tone. Why HAD she ordered that again! This was the third time she had ordered chicken salad while dining with him.

He would think she didn't know how to order a dinner. Well, did she? No. She didn't know how to pronounce those French words on the menu. And she didn't know how to use the table appointments as gracefully as she would have liked; found that she couldn't create conversation—and was actually tongue-tied; was conscious of little crudities which she just knew he must be noticing. She wasn't sure of herself, she didn't KNOW. And she discovered, as we all do, that there is only one way to have complete poise and ease of manner, and that is to know definitely what to do and say on every occasion.

Are You Conscious of Your Crudities?

It is not, perhaps, so serious a fault to be unable to order a correct dinner. But it is just such little things as these that betray us—that reveal our crudities to others.

Are you sure of yourself? Do you know precisely what to do and say wherever you happen to be? Or are you always hesitant and ill at ease, never quite sure that you haven't blundered?

A Social Secretary for Life!

The famous *Book of Etiquette*
Nearly 500,000 Sold for $3.50
NOW ONLY $1.98

We have on our shelves at the present time several thousand sets of the *Book of Etiquette* in the regular $3.50 edition.

To clear the shelves quickly and make room for new editions now being printed, Nelson Doubleday, Inc., makes this unusual offer: To the next few thousand people who order the *Book of Etiquette*, the special bargain price of $1.98 will be extended. In other words, if you act without delay you can secure the complete, two-volume set of the *Book of Etiquette* at practically HALF the usual cost.

Use the special coupon. It will bring the *Book of Etiquette* to you promptly, at the special bargain price.

Every day in our contact with men and women we meet little unexpected problems of conduct. Unless we are prepared to meet them it is inevitable that we suffer embarrassment and keen humiliation.

Etiquette is the armour that protects us from these embarrassments. It makes us aware instantly of the little crudities that rob us of our poise and ease. It tells us how to smooth away these crudities and achieve a manner of confidence and self-possession. It eliminates doubt and uncertainty, tells us exactly what we want to know.

There is an old proverb that says "Good manners make good mixers." We all know how true this is. No one likes to associate with a person who is self-conscious and embarrassed; whose crudities are obvious to all.

Do You Make Friends Easily?

By telling you exactly what is expected of you on all occasions, by giving you a wonderful new ease and dignity of manner, the *Book of Etiquette* will help make you more popular—a 'better mixer'. This famous two-volume set of books is the recognized social authority—it is a silent social secretary in half a million homes.

Let us pretend that you have received an invitation. Would you know exactly how to acknowledge it? Would you know what sort of gift to send, what to write on the card that accompanies it? Perhaps it is an invitation to a formal wedding. Would you know what to wear? Would you know what to say to the host and hostess upon arrival?

If a Dinner Follows the Wedding——

Would you know exactly how to proceed to the dining room, where to seat yourself, how to create conversation, how to conduct yourself with ease and dignity?

Would you use a fork for your fruit salad, or a spoon? Would you cut your roll with a knife, or break it with your fingers? Would you take olives with a fork? Or how would you take celery—asparagus—radishes? Unless you are absolutely sure of yourself you will be embarrassed. And embarrassment CANNOT BE CONCEALED.

***Book of Etiquette* Gives Lifelong Advice**

Hundreds of thousands of men and women know and use the *Book of Etiquette* and find it increasingly helpful. Every time an occasion of importance arises, every time expert help, advice and suggestion is required—they find what they seek in the *Book of Etiquette.* It solves all problems, answers all questions, tells you exactly what to do, say, write and wear on every occasion.

(in very small type)

If you want always to be sure of yourself, to have ease and poise, to avoid embarrassment and humiliation, send for the *Book of Etiquette* at once. Take advantage of the special bargain offer explained in the panel. Let the *Book of Etiquette* give you complete self-possession; let it banish the crudities that are perhaps making you self-conscious and uncomfortable when you should be thoroughly at ease.

Mail the coupon NOW while you're thinking of it.

The *Book of Etiquette* will be sent to you in a plain carton with no identifying marks. Be among those who will take advantage of the special offer.

Nelson Doubleday, Inc.,
Dept. 3911 , Garden City, New York.

Nelson Doubleday, Inc. Dept. 3911, Garden City, New York (*fine print*)

I accept your special bargain offer. You may send me the famous two-volume *Book of Etiquette*, in a plain carton, for which I will give the postman only $1.98 (plus delivery charges) on arrival—instead of the regular price of $3.50. I am to have the privilege of returning the books within 5 days and having my money refunded if I am not delighted with them.

Name ....

Address ....

☐ Check this square if you want these books with the beautiful, full-leather binding at $2.98 with the same return privilege.

(Orders from outside the US are payable $2.44 cash with order. Leather binding outside the US, $3.44 cash with order.)

2. They Laughed When I Sat Down at the Piano . . . But When I Started to Play!—

Check out this ad on p. 189. It was written by John Caples for the US School of Music.

Text

Arthur had just played *The Rosary*. The room rang with applause. I decided that this would be a dramatic moment for me to make my debut. To the amazement of all my friends, I strode confidently over to the piano and sat down.

"Jack is up to his old tricks," somebody chuckled. The crowd laughed. They were all certain that I couldn't play a single note.

"Can he really play?" I heard a girl whisper to Arthur.

"Heavens, no!" Arthur exclaimed, "He never played a note all his life . . . . But just you watch him. This is going to be good."

I decided to make the most of the situation. With mock dignity, I drew out a silk handkerchief and lightly dusted off the piano keys. Then I rose and gave the revolving piano stool a quarter of a turn, just as I had seen an imitator of Paderewski do in a vaudeville sketch.

"What do you think of his execution?" called a voice from the rear.

"We're in favor of it!" came back the answer, and the crowd rocked with laughter.

Then I Started to Play

Instantly a tense silence fell on the guests. The laughter died on their lips as if by magic. I played through the first few bars of Beethoven's immortal *Moonlight Sonata*. I heard gasps of amazement. My friends sat breathless—spellbound.

I played on, and as I played, I forgot the people around me. I forgot the hour, the place, the breathless listeners. The little world I lived in seemed to fade—seemed to grow dim—unreal. Only the music was real. Only the music and the visions it brought me. Visions as beautiful and as changing as the wind blown clouds and drifting moonlight that long ago inspired the master composer. It seemed as if the master musician himself were speaking to me—speaking through the medium of music—not in words but in chords. Not in sentences but in exquisite melodies!

A Complete Triumph

As the last notes of the *Moonlight Sonata* died away, the room resounded with a sudden roar of applause. I found myself surrounded by excited faces. How my friends carried on! Men shook my hand—wildly congratulated me—pounded me on the back in their enthusiasm! Everybody was exclaiming with delight—plying me with rapid questions . . . "Jack! Why didn't you tell us you could play like that?" . . . "Where DID you learn?"—"How long have you studied?" "Who WAS your teacher?"

"I have never even SEEN my teacher," I replied. "And just a short while ago I couldn't play a note."

"Quit your kidding," laughed Arthur, himself an accomplished pianist. "You've been studying for years. I can tell."

"I have been studying only a short while," I insisted. "I decided to keep it a secret so I could surprise all you folks."

Then I told them the whole story.

"Have you ever heard of the US School of Music" I asked.

A few of my friends nodded. "That's a correspondence school, isn't it?" they exclaimed.

"Exactly," I replied. "They have a new, simplified method that can teach you to play any instrument by mail in just a few months."

How I Learned to Play Without a Teacher

And then I explained how for years I had longed to play the piano.

"A few months ago," I continued, "I saw an interesting ad for the US School of Music—a new method of learning how to play which only cost a few cents a day! The ad told how a woman had mastered the piano in her spare time at home—and WITHOUT A TEACHER! Best, of all, the wonderful new method she used required no laborious scales—no heartless exercises—no tiresome practising. It sounded so convincing that I filled out the coupon requesting the Free Demonstration lesson.

"The free book arrived promptly and I started that very night to study the Demonstration lesson. I was amazed to see how easy it was to play this new way. Then I sent for the course.

"When the course arrived I found it was just as the ad said—as easy as ABC! And, as the lessons continued, they got easier and easier. Before I knew it I was playing all the pieces I liked best. Nothing stopped me. I could play ballads or classical numbers or jazz, all with equal ease! And I never did have any special talent for music!"

Play Any Instrument

You too can now TEACH YOURSELF to be an accomplished musician—right at home—in half the usual time. You can't go wrong with this simple new method which has already shown 350,000 people how to play their favorite instruments. Forget that old-fashioned idea that you need special 'talent'. Just read the list of instruments in the panel, decide which one you want to play, and the US School will do the rest. And bear in mind, no matter which instrument you choose, the cost, in each case, will be the same—just a few cents a day. No matter whether you are a mere beginner or already a good performer, you will be interested in learning about this new and wonderful method.

Send for Our Free Booklet and Demonstration Lesson

Thousands of successful students never dreamed they possessed musical ability until it was revealed to them by a remarkable 'Musical Ability Test' which we send entirely without cost with our interesting free booklet.

If you are in earnest about wanting to play your favourite instrument—if you really want to gain happiness and increase your popularity—send at once for the free booklet and Demonstration lesson. No cost—no obligation. Right now we are making a Special offer for a limited number of new students. Sign and send the convenient coupon now—before it's too late to gain the benefits of this offer. Instruments supplied when needed, cash or credit. US SCHOOL OF MUSIC, 1031 BRUNSWICK BUILDING, NEW YORK CITY.

Pick Your Instrument

Piano/'Cello/Organ/Violin/Drums and Traps/Banjo/Tenor Banjo/Mandolin/Clarinet/Flute/Saxophone/Harmony and Composition/Sight Singing/Ukulele/Guitar/Hawaiian Steel Guitar/Harp/Cornet/Picolo/Trombone/Voice and Speech Culture/Automatic Finger Control/Piano Accordian

Coupon

US School of Music, 1031 Brunswick Bldg., New York City. Please send me your free book *Music Lessons in Your Own Home* with an introduction by Dr Frank Crane, Demonstration Lesson and particulars of your Special Offer. I am interested in the following course:

....

Have you the above instrument? ....

Name/Address/City/State ....

3. To Men Who Want to Quit Work Some Day

The Phoenix Mutual Life Insurance ad was the brainchild of John Caples and Bruce Barton of BBD&O.

Text

This page is addressed to those thousands of earnest, hard-working men who want to take things easier some day.

It tells how these men, by following a simple, definite plan, can provide for themselves in later years a guaranteed income they cannot outlive.

How the Plan Works

It doesn't matter whether your present income is large or merely average. It doesn't matter whether you are making fifty dollars a week or five hundred. If you follow this plan you will some day have an income upon which to retire.

The plan calls for the deposit of only a few dollars each month—the exact amount depending on your age. The minute you make your first deposit, your biggest money worries begin to disappear. Even if you should become totally and permanently disabled, you would not need to worry. Your payments would be made by us out of a special fund provided for that purpose.

And not only that. We would mail you a check every month during the entire time of your disability, even if that disability should continue for many, many years—the remainder of your natural life.

Get This Free Book

The Phoenix Mutual Company, which offers you this opportunity, is a 125-million dollar company. For over three-quarters of a century it has been helping men and women to end money worries.

But you're not interested in us. You are interested in what we can do for YOU. An illustrated, 36-page book called *How to Get the Things You*

Want tells you exactly that. It tells how you can become financially independent—how you can retire on an income—how you can provide money for emergencies—money to leave your home free of debt—money for other needs.

This financial plan is simple, reasonable and logical. The minute you read about it you will realize why it accomplishes such desirable results—not for failures, not for people who can't make ends meet, but for hard-working, forward-looking people who know what they want and are ready to make definite plans to get it. No obligation. Get your copy of the book now.

NEW RETIREMENT PLAN

Here is what a dividend-paying $10,000-policy will do for you:

IT GUARANTEES WHEN YOU ARE 65

a monthly income for life of $100, which assures a return of at least $10,000, and perhaps much more, depending on how long you live, or, if you prefer, a cash settlement of $12,000.

IT GUARANTEES UPON DEATH FROM ANY NATURAL CAUSE BEFORE AGE 65

a cash payment to your beneficiary of $10,000, or $50 a month for at least 24 years and eight months.

Total $14,823

IT GUARANTEES UPON DEATH RESULTING FROM ACCIDENT BEFORE AGE 60

a cash payment to your beneficiary of $20,000, or $100 a month for at least 24 years and eight months.

Total $29,646

IT GUARANTEES THROUGHOUT PERMANENT TOTAL DISABILITY WHICH BEGINS BEFORE AGE 60

a monthly disability income of $100 and payment for you of all premiums.

Plans for women or for retirement at ages 55 or 60 are also available.

Phoenix Mutual
Life Insurance Company

Hartford office: Hartford, Conn. First policy issued 1851 . . . .

. . . .

. . . .

. . . .

Coupon for Free Booklet

Name/Business address/Home address/

Date of birth. . . . .

. . . .

. . . .

. . . .

. . . . City/State . . . .

Once you have soaked yourself in these ads and the reasoning behind them, you might find these points helpful when you set out to write your own mailers. Apply Glim's Six-Step Body Copy formula to the text. Does the story follow (broadly) the logical selling sequence—Arresting Power, Substantiation, Transition, Competition, Product and Business Ending? If not, why not?

Remember, once you know the rules, you are at liberty to break them, if you can do so brilliantly!

On Writing Mailers

- The envelope should be interesting, intriguing enough to be opened. Otherwise it ends in the wastepaper basket. Try to let your direct mailer sneak in as a personal letter.
- The cover headline should provoke, tease the reader into reading on. This is the only chance to grab attention, so give a hint as to what is being offered.
- Inside: the main heading or subhead should provide the answer to the teaser on the cover. Get straight into the body copy with a bomb of an opening sentence. Now you have set the pace, keep it going.
- Take your story upwards and onwards, building up to the announcement of your product. Do not oversell your product, let it speak for itself. Seduce your prospect into reading on.
- Do not try to sell anything at this stage, but offer a chance to see/taste/touch—without having to pay anything. People get turned off if they think they are being sold a bill of goods, but they are willing to try something new if they feel they have nothing to lose.
- If you are making a special offer, do it now, and keep your promise. You might have begun a dialogue with the reader, so you have to impel the person to act. Something like having a big fish on a line . . . you have to play the fish, give the line slack, then draw it in again.
- Anticipate objections, fears, trepidations, mental blocks . . . and try to reassure the reader on all counts. Here is where Tone of Voice comes into play. Also Brand Image, and Glim's Appeals. Go to work with a vengeance.

Basic Structure for Direct Mailers

- Interesting envelope
- Provocative headline on cover (first page)
- Inside headline (answer to cover)
- Hit them with a good opening paragraph
- Get into your product story
- Build interest in product attributes by anticipating/creating consumer needs
- Suggest course of action at no cost to reader
- Special offers, if any
- Reassurance (company name, history, satisfied consumers)
- Attach coupon and business reply card

Tips on Crafting the Copy

- Formulate the subheads so that just by reading these rapidly the consumer gets an idea of the whole story. If he is hooked, he will read the fine print.
- Use present tense/imperatives to encourage action.
- Be believable, move from the known to the unknown.
- Identify with the target audience.
- Identify with the consumer's problems/needs.
- Use testimonials where possible.
- Make it easy for the reader to take action.
- Use the sequence of subheads to tell your story briefly.

Warm-up

Make a note of how many direct mailers you get in a week/a month.

Which ones have you opened? Why? Which have you responded to?

What was the nature of your response? Why do you suppose you have been put on the advertiser's mailing list? How do you think they got your name and address? How many of the mailers follow the guidelines suggested above? Is there room for improvement? How?

Workout

Write a direct mailer for one of the following:

- Kitchen air purifier (invent a name)
  Looks something like an exhaust fan
  Costs around Rs 1500 with installation

- Executive swivel chair
  Specially designed for maximum comfort
  Costs around Rs 7,800 per piece
- *Children's Encyclopaedia Britannica*
  Set of 20 volumes, hardbound, colour
  Costs around Rs 15,000

Remember to apply all the rules of crafting and selling. Before getting down to writing, study the sales argument/copy structure in the mail order ads featured earlier:

- Again she ordered, "Chicken salad please . . . ."
- "They laughed when I sat down at the piano . . . ."
- To men who want to Quit Work . . . .

21

Writing for Television

If direct mail is like a salesman's foot in the door, the *TV Commercial* is having him partake of the family dinner. Whether you like it or not, he is there interrupting your conversation, and worse still, he talks about himself!

People tolerate TV commercials because they come with the packaged product . . . their favourite programmes, the news at nine, old movies and the rest of TV fare. But though they are a trapped audience, they may not always listen to this not-too-welcome guest. If he is amusing, or informative, or has a striking personality, they will stop what they are doing and give him a hearing—for a while. But they would just as easily turn him off if the World Cup is on, or if the toast is burning, or something better turns up.

The TV salesman has taken up almost permanent abode in their homes, a sort of non-paying guest who mooches about trying to gain some attention, even if it is just the dog's. (I once had a cat who loved commercials and sat adoringly before the idiot box for hours.)

Yet, the household has a sort of repellent fascination for their guest. Sometimes, quite against their grain, they sit through what seems like hours of TV ads, hoping the next one is going to be better. The more steely-nerved up and walk away—to fix dinner in two minutes or to write that letter—before settling back to the soap opera. TV has joined the ranks of death and taxes.

As for the copywriter, so far so good. Depending on budget and other considerations, your product may be designed to reach the target audience through a single medium or a combination of a few: press/press and film/press and TV/press, TV and outdoor/outdoor alone/film alone/TV alone.

This decision is arrived at in the Creative Strategy jointly with the account/media planners and the research group. Indeed, it cannot be stressed enough that advertising is *teamwork*. Great ideas can come from anywhere and anyone. That is why some agencies accept awards and other honours in the name of the whole organisation rather than individuals.

Even so, the copywriter has to know how to think up an idea and write the script for a TV commercial: 20-second, 30-second or 60-second. Assume your brand is being advertised through a successful three-ad press campaign, and the client is encouraged to spend another huge sum on TV. But the same results-oriented positioning statement needs to be reflected in this medium as well. The client is thoroughly aware of the long-term benefits of brand building and is not taking chances.

You take another look at the Creative Brief and Strategy for the product. Here is the Positioning, the Proposition, the Tone of Voice, the desired Brand Image, the Target Audience, all nicely wrapped up and presented in a striking four-ad press campaign. The press ads are stirring up a storm in the market and sales are soaring. The client is jubilant—the TV idea must double the impact of advertising and treble sales!

What next? In some agencies the copywriter/art director on the account pull out their rough pads and get to work. In others, an outside film-maker is called in and briefed, in consultation with the creative team. Either way, the copywriter had best be prepared with some ideas.

The client's budget luckily runs to a 60-second commercial—in colour. Do not laugh, it could be a creative idea to do a film in black and white, just to stand out of the clutter. A TV commercial for Tuk Biscuits I saw in England years ago is etched indelibly in my memory. Full-screen close-up of man's face and hands holding a biscuit. He is talking in a whisper about the virtues of Tuk. So crisp, so fresh, when you break it in half, it goes . . . "Tuk" . . . he says, and breaks the biscuit. By this time you have actually turned up the volume on the telly, straining your ears to hear the *sound* of the biscuit crumbling! What a commercial!

If you have to base the commercial on the press campaign, it is best to study the ads for a while and then *put them away*. This way, you give your mind a chance to stretch and think filmically.

The difference? Two new elements have entered the picture, quite literally. They are called *Audio and Video* (moving visuals). Audio is not to be confused with Tone of Voice—though that too has its place in a commercial.

The blend of these two elements is what makes TV (and film) so exciting. *Sight and Sound* that moves and flows . . . a far cry from the static, though less ephemeral, press ad. Imagine, 60 whole seconds to play with music/words/sound/speech in order to persuade a trapped target audience to at least notice, if not buy your brand! If you fail to achieve this, it would be a shame.

In TV or film, you have a whole minute to make an impact on the viewers . . . through their ears and eyes. Close your eyes, and set your stop watch for 60 seconds. Get the feel of a minute?

The Single Big Idea

Once again you are up against what copywriters are paid to do—*think up Big Ideas!* What an opportunity! You have a successful press campaign running, you may even have your message splashed across hoardings, and most certainly your product is being backed up by Point of Sale material. Now to round up the gig with a clincher on TV.

Great TV commercials are generally those where a *Single Big Idea* leaves its impression. Someone says, "Hey, did you notice so-n-so ad on TV for Brand X?" And the friend replies, "No, what was it all about?" And Someone says, "Well, er, I can't exactly say, but it was fantastic!"

Or a conversation might go like this.

"Saw this absolutely stunning commercial last night. This guy is driving this fantastic car, and this girl in short shorts hitches a ride, and she has fabulous hair, and they get talking, and suddenly the cops stop them for speeding, and this girl—gosh you should've seen her eyes, flashing fire, and then the cop lets them go. And how they laugh!"

"Great, *yaar*. I was caught for speeding last week."

"Yeah, the ad really broke me up!"

"By the way, what was the product being advertised?"

"Product? What product? I was telling you about this chick, man. You dumb or something?"

That is not what Big Ideas are about. Unfortunately, how many ads like this does one see cluttering up the box? How many are based on a *Single Big Idea*? How many will stand the test of time and be remembered long after the brand dies? What brings a TV commercial immortality?

Again and again we come up with the 64-million dollar question: how do you get a *Big Idea*? In film and TV, even more so than in the creation of a press ad, the marriage of copy and visual becomes paramount. The *Big Idea* can spring from either or both elements with equal impact. Sometimes the brief calls for only TV as the medium for the campaign, sometimes TV is part of a multi-pronged campaign. If the latter, it is reasonable to suppose that the TV idea will reflect the current campaign proposition. For instance, if a toilet soap is expressing 'freshness of limes' through a waterfall mnemonic, the waterfall has to be retained in the press, TV and film. The 'complete man' in a campaign for men's suiting is featured in both press and television.

This consistency in advertising, a hanging together of media, all pulling in the same direction, is part of Brand Building. The *Big Idea,* therefore, must constantly be a memorable expression that is consistent with the Brand Image of the product. When this is done exceptionally well over decades, you get the makings of an advertising classic.

Warm-up

Jot down as many top-of-mind TV commercials as you can—in five minutes. Just five minutes, please!

Why do you remember them? What is the Single Big Idea in each?

Have you seen the same product or service advertised in the press, or on hoardings? Anywhere else?

Use the space provided for your notes:

Brand

Examples

- SMIRNOFF VODKA
  The Big Idea: Visual mnemonic of see-through glass bottle and distorted images/ comic element
- TITAN WATCHES
- ERICCSON CELL PHONES
- BACARDI RUM
- APOLLO TYRES
- SURF EXCEL
- SERVO ENGINE OIL
- NESCAFE
- BRITISH AIRWAYS
- CITIBANK

(You may select your own favourites, of course!)

Another Warm-up

Soak in TV-watching for a week. Make a note of the commercials you think are good. What appeals do they use? Who do you think they are aimed at? What makes them different from the less memorable ones? Could you improve on them? How?

Yet Another Warm-up

You have already seen how there may be many techniques used in creating press ads. Similarly, there are many techniques to be found in the TV commercial. Try and figure out what they are while you are doing the previous exercise. Make a list of them for future use.

Note down the TV commercials you think are good in the appropriate technique category. Make this exercise a habit for a few months till it becomes part of your subconscious thinking.

TV Spot Techniques

Some common techniques employed by TV producers and directors are given here:

- ***The Demonstration*** Show the product in use. Actually *show* dirty clothes get clean after being soaked in Brand X detergent powder. Very powerful persuader.
  Example: Whisper sanitary napkins
- ***The Testimonial*** Very believable when someone you know or admire appears on the box and swears that Brand X is the ONLY one for him/her.
  Examples: Nawab of Pataudi for Gwalior Suitings
  Vishwanath, the chess champion, for NIIT
  Sachin Tendulkar for Visa Credit Cards
- ***Slice of Life*** Actual real-life situations which the viewer can easily identify with (the ma-in-law/daughter-in-law scenes, the child winning a race in school sports, the husband gulping down his breakfast before he leaves for work).
  Example: Maruti Esteem (father/son)
- ***Humour*** Never fails to appeal, if used with taste and flair. Subtlety preferred to corn. Must be relevant to the Brand. It should spring naturally from the situation, not forced.
  Example: Nokia's talking statues
- ***Visual Mnemonic*** The frequent use of a visual burr (device to aid memory), that becomes a part of the Brand property. Like the dilated images in the bottle of Smirnoff Vodka. Unforgettable!
- ***The TV Jingle*** A tune that becomes identified with your brand, so catchy everyone's humming it. Most commonly used technique, but very effective, given our national love of music.
  Examples: Titan watches
  Apollo Tyres
  Bacardi rum
- ***Computer Graphics*** This is effective when technology is used not just for its own sake but as a vehicle for the Big Idea.
  Example: The cheetah morphs into a Bajaj bike
- ***Comparison*** A seldom exploited technique which could be very powerful in bringing out a brand's competitive edge.
  Example: Captain Cook salt vs Tata salt

- ***Lifestyle*** Consumer parity products, such as cigarettes, cold drinks and textiles have to depend on unique selling lifestyles rather than on unique selling propositions!
  Example: Weekender jeans/casual wear
- ***Problem–Solution*** Where the focus is on a consumer problem and presents a demonstrable solution.
  Example: Clinic All-clear dandruff shampoo
  Clearasil ointment for pimples
  Fair and Lovely cream for a fairer complexion

Presenting the Idea

Mubi Ismail, the late films chief of Lintas, had a neat way of presenting a film idea. She called it The Treatment. In the process of writing the treatment, she clarified her own thoughts, and thereby gave the client a good notion of her TV commercial even before doing the story board. This is how a Film Treatment goes. It works equally well for TV.

Let us say we are doing a film/TV treatment for NEW DENTIUM toothpaste. We are going to base the film/commercial on the proposition used in the press ad— "New Dentium with calcium protects tooth enamel while it cleans." The Big Idea is—Dentium is your lifetime guarantee against wearing dentures.

The Treatment: No Dentures!

Film opens with MS (medium shot) of grandfather at dining table. As he eagerly bites into a large red apple, his dentures stick in the fruit, leaving him toothless. He grimaces into camera. Pan to six-year-old girl also seated at the dining table, who is biting into a *'bhutta'* (corn on the cob). Child giggles and drops her *'bhutta'*. Match cut to child's hand picking up—not the 'bhutta' but a toothbrush. She squeezes some Dentium toothpaste onto it and begins to brush her teeth.

Announcer: You won't have to wear dentures when you are sixty . . . if you start taking care of your teeth when you are six.

SFX: Giggles

Anncr: New Dentium is reinforced with calcium to prevent wear and tear on tooth enamel . . . while it keeps teeth sparkling clean! Pan to CU of pack on bathroom shelf, and pull back to girl's smiling face, all her teeth showing.

SFX:	More giggles
	Freeze on pack shot/logo.

Note: The Treatment is a perfect vehicle when you want to test out an idea quickly. It allows for flexibility and concentrates on a Single Big Idea. It lends itself to a 30-second or even a 20-second commercial, very important when talking budget. Easy to visualise, the treatment can be worked out in detail with the producer after the client has approved of the idea.

A rule of thumb in presenting TV scripts is that Video always comes first. Audio (script and sound effects) is presented after or alongside. Perhaps this comes from the fact that we always see the lightning first, and hear the thunder a few seconds later!

The Film/TV Presentation

Client: Memorex Media Products Group
Agency: Doyle Dane Bernbach, San Francisco, CA
Writer: Michael Litchfield
Art Director: Herb Briggs
Director: Tom Barron

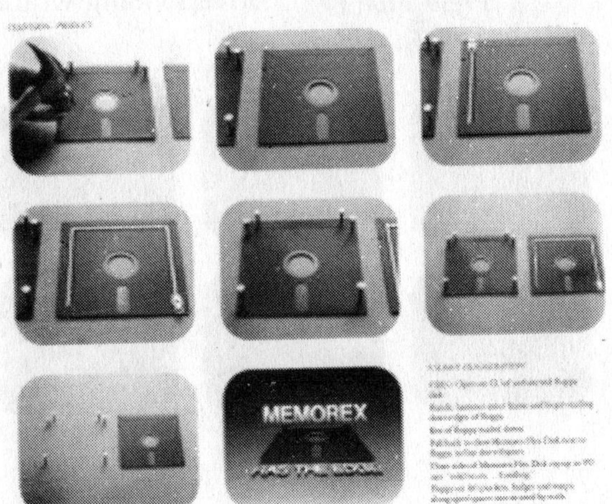

A Slight Exaggeration

VIDEO Open on CU (close up) of unfastened floppy disk.

Hands, hammer enter frame and begin nailing down edges of floppy.

Rest of floppy nailed down.

Pull back to show Memorex Flex Disk next to floppy in first three frames.

Three sides of Memorex Flex Disk zip up as VO (voice over) says, "Solid seam . . . bonding."

Floppy on left puckers, bulges and warps, along open spaces not secured by nails.

First word of super (superimposed letters) comes up.

Rest of super comes up.

AUDIO:

Announcer: Memorex brings you . . . a slight exaggeration.

Anncr: Most floppy disk makers seal their edges just here . . . .

SFX: HAMMERING

Anncr: . . . and there.

SFX: HAMMERING

Anncr: But not Memorex. We seal every inch of every disk with . . . .
. . . Solid . . . Seam . . . Bonding.

SFX: ZIP . . . ZIP . . . ZIP

Anncr: So a Memorex edge fights bulges (*SFX:* (BLOOP)), puckers (*SFX:* (BLOOP)), and warps (*SFX:* (BLOOP)).

Anncr: Because if all that (*SFX:* (BLOOP, BLOOP, BLOOP)) jams your disk drive, you can lose all your data. And that's no exaggeration.

Anncr: Memorex . . . has the edge.

(*Source:* ADLA:2, Art Directors Club of Los Angeles)

The Storyboard

Another Way to Present the TV/Film Idea

The script is rendered visually through this method. Each frame represents an important point in the action and is accompanied by the corresponding words and sound effects.

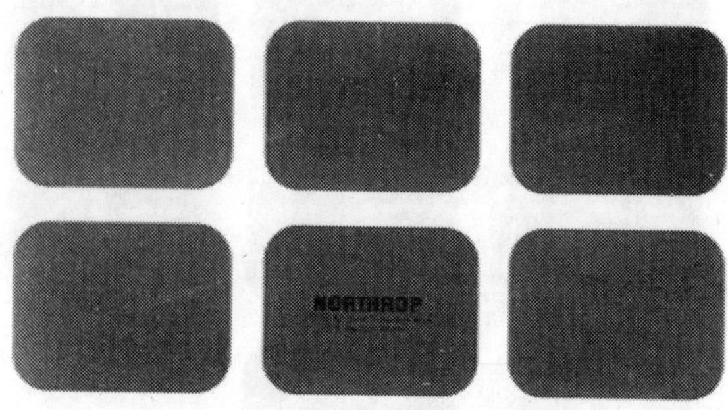

Client: Northrop Corporation
Agency: Philips-Ramsey, Los Angeles, CA
Writer: Mark Deschenes & Northrop Corporation
Photographer: Marc Coppos
Art Director: Jim Cox

Air

VIDEO		AUDIO
1. Open on blue sky.	*SFX:*	Wind
2. ELS (Extreme long shot) of jet plane entering frame from left.	*SFX:*	Distant jet engine
3. As the jet moves across the frame, we see the contrail.	*Anncr:*	Our way of life in America is defended by a select few. At Northrop Corporation we never forget that those few depend on the products we make to

		help safeguard the way of life we all enjoy.
4. FADE IN SUPER: NORTHROP Making advanced technology work for America's defense. FADE OUT SUPER.	*Anncr:*	Northrop. Making advanced technology work for America's defense.
5. Flock of birds fly across frame.	*SFX:*	Birds flying by

(*Source:* ADLA: 2, Art Directors Club of Los Angeles)

TV Commercials: A Team Effort

Bahadur Merwan, who has done all the cartoons for this book, offers copywriters a few tips when it comes to making TV commercials. He says, "Though a TV/film idea or concept may be the brainchild of either the copywriter or art director, the commercial only takes shape with the participation of the team. Here your partner, the art director, scores as he is gifted with visual capabilities backed with an illustrator's talents. But both copy and art should clearly understand the techniques used in shooting and editing a commercial. This will help you to put across your ideas more professionally to the film or TV producer."

Given below are some common terms used in TV/filmmaking. Understanding them will help you create effective commercials.

Terms Used for Camera Movements

ECU: extreme close up
CU: close up
ELS: extreme long shot
LS: long shot
MLS: medium long shot
Pan: camera movement to the right or left on the horizontal axis
Tilt Up/Tilt Down: camera moves up or down on the vertical axis at 90°
Zoom In: move closer to an object by using a zoom lens
Zoom Out: move away from the object by using the same lens
Wide-angle Shot: a wider view covered by using a wide angle lens. This could be an extreme wide angle shot or a 'fish-eye' effect of 180°; the entire view then appears in circular form

Tracking: shot taken while following an object either by placing the camera on a trolley (rail track) or by a hand-held camera

Crane Shot: shot taken by the camera placed on the crane to take a top angle shot with movement

Helicopter Shot: shot taken from a chopper. This shot gives flexibility and speed and adds drama in bird's eye view photography

Soft Focus: produces softer effect with a special lens

Split/Prism Effect: multiple effects produced by using a special lens

Spot Focus: centre image remains clear while the area around it goes out-of-focus or is slightly blurred

Terms Used in Editing

Cut: abrupt end of one shot to start another shot

Match Cut: abrupt change of shot but the next shot matches with the previous one in form/shape/colour/speed or movement

Dissolve: one scene merges with another. The duration of a dissolve could be fast or slow, depending on the mood you wish to create

Match Dissolve: one scene dissolves into the other, but the previous shot matches the following shot in shape or angle or colour or movement. Here again the duration of the dissolve could be faster or slower depending on the mood of the scene

Wipe/Flip: change of one scene to another by revealing the next either by (a) turning a page type of effect, (b) a ripple effect, or (c) breaking one scene into splinters to reveal the other, and so on. There are any number of special effects available on the editing table

SFX: special sound effects used to enhance or create the mood of a scene

CG: computer graphics (images created by use of special computer software)

FVO: female voice over

MVO: male voice over

Anncr: announcer

FO: fade out

Workout

1. Accompany the TV/film crew in your agency on a shoot—preferably outdoors!
2. Write a 30-second TV script for *Dentium Toothpaste*, based on the information you have about this purely imaginary brand (read the previous chapters again to refresh your memory).
3. Watch ZEE, Star Plus and [V] channels for a week. Select what you consider the five most outstanding TV commercials. Are they supported by press campaigns? Derive propositions for the product, based on the commercial. Is this proposition reflected in the press campaign?
4. Turn a TV commercial into a press ad, and vice versa.

22

Writing for Radio and Multimedia

In the early twenties, before the arrival of television, *Radio* was king. People were glued to their sets—not just to listen to favourite programmes but also to hear the news of the world. Radio was so much a part of life that people set their watches by Radio time. It was the backdrop for domestic life. Housewives went about doing their chores with the radio or transistor playing all day long, and cricket fans still depend on this aural and portable medium for the latest scores. The signature tune for All India Radio has stayed unchanged for the last 70 years. And anyone can recognise the BBC, Radio Ceylon (now Sri Lanka Broadcasting Corporation) or Radio Kuwait at the flick of a button.

Today, although Radio has become a *reminder* medium, it still plays an important—and economical—role, especially in rural India.

It takes greater skill and imagination to think up Radio Spots—as they are called—which may be 10-second, 20-second or 30-second spots. Radio-sponsored programmes are also used, like the old Binaca Hit Parade (now Cibaca Hit Parade), at fixed times. Tone of voice and brand image become crucial in writing for radio.

Writing for Radio comes somewhere between the rigidity of the press ad and the 3-dimensional appeal of the TV commercial.

You are appealing to the human EAR, a sensitive organ that works even when you are not aware it is. Hearing responds to the oddest things. If you wear spectacles, notice how your *hearing* improves when you put them on? Try watching TV on *Mute*. How much can you gauge of what is going on? Why are the more progressive helmets for bikies designed to *expose the ears?* How did Beethoven compose great music which he could not hear?

If you want to get an idea of how important your hearing is, stuff your ears with cotton so you block out as much sound as possible. Do this for a whole day. How did you feel when you got the cotton out of your ears again?

The English language is glutted with idioms, phrases, slogans and proverbs that make reference to ears/hearing/sound. Just for fun, fill in the blanks below with the appropriate aural words:

1. As . . . as a bell.
2. Making a silk purse out of a sow's . . .
3. Ever . . . the one about the farmer's daughter?
4. Word of . . .
5. Stop, look, . . .
6. Grinning from . . .
7. He's all . . .
8. H . . . ! H . . . ! (after a good speech).
9. Empty vessels make the most . . .

10. No action . . . only.
11. The . . . of silence.
12. Keep one's . . . open.
13. To have a musical . . .
14. To be a good . . .
15. Prick up one's . . .
16. You could . . . a pin drop.
17. "Friends, Romans, countrymen, lend me your . . ."
18. A . . . of laughter.
19. Under one's . . .
20. Out of . . .

Do you ever wonder what people did before the radio came?

The challenge of writing for Radio is to create images in the listeners' minds which will evoke a desired mood. This mood or response must be sharp enough to give the product being advertised a place in the listener's limited memory box.

Just as in writing for press or TV, tried and true techniques work well for Radio: slice of life, demonstrations, humour, testimonials, talking heads, problem-solution. Obviously you can add to this jingles, mimicry and musical vignettes as endemic for this medium. Here is a tip. Try and adapt TV treatments to Radio, while omitting the pictures.

Creating a Radio personality or character to sell your product is another good idea. This person, like Surf's Lalitaji or Asian Paints' Gattu, could be used to announce special offers, break news or give other information about the brand.

The simplest way to be effective on Radio, and this may come as a surprise, is to adapt Aesop Glim's Six-Step formula for writing body copy for press ads to the "sound only" medium. Radio spots are also time-bound, like TV commercials. There is only so much you can say in so much time (20 seconds, 30 seconds, 60 seconds).

- ARRESTING POWER — Use a signature sound or tune, or a phrase or catchy slogan that heralds your product.
- JUSTIFY/SUBSTANTIATE — Give the listener a strong reason to keep listening.
- GET INTO STORY — Introduce brand name.

- TALK PRODUCT — Extol its virtues.
- ELIMINATE COMPETITION — Ignore them with a phrase such as: "Only Brand X can do/give!"
- IMPEL ACTION — "Hurry! Last day today!" "Stocks limited!" "At your nearest chemist!" "Free with every pack . . . !"

For example, here is a make-believe 30-second spot called *Castanets*.

Castanets

SFX (sound effects): Click click click of castanets beating out a brisk tune.

Small boy: Hey, Gramps, I didn't know you could play the castanets.

Gramps: These are not castanets. They're my dentures.

Small boy: Oh.

Announcer: You can spend your old age playing with your dentures . . . or you can start using New Dentium toothpaste.
Only Dentium is reinforced with calcium—to keep tooth enamel strong and healthy.
So, your teeth last . . . as long as YOU do.
The choice is yours.
Brush with New Dentium every day.
Or brush up your castanets.

SFX: Click click click.

Note: In a Radio Spot, use easy-to-say, easy-to-understand words and short sentences packed with punch. Time your commercial by reading the words out loud and mimicking the sound effects. After a while, you will easily judge how many words go into a 20-second, or 30-second spot.

Points to Consider

Tone of Voice

As discussed earlier, tone of voice can be used most effectively to coax, admonish, reassure, soothe. Choose the one you think is most suitable to get your message across.

The Voice Over

Too many voices clutter up the message. The announcer's voice could be enough, if you have a strong line to deliver. This, accompanied by a signature tune, could really make an impact.

Voice Contrasts

If using more than one voice over, try and introduce man/woman or woman/child, or high-pitched voice/low gruff voice of the same sex. Try for a voice mnemonic, if possible i.e., a unique voice (aural burr) that becomes associated with your brand.

Signature Tune

Where a distinctive bar of music gets associated with the brand. Good examples are jingles for Lifebuoy, Nirma and Britannia biscuits.

Use of Humour

A funny story told over the air could get your audience smiling, but let it reinforce your brand, not obliterate it (a good example, Maggi Sauce: It's different).

Sound Effects

An aural "burr" that becomes associated with your product—school bell, dinner gong, ambulance siren, call of the *muezzin*, cowbells, train whistle, thunderclap (e.g., Castrol engine oils).

Nostalgic Tunes/Sounds

Lullabies, old favourite melodies, watchmen's whistle evoke a sense of familiarity which strike a sympathetic chord in the listener.

Film Songs

Indians love music, especially film music. Cash in on this, e.g., Uncle Chipps (*Bole mere lips*), Coke (*Aati kya Khandala*), Onida Black & White TV (*Yeh black and white*).

Radio Programmes

Budget permitting, you might get lucky enough to find a client to sponsor a radio show. Good examples, the Cibaca Hit Parade, the Bournvita Quiz, Close Up Round Up, Lux Filmi Sitaron ka Sargam.

Scripting an Audio-Visual

In my youth (as Father William said to the young man) the humble carousel and single projector pulsed with a tape recorder, were the once-exciting precursor to super-8, computer graphics, and multimedia shows. Creative teams reached heights of ecstasy moving from a single projector to multi-projectors, 18-screen AVs and video walls!

Writing for *Audio-Visuals* is a logical stepping stone from writing radio commercials. Actually they are a chicken and egg sort of thing, both disciplines feeding each other. Radio trains you to write so that the audience imagines the visual . . . in the AV, you have to write so that your partner, the art director, can imagine the visuals. Audio-Visuals forced copywriters to refine and focus the art of writing a script that was taut, laconic and which jelled with the visuals.

I loved AVs and had a lot of fun learning at the knees of Mubi Ismail (mentioned earlier), who surrounded such events with much fanfare and razzmatazz. Lintas was lucky to have an admiring audience in the client, Hindustan Lever, for whom Ms Ismail masterminded many intricate Audio-Visuals often involving as many as 16 projectors! She always brought an element of surprise to her performances. Once a live but leashed black panther was dragged on stage during a show for a visiting dignitary. The Lever executives and their guests jumped up as one man, resulting in 500 auditorium seats springing back in a thunderclap of Jovian proportions . . . which made the poor panther turn heel and piddle all over its master's trousers!

My very first solo Audio-Visual job, complete with a throwaway idea, was handed me by my boss Alyque Padamsee—a tiny curtain-raiser for Reckitt and Colman India's sales conference. It was just 40 slides dropping in the carousel every five seconds (200 seconds—an AV lasting a mere 3 minutes 20 seconds) but I have kept the script to this day—I was so proud of it!

Here is the RCI script. Forty cartoon drawings were used and made into slides for this. It was based on Henry Ford's famous belief that "History is Bunk!"

Partners in Profit
Slide Sequence/Script

1. Though most people don't know it, some of the world's greatest figures have been salesmen.

2. Some people sell products, others sell ideas. And each person has his own individual selling technique.
3. Take Adam. After he was banished from the Garden of Eden, he had to earn a living, so he became a salesman.
4. Naturally, he sold apples. He knew all about them.
5. His technique was simple. He always took Eve along with him on a sales trip! While the dealer was busy staring at Eve, Adam got him to sign an order for 10,000 apples.
6. But soon he realised that Eve's fig leaves were attracting more attention than his apples.
7. Smart salesman that he was, Adam switched over to selling fig leaves!
8. Then there was Marco Polo. Besides being an explorer, he was the world's first travelling salesman, and the originator of travelling salesman jokes.
9. Marco made a great hit in China, where he built up a fortune selling spices.
10. In China, where everybody looked alike, dressed alike, and read the same book (Mao's Thoughts) . . .
11. . . . Marco found it easy to convince the dealers that spices were the variety of life!
12. The world's first sales lady was Cleopatra of Egypt. This enterprising woman sold pyramids . . .
13. . . . a thriving business, because there was always somebody drowning in the Nile.
14. Cleopatra did not do much travelling, partly because the pyramids were too heavy for her to lug around on sales trips . . .
15. . . . and partly because she believed that more deals are made reclining on a couch than this world dreams of.
16. As a sales lady, Cleopatra was very popular. She had so many cute little tricks up her sleeve, the dealers were never quite sure what she was selling!
17. This only added to the fun. What's more, they appreciated her expensive giveaways like *Ooomph*, an exotic, rare perfume.
18. While Cleopatra was doing her bit for Egypt, the Rani of Jhansi was very busy in India.
19. She believed that a Rani on the *ghoda* is worth two on the *gaddi*—which means that a queen on a horse is worth two on the throne. Her dealers agreed.
20. Even though the Rani's technique was one of feminine warfare.

21. Her chief weapons? A shining, bright-edged . . . smile . . .
22. A keen, sharp . . . sense of humour . . .
23. . . . Her dazzling good nature!
24. The dealers were captivated, and vied with one another to place their orders with her . . .
25. . . . and they were some orders!
26. Another famous salesman was Samson the Strong. He always put tremendous punch into his sales talk . . .
27. . . . and this got him many orders. Dealers liked Samson—they could always depend on . . .
28. . . . his prompt deliveries!
29. For many years, Samson was in the real estate business . . . .
30. . . . but when the crash came, he switched to selling insurance.
31. Like all strong men, Samson had one big weakness—his was lady Deal-i-lers!!
32. So much for history. But today's world offers a more up-to-date example of good selling. Take the case of Reckless Reckitt and Cautious Colman. (By the way, any similarity these chaps' names to that of a reputed national company is purely intentional!)
33. Dealers would close shop and take the day off when they heard Reckitt and Colman were in town!
34. Reckless was the sort of guy who would promise them the moon . . . .
35. . . . but it always turned out to be stale, green cheese!
36. While Cautious, on the other hand, would make no promises at all . . . much to the dealer's despair.
37. Customers walked off in a huff because the products they wanted were always out of stock. Sales dropped and dropped . . . till one day . . . .
38. . . . Reckless Reckitt and Cautious Colman decided to join hands and modify their selling techniques. Reckitt promised not to do anything rash, and Colman ventured to set up a window display!
39. Reckitt's smile became more genuine, and Colman began to listen to dealers' problems. They started getting more orders . . . and remembered to fulfil them. Sales began to soar and soar . . .
40. That was many years ago. Today Reckitt and Colman are a mature, experienced company. They enjoy the fullest confidence of their dealers . . . with whom they have become true Partners in Profit.

Those simple, charming days! I hope RCI does not mind being used as an example . . . it was so many years ago.

No chapter on Multimedia can be complete if it does not mention that most marvellous one of all . . . the Internet. Former HTA copywriter and my dear friend, Seema Bakshi, who with husband Arindam Ganguli, now runs Communications Centre in New Delhi, was persuaded to share her experience of Internet sourcing.

You and the Internet—Made for Each Other?

by Seema Bakshi

Being a copywriter is just great.

You're never on the same job for long. (An attention span of five minutes is quite acceptable.)

The process of collecting irrelevant information is highly respected as a research activity—and supported. (Like going to a film or art show.)

You can look busy while inspecting the dirt under the nails. (Or the tesselations of the screen saver.)

You often get your best headlines from the bin. (Note how miraculously a headline written for butter does the job for a lathe machine.)

Basically, you've got a temperament. And now, virtually made to order, is a universe that offers you your kind of gratification!

To Start with, the Learning of the Medium

You can float, flit and fly from site to site, with John Lennon's, 'Imagine There's No Country' strumming in your head. Experience the thrill of a bungee jump, leaping from Iceland to Argentina in one swoop. Learning the ins and outs of the Internet can be a fully satisfying experience with the hours fluidly melting away from sunrise to sundown. And effortlessly you can come to grips with the *friendliness* of the medium, the *informality* of address to customers and clients, the *classlessness* of the cyber society. (Where even a flea may talk with authority.)

A State of Total Irreverence

The Internet is maintained by geeks who transcend rules they themselves make. But it is used by us folks who don't know baud from baudy! The very environment calls for audacity, courage and irreverence. Anything can be done, if not today, then who knows, tomorrow? It's a place which encourages you to let your creative juices flow, without fear of rejection or scorn.

Mozilla, What's That?!

Much of the time the Internet confronts you with technospeak and such gorillas. But as with marketing jargon, you can give it all a friendly toss! Just stick to your guns with the ammo you've gathered and apply your copywriting fundas to ads, promos, web sites, or whatever you're at. Target Audience, Tone of Voice, Personality, Positioning, et al. *Because the medium may change, but the message may not.*

The Inspiration's All Around

The Internet is better than the Black Book, more meaty than an encyclopaedia, less time consuming than a library, more picturesque than Art Direction, an absolute universe of ideas, information and inspiration. If you need it, *you've got a friend.*

Warm-ups

1. Put on earphones and listen to the radio for a whole day. Listen to the commercials. Which ones appeal? Which bore you to tears? Make a note of any aural burrs (school bell, train whistle, dinner gong, factory siren, ambulance siren, police siren) that listeners would recognise easily, and which you could employ in your radio commercials.
2. Open a special file for radio ideas.

Workout

1. Write a 60-second radio spot for Dentium toothpaste! Then boil it down to a 20-second spot, using the same idea.
2. Try to visualise the 40-cartoon drawings used to supplement the Partners in Profit AV script you have just read. Then suggest another visual which could replace each cartoon, using real-life photography. In your view, would this improve the AV? Ask yourself, can I think in cartoons? Or do I always think real-life?
3. Convert the RCI audio-visual script into a short Radio programme aimed at housewives who use Dettol.

23

Writing for In-Shop Media

When we were children we learnt a poem which went something like "I have a little shadow, he goes everywhere with me." We also learned about Mary's little lamb . . . everywhere that Mary went the lamb was sure to go. Meet the salesman who dogs you when you go out shopping. Unlike the salesman with his foot in the door, or the one who hangs around your living room, or the one who sings to you on the radio, this one is harder to resist.

Because he is right beside you when you open your purse!

Here you are, casually browsing in a supermarket while waiting for a friend—and an attractive poster (or dangler, or counter dispenser) catches your eye. You take a closer look—and hey, you are reaching for your wallet. Perhaps it is something you have forgotten you wanted, or perhaps you have impulsively decided to try something new. Whatever the reason, *Point of Sale or Point of Purchase* material really works!

Remember precis-writing at school? Well, here is your chance to practice it now—and make money doing so. Point of Sale/Point of Purchase (POS/POP) are crisp contractions of the main advertising message. They are generally short and compelling; the objective is to give the unwary consumer a last shove to buy a brand he had not earlier intended to buy.

Most shopkeepers are possessive about space. Every inch is used to stock their wares. So POP must be really exciting and practical to tempt him to have it in his shop. The copywriter and art director have to be really ingenious in their designs. The colours must be chosen with care. The type used must be clear and legible.

Walk around the shops in your locality. Notice the in-shop material being used. Look out for new places where you could recommend further use of POP. Windows, shelf space, cardboard cutouts, fringes, awnings, wallpaper. Many smaller shops look gay and inviting because of the POP material supplied to them by advertisers.

Copywriters, strictly speaking, do not have a strong role to play in designing POS once the main copy message is arrived at. The same message (naturally based on the ongoing press/TV campaign) is adapted for use in retail outlets. The logo and the company colours become centre stage. Mnemonics are useful here and can be made to highlight the brand in ingenious ways. The Surf 'dazzle motif' or Air-India's Maharajah are cases in point. For example, a grocery store could be provided with an awning painted with the dazzle motif; or a travel agency foyer could display a life-size cutout of the Maharajah. Some cigarette vendors and *panwala* shops are given umbrellas with the product message printed on them.

The danger, of course, is clutter. Everyone is vying for attention. So the challenge is always—*something new, something different*. Today, more than ever before, the medium is the message. Thank you, Marshall McLuhan.

Sales Promotions

Ad agencies use long-term and short-term strategies to sell brands. Long-running (annual or more) press campaigns, supported by TV, film, radio and outdoor are known as *theme* advertising. Sales promotion today increasingly uses conventional media like TV. But it is mainly done through POP, POS, mailers, flyers and event management as part of what is known as *scheme or tactical* advertising. Theme advertising is familiarly called *above-the-line*, and scheme advertising is known as *below-the-line*. These are the differences between a war and battles. The war goes on and on; the battles are fought in different areas—on the ground, in the air, on the ocean.

It seems reasonable to speak of this marketing tool here as it generally requires a greater involvement by the retail trade/shopowners/shopkeepers . . . as well as the use of in-shop and other advertising material. Copywriting skills most definitely come into play in the area of sales promotion.

A Temporary Incentive

Sales promotion exploits the consumer's interest in getting something at a discount! It appeals to the incipient desire in all of us to *gamble*, to take mild *risks*, to respond to a challenge, and to make *easy money*. It recognises consumer psychology and behavioural habits: the impulse to buy, the solace of spending money . . . it effectively uses Aesop Glim's nine basic buttons to impel purchase.

Like in the other media, advertising done for sales promotions makes use of:

The four instincts: Sex/Love. Fear. Anger/Rage. Hunger.
The five senses: Touch. Sight. Hearing. Taste. Smell.

The consumer feels he is getting a good deal, and the advertiser of the brand is getting an even better deal!

Sales Promotion Incentives

- free sampling (sachets)
- mail-ins for free gifts/samples
- free containers/reuseable jars
- promotional games
- contests and competitions
- lucky draws
- coupons, distributed in various ways
- cash refunds
- extra product free (piggy back)
- extra quantity for same price
- gift items

The consumer needs to be informed about these incentives—through POP/POS, mailers, posters, localised ads, 10-second TV or radio spots. When this is the objective, you are engaged in 'scheme' advertising, bearing in mind the brand's overall 'theme' advertising. The brand builders have to be like a good general who thinks out tactical manoeuvres in the light of a larger plan.

The sales promotion must be legal, easy to implement by the trade, easy to understand and seen as honest and above board by the customer. Exchanging five bottle caps for a free bottled drink, or getting a small sachet of washing powder when you buy a 2kg-pack . . . these are simple sales offers. When it comes to contests, magazine subscriptions, mail-ins for free gifts . . . things can get more complicated. The marketing team must carefully calculate the costs of these in terms of infrastructure, energy levels and budget. There is also the time factor to be considered; most promotions are effective in a short time span.

Planning a Promotion

If the client's strategy for the brand excludes conventional media such as TV, radio and others but is based solely on promotions, follow the same logic as when planning a campaign in these media. Make sure you have a comprehensive Agency Brief—product, market, consumer, marketing goals, advertising goals, budget considerations, research results, past promotional efforts.

It might help to assess the brief in terms of asking the questions—(a) Where are we? (b) Why are we here? (c) Where do we want to be? The sales promotion and its implementation answers the question—(d) How do we get there?

Where Are We?

As in the case of planning a press campaign, the client brief to the agency must provide all information about:

1. Product: its usage, its sales, its strengths and weaknesses, its price
2. Competition: what they are saying and doing, their strengths and weaknesses

3. Consumer: the target audience, attitudes to the brand, buying habits, etc.
4. Market: in terms of cash value/sales of the product and area covered
5. Marketing: distribution network and sales policy, average monthly or quarterly penetration, trade and retail pricing, breakdown of sales by pack sizes, number of packets per case, size and structure of sales force
6. Company Policy: towards sales force involvement, towards the trade/trade's policy, toward product category
7. Past Promotions: description/results/conclusions
8. Reasons: e.g., to help overcome retailer reluctance to stock a particular size of the brand

Why Are We Here?

Good clients also tell you *why* the brand is where it is. This means going further than the cold facts and figures of market share, penetration, distribution and pricing. It has to do with motivations, influences and consumer behaviour.

Your brand may be regarded by both trade and consumer to be rather up-market, as having snob value. The 'opportunity' here is for your brand to occupy a unique position where it does not directly compete with more popular brands. The 'danger' is that it may appeal to only a narrow segment of consumers. These *qualitative* rather than *quantitative* values may help explain why the brand is able to maintain a slight premium price over competitors, or why it is stocked by fewer outlets than competition.

Knowing this, you will avoid unsuitable sales incentives like offering retailers prizes such as a month in a five-star hotel. Far from encouraging them to stock your brand, this may well convince them that they were right to regard it as one meant for an elitist minority—which did not shop at their stores!

Where do We Want to Be?

The client must *set down in writing* what he hopes the sales promotion will achieve for the brand. The sales promotion exercise and execution could involve many people within the client's company: product managers, packaging buyers, distribution staff, sales force, legal department and others. All need to be apprised of the marketing intention, so a formal proposal should be fleshed out. The client must also justify to his marketing team why a promotion is needed to meet the objective . . . rather than some other sales technique.

Sales promotion may be undertaken:

- to clear extra stocks
- to shore up brand image
- to create goodwill
- as a hedge against competition
- as a response to falling sales
- to build brand identity
- to encourage retailers to stock a new product
- to encourage them to stock larger quantities
- to encourage them to give the product special display
- to encourage repeat purchases
- to optimise advertising expenditure
- to localise brand usage
- to increase brand usage among a specific target consumer

Be sure you know your client's reasons.

How do We Get There?

Once you have a clear idea of the client's sales and marketing objectives you can get down to work on the promotion. You may want to enlist your research team to compile a list of questions, or suggest a suitable modus operandi depending on what you want to achieve. Here is a checklist:

- What should the key consumer message be?
- What should the trade proposition be?
- What should the consumer be offered?
- How should the offer be expressed?
- What medium (leaflets/mailers/handbills/contests) should be used?
- How is the consumer to avail of the offer?
- How is the sales force to be equipped?
- How is the trade to be informed?
- What is the rationale behind the promotion?

- What evidence is there for believing it will work?
- How much should the budget be?
- What about timing? Start date/finish date/dates for decision and action in lead-up period should all be considered.
- What results are expected (in figures preferably)?
- What is the estimated payout/income/profit?
- How should the results of the promotion be evaluated?

When you have the answers, it is easier to formulate a statement of how to gauge the success of the promotion in order to optimise its use in the future.

Pre-Testing

If the client can afford it, pre-test the communication message of the promotion with a cross-section of the target audience. One expression of the offer may work much better than the other. For instance, you may want to select one of the following alternatives:

- Normal price Rs 20—now Rs 15!
- Rs 5 off!
- 25% discount!
- 4 weeks supply for the price of 3!
- 12 units for the price of 9!

A Rs 5-off promotion may well work harder than a Rs 7-off scheme which is less powerfully worded. Some of the common methods of testing used in consumer research are given below:

Hall Tests

Consumers are asked to look at a range of attractive premiums and rank them in order of preference.

Group Discussions

For example, to test whether a premium is compatible with the consumer's perception of the brand to be promoted.

In-Store Tests

When the aim of the promotion is to increase short-term sales, a careful monitoring of brand sales in the test stores for some months (rather than weeks) before the promotion is launched becomes essential. This helps to gain an accurate interpretation of the promotion's sales results. You could also compare sales in the stores where the promotion was offered with sales in a matched panel of control stores in which you do not offer the promotion.

Cost and Scale of Pre-testing

This should be related to the size of the budget. In all forms of pre-testing avoid comparing apples with oranges. For instance, do not hall-test against each other a series of products of widely different costs, unless you agree on a method of weighing the results to take into account these cost variations.

The agency's role and the client's role may overlap where sales promotions are concerned. Some agencies have begun to take over the entire operation. In some cases there is a 50:50 collaboration. What is important is that you, the copywriter, are not just a crafter of words, but a seller of brands. Your particular skill is presenting the ideas in words, but the ideas can come from anywhere and from anyone, even the client himself.

Slogans that Sell

Free with Every Jar/Pack/Bottle
Hurry! Stocks Limited
Enter the Free-For-All Contest
Exchange Your Old TV for . . .
Offer Open Till . . .
The Early Bird Gets the . . .
Special Offer for this Week Only
Win! Win! Win!
Fabulous Prizes Worth Rupees Fifty Thousand to be Won

Warm-ups

1. Start a file on sales promotions you have noticed. A few are listed here. What appeals have they used? What made them success stories? Instead of going to the movies one weekend, spend the time with dealers, retailers and salesmen who have to implement the promotions.

Make a note of their comments and any ideas they might have to improve sales of the brands. What consumer feedback did they get?

Current Promotions

Pizza Hut/Pepsi promotion
Tata Cafe in PET jars
Surf plastic bucket
Pepsodent toothpaste free samples
Nescafe contests
Horlicks family's favourite health drink contest
Boomer sticker schemes
Maggi Club
Bournvita Quiz
Thums Up cricket souvenirs
Milkmaid recipe coupons and booklets
Welcomgroup's executive club spouse offer
Airlines frequent-flyer programmes
Airline/Hotels clubbed offers (Sahara airlines)
Arrow shirts—buy one and take one free
Lee shirts—one tee shirt free
AIWA exchange programmes (TV/audio systems/CDs/LDs free)
AKAI—ditto
Magazine promotions (*Time, Femina, Cosmopolitan, India Today*)
World Cup promotions

2. Think of ideas to promote sales of Dentium toothpaste in Bangalore over a period of three months (June–August). The client expects the sales to treble.

24

Writing for Outdoor Media

Once you have mastered the disciplines of writing a press ad and a TV or radio commercial, you will find *Outdoor Media* a breeze. These are the cherries on your cake—hoardings (billboards), banners, posters, wall paintings, car stickers, bus panels and all the 'jazzmatazz' that ornament the highways and byways of city and countryside. (That they are the bane of environmentalists and often of nuisance value to residents are points often glossed over by advertisers and their agencies.)

American humorist Ogden Nash put it like this:

I think that I shall never see
A billboard lovely as a tree.
Indeed, unless the billboards fall
I'll never see a tree at all.

Hoardings/Billboards

Hoardings and their ilk are *reminder media.* Sometimes they may form the *only* media in a small-budget campaign, or where the marketing is localised. If they are part of a larger multi-media campaign, the advertiser's message is adapted to suit the medium.

Guidelines for Hoardings

Lots of white space
Not more than 11 words
Eye-catching colours
Legible type
Good location
Make use of the medium

Some brands have permanent sites for their hoardings. This is an advantage. Like the Air-India hoarding space at Mumbai's Nariman Point. Traffic lights at this corner make it impossible for drivers to ignore the weekly change of message, sporting the evergreen Maharajah. Amrutanjan (pain balm) has its name straddling the hills near Lonavala (a holiday resort between Mumbai and Pune) in giant letters. Just the name, no message, but it stays in your mind. Hoardings are a wonderful way to be creative. Unfortunately few copywriters take the opportunity to literally 'show off'. Here are some examples of memorable hoardings:

- ARALDITE—It also sticks handles to teapots.

My fareway to Japan
TOKYO
OSAKA
RS. 34515
Contact your travel agent or nearest Air-India office.
एअर-इंडिया
AIR-INDIA

- Mellwood Bacon belongs to all the best clubs.
  (visual shows three giant club sandwiches)
  FISCHER'S
  the bacon-makin' people
- Whenever you see colour think of us.
  JENSON & NICHOLSON
- AMUL—utterly, butterly delicious billboards!
- AIR-INDIA—weekly change at Nariman Point, Mumbai.
- 555 CIGARETTES—backlit hoardings.

Billboards can be used very effectively not just to promote a brand, but also to draw attention to public causes and current topics.

Innovations in Media

Two examples stand out for me. The Dettol Show Window in Akbarally's department store (Mumbai). And the Red & White cigarette hoarding across the overhead pedestrians bridge (now replaced by an underground passageway) at Churchgate. Both were firsts of their kind.

The Dettol show window drew crowds. It used 'mobility' instead of the usual static display. It was like the interior of a large doll's house . . . bedroom, bathroom, playroom. A little mother-doll dressed in a sari would come trundling along on rails, holding a big bottle of Dettol Antiseptic liquid. In each room she would stop and 'pour' some imaginary Dettol into (a) the father-doll's shaving mug (b) the baby doll's bath water, and so on and so forth. It was a way of making people aware of other occasions and uses for Dettol than just to wash hurts and bruises. Needless to say, Dettol sales soared.

The Red & White man in his famous top hat and striped shirt was also a 'mobile'. He was a large cut-out and held a cigarette in his hand. By some marvel of engineering, he kept raising his arm and 'smoking' his cigarette—and lo and behold, real smoke came out of his mouth! He was the talk of the town for a long time.

These ideas may seem simple and childish. But in the early '70s they were pathbreakers. A more up-to-date example: the live hair-style/fashion show in front of a digitally backlit billboard for Organics Shampoo.

Neon signs, balloons, sky writing, badges, tee-shirts and caps, kiosks, trees, bus panels, and everything that goes under the umbrella of 'street furniture' is used to advertise your message out of doors. You name it—and you can use it . . . !

Any uncovered space is fair game. There are notices everywhere—in trains, buses, cars, taxis. Only airplanes have not yet been invaded! However, I have heard of a live fashion show held on one of the private carriers. Consumerism is growing by leaps and bounds in India, and the battle for the buyers' attention is an endless one.

Since most outdoor messages are short and crisp, they may just highlight the brand name and logo—like ONLY VIMAL on bus panels.

Exhibitions, Events, Etcetera

Today the boundaries of what is known as outdoor advertising are being stretched. Needs change, the industry has changed, the consumer is more savvy, the competition more ferocious, the market wider and deeper, the clients a mixed bag. Fortunately, *plus la change plus c'est la meme chose* (which freely translated means the more it changes, the more it is the same thing).

Exhibitions and trade fairs are still known by these appellations. But a new term has entered the advertising lexicon: *Event Management*. This can cover anything—road shows, stage shows, book readings and signings, beauty contests, TV quizz shows, sponsored programmes, street shows, sound-and-light shows, song-and-dance shows, fashion shows. Fund-raising efforts like White Cane balls (to raise money for the blind), promoting CRY cards, schemes to Save the Tiger, Save Depressed Mothers, Feed the Hungry, Give a Dog a Home, or Adopt an Oldie often employ promotional methods that entail Event Management.

Copywriters are expected to turn a trick or two even in these areas. You have to know what is 'happening' out there in a world inhabited by yuppies, puppies and dinks. Promos and events target mainly the under-20s. They are the MTV generation exposed to different media and whose attention span is not more than 30 seconds, the length of the average commercial!

What appeals to this segment? Who and what do they identify with? Should the advertising message be more visual? Should it be in 'Hinglish', more and more the preferred idiom of teenagers? Should it be shouted or sung or whispered in their ears?

Research shows that teens spend the maximum time out of the house. So where would they receive the advertiser's message? Logically, in the street, in a shop, in a restaurant or cinema hall. Now event branding has become the name of the game. Road shows, street shows, stage shows, retail promos demand bright insignias to attract the young. Successful examples are the MTV/Channel [V] road shows, the Coke road shows with Daler Mehendi, Pepsi stage shows with multiple activities tied up with Channel [V] and the McDonald's in-shop promotions.

A promotion for Crush orange drink from Cadbury Schweppes tied up with English and Hindi films in metros for instant brand identification. More recently, Charms cigarettes followed the same route with a tie-up with the movie *Hyderabad Blues* (these cigarettes come in a denim-look pack and the famous Charminar is located in Hyderabad!). The film, which had a highly unconventional theme, became a hit with yuppies—the Charms target audience. Another example is the already mentioned unconventional idea thought up by a young media person for Fevicol: five-second flashes during the screening of '*Sholay*'.

Tomorrow's copywriter may be asked to play a role in any type of communication which requires ideation and the written word. Till now we have dealt mainly with writing for profit, i.e., either your own, or the agency's, or the client's. We have driven home the point it pays to advertise. The art and craft of copywriting, however, need not be restricted to lining the client's coffers. Advertising can promote a brand and make it a runaway success—and may also earn a client much goodwill for his company.

Good Citizen Advertising

As consumerism grows by leaps and bounds, I believe there is a parallel need for advertisers to channel some of their profits into what is known as public service advertising. Frankly, I dislike that term. It sounds too much like the advertiser is doing people a favour. I prefer to call it *Good Citizen Advertising,* to remind ourselves of *noblesse oblige*. Of course, advertisers do drop something in the box now and then, but it is just a drop in the ocean.

Why is there no single agency devoted wholly to Good Citizen Advertising? Or a TV channel meant exclusively for sponsored programmes to raise funds and resources for worthy causes? So much money is spent on goods and services. So little on those that offer a tax write-off.

It is an interesting corollary that the films, commercials and press campaigns that win international awards are very often those which are designed for some public cause. Why? They pull at your heart-strings. And open your pursestrings.

As you mature as a copywriter, you might try to spread the idea of Good Citizen Advertising in your agency or among your clients. It is amazing how good one feels when one has done something for someone, at not much cost to oneself. And the rewards are enormous in terms of goodwill. I believe that what goes out must come in again. *The Bible* has a verse, "Cast your bread upon the waters, for you will find it again after many days" (Ecclesiastes 11:1), which I have experienced as truth.

And, so, it would appear has Alyque Padamsee.

No Free Lunch

by Alyque Padamsee

My interpretation of 'there is no free lunch' means that corporates who make a profit out of society must put a little of those profits back into society.

In that sense, the Tata Group, the Birlas, MRF and Britannia are among the companies in India that have always been at the forefront of public service activities. But I often feel that not enough is done by our advertising fraternity. Since we have developed skills in mass communication, we should be at the forefront of changing attitudes. From awareness comes change, as we know. Why should we only motivate people to change from using charcoal to using toothpaste? We can use our skills for other purposes, for instance, to improve the status of women in India. Work with the *mahila mandals,* give them of our time, and our experience in the area of motivation.

When I was the chief executive of Lintas, I realised I had the power to do something. So when UNESCO declared the International Year of the Disabled we came up with a public service film called *The Story of Hope.*

A very simple script. It opens on the hand of a little girl drawing on a slate with a piece of chalk. She draws a stick figure, complete with head, hands and legs, and says out loud, "This is my Daddy." Then she draws another similar figure and says, "This is my Mummy." She finally draws a slightly smaller figure and says, "And this is me." Then she thinks for a moment, wets her finger and erases one of the legs. "No. *This* is me." And the voice-over says, "The disabled don't need your pity. They need your understanding." This film, produced by Kailash Surendranath (who also pioneered the Liril film), was voted into the Clio Hall of Fame (the Oscars of world advertising). The idea was based on a consumer insight that came from my habit of watching the way people behave. Whenever a child was introduced as disabled, everyone would go, "Tsk. Tsk. Tsk." Horribly demeaning for the child. Pity is a humiliating experience. It destroys confidence.

These days a lot of public service advertising is not well thought out. Any advertising, even the public service kind, must have *a unique consumer insight* to motivate the target group into action. It is not enough to just shock the public in the hope of picking up an award at the annual ceremonies.

My first involvement with public service communication began many years ago. Jayaprakash Narayan was very active with the Sarvodaya Mandal and had asked the public to contribute funds for the relief of famine in Bihar. I read in a newspaper article that while Bihar traders were sitting on mounds of rice and wheat, the rural poor were reduced to eating the bark of trees. It brought tears to my eyes. But what's the good of tears if I can't turn them into action, I thought. And that is how I first got the idea of *using emotional triggers* for social service action.

I wrote an emotional appeal to a thousand of my friends and acquaintances, telling them that J P Narayan was raising funds for famine victims in Bihar *"who were eating the bark of trees".* We managed to get together about two and a half lakh rupees, which at that time was a lot of money. Just through a simple letter. People have big hearts. You've got to know how to unlock them.

An NGO that I've been involved with for a number of years is Akansha (meaning aspiration). A simple but brilliant idea dreamed up by Shaheen Mistry—a young St Xavier's College student. She believed that the most important thing—more than food, shelter and clothing—the children living in slums were deprived of was education.

Why not take the slum children to nearby unused school classrooms and teach them "the three Rs"?

She and her friends got permission from the priests at Holy Name School and transported some children from the Cuffe Parade slums to the empty classrooms every day at 4 pm. Then for two hours, Monday through Friday, they taught the children to read and write. And from humble beginnings of just 20 children in the first year at the Holy Name School, they've now grown to over a thousand children in about 12 to 15 schools. Dreams do come true as long as you have *the energy and a plan of action.*

Let me tell you about my theory of second citizenship. Your first duty as a citizen, of course, is to help defend your country in time of war and pay your taxes regularly in peacetime. Your second citizenship is what you owe to the community in which you live. Not just to donate money, but also your time, energy and skills. Every educated Indian should be duty bound to get involved with community service. Like volunteering a few hours a week to help NGOs, for instance, National Association for the Blind or Spastics Society of India. Or organising a street committee to help keep your road clean. When Mrs Gandhi was assassinated, I was very upset. I suppose out of grief comes insight. I sat down and wrote the following lines, "I am an Indian, not because I am a Hindu or a Muslim or a Sikh or a Christian or a Parsi or a Jew. I am an Indian because if I am not . . . who am I?"

Several people in the office felt that these lines were very apt for the troubled times we were all going through, what with the Sikh riots in Delhi. So that year, for the Lintas annual memento, we printed these lines on a small mirror and sent it out to clients, suppliers and other people who interacted with us.

In its own way, it was a message of communal harmony, because no matter what community you hail from or what religion you follow, as soon as you step out of the country, you are an Indian. And this is the only identity you have.

Public service is actually private satisfaction.

Warm-ups

1. Think of as many suggestions and ideas as you can to encourage motorists to drive safely. Write a paragraph on each idea. What media would you use? How expensive is it to execute? How practical? Would it be acceptable to your local municipal corporation? Who could you get to bear the expenses? Is it a long-term or a short-term campaign? Does it involve the co-operation of the motorist in any way? Who else does it involve? You should be able to give at least 10 ideas.
2. Plan an event to create public awareness about AIDS and raise funds to fight the disease.
3. Write an impactful line for the Air-India hoarding at Nariman Point impelling Mumbai's citizens to SAVE WATER.

25

Presenting to Agency Big Dads

If you have got this far, you are now familiar with the basics of a campaign, whether single or multi-pronged. But the proof of the pudding is in the eating; the agency *Big Dads* have to get a taste of the dish before they pronounce it good enough for the client. The art of *presentation* is the art of selling—tuned to perfection. Indeed, every stage of agency life is sell, sell, sell.

Copywriters sell their ideas to the art directors. Art directors sell their ideas to the production guys. Account executives have to sell theirs to their supervisors. Creatives have to sell their work to client servicing, to the copy and art chiefs, to the film and radio people, to the model co-ordinator, to anyone who will listen and some who will not. No wonder the agency is like a fish market! Or the stock exchange!!

No campaign goes out into the market without everyone having put their stamp on it. Some agencies have something called a Plans Board, or a Review Board. The Big Dads sit on these boards. They represent creative, media, research and other disciplines. They are the judges. If your campaign passes the Plans Board, chances are it will do well at the Client Presentation. It is like the dress rehearsal for the Opening Night.

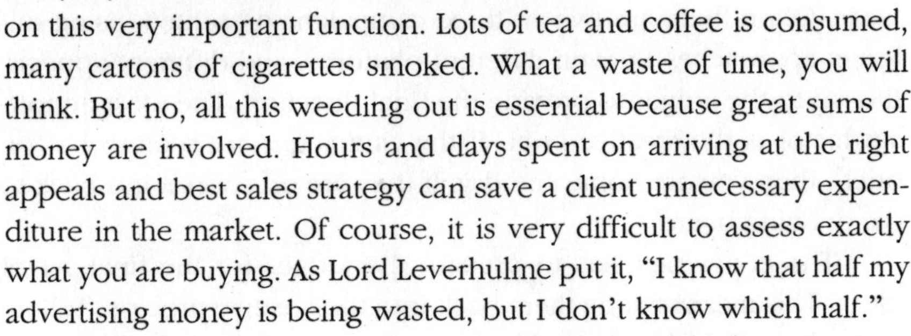

Presenting (or selling) campaigns are an everyday affair. Hours and hours are spent on this very important function. Lots of tea and coffee is consumed, many cartons of cigarettes smoked. What a waste of time, you will think. But no, all this weeding out is essential because great sums of money are involved. Hours and days spent on arriving at the right appeals and best sales strategy can save a client unnecessary expenditure in the market. Of course, it is very difficult to assess exactly what you are buying. As Lord Leverhulme put it, "I know that half my advertising money is being wasted, but I don't know which half."

Many experts have tried to come up with methods to measure advertising effectiveness. There are books on this subject which you would profit from reading. It is not the scope of this one. For the moment, concentrate on learning how to sell your work to meet the approval of those who know more than you do. Creative judgement is not learnt in a day. It comes with practice, with experience, with knowing your market and your consumer, with having a 'nose' which can sniff out a good campaign idea from a not-so-good one. This too requires a book—perhaps my next one!

The Plans Board

As a copywriter, you will constantly be asked to submit your work to greater minds than yours. Of course, you wili be given a chance to present and defend your ideas. So go armed into the lion's den. Here are a few pointers:

Take, for example, a major in-house presentation. The conference room is booked for the whole morning. Pads and pencils are laid out on the huge table. The audio-visual accoutrement, recorders, etc., are in place. The creative brief is smartly bound and placed in front of each 'judge'. They are reading it diligently, arming themselves with the facts and figures.

The creative team enters, accompanied by account executives, media planners, research representatives. They are carrying piles of artworks, copy sheets, storyboards and other material.

The account executive/supervisor normally starts the ball rolling. Gives the background and leads up to the creative strategy. The judges listen in interested silence, asking a question here or there.

Then creative gets into the act. Either the art or copy person (the braver or more eloquent of the two) is chosen to 'sell' the campaign ideas. Often there are two or three campaigns presented, using different approaches or even different platforms and different appeals. It is up to the judges to provide the final direction. The most important factor is the creative brief. If the campaigns are seen to be 'on brief', then you are home and dry. If they are off course, it is back to the drawing board.

The copywriter has to prepare the judges for the final set of ideas. This means taking them back into the creative process. Telling them about how they arrived at the proposition. Taking them through all the stages of the creative strategy.

It is important to listen to the views of the Plans Board carefully. They are on your side but they are also on the client's side. They want the campaign to sell as much as you do but they have to be the devil's advocate. You can be comfortable with these judges, because they are there to help you, not demolish you. They will impart their wisdom and experience. So there is no need to feel nervous.

I used to get tongue-tied at every presentation. All my carefully marshalled arguments would fly out of my mind. Sometimes a senior colleague would give me a kick under the table. Or a judge would kindly help me out. Slowly, as confidence increased, I learned to put across my points logically. To build up to the final argument before unveiling the Big Idea.

Imagine you are on a "how to make tasty biryani" programme on TV. You have got all the ingredients nicely laid out. The raw rice, the little heaps of masala, the bits of meat cleaned and chopped, the utensils ready, the cooker waiting. You go about mixing your ingredients, step-by-step. From time to time you look up at the audience. But basically you are engrossed in the making of the biryani. You want it to taste real good; in fact, you are sure it is going to taste good because you have got all the right ingredients, and you are doing the right things.

A presentation is similar. Place all the ingredients of your campaign candidly on the table—within the parameters of the creative strategy (Tone of Voice, Target Audience, Brand Image, Proposition). You might want to use slides, flip charts, laptops or just read from a document. Because this is a dry run, you do not have to go to great lengths in using expensive materials for your presentation, which are better saved to 'wow' the client with.

Points to Consider

1. Even if you know the tricks of selling, the judges know them better.
2. They know you are saving the best for the last.
3. They can tell if you have done your homework.
4. They can sniff a good idea when they see one.
5. They start looking at their watches if you are longwinded.
6. They lean forward if they are interested.
7. Speaking clearly and slowly helps the judges to concentrate.
8. Saris which keep slipping, or hair that falls across your eyes distract the judges.
9. When flustered, sip some water.
10. Even if you flunk this one, there is time for reworking.

Preparing to Present

1. Have all your material at hand.
2. Work out a rationale.
3. State the objectives clearly.
4. Proceed from the known to the unknown.
5. Be logical.
6. Build up to the finale.
7. Reveal the Idea.
8. Wait for applause.

The Philadelphia Cheese Story

In-house presentations can be a lot of fun. Many years ago in JWT London (as a mere junior writer getting familiar with films) I was involved in a major presentation by sheer accident. Jill Firth, one of the several creative group heads in that enormous shop, had to rush off to Europe for a shoot and asked me to take her place in the Kraft Philadelphia Cheese workshop. Was I thrilled!

Now the clients were America-based and wanted to experiment with an international campaign with a common platform that would make Philadelphia soft, fat, cream cheese (or 'Philly' for short) acceptable across global markets. As this was 1977, the notion was something of a novelty.

Creative teams (pairs of copy/art) were drawn from France, Italy, UK and USA. Jill was in the UK team, but since she was pulled away, an English-speaking Indian copywriter plugged the last- minute hole. The modus operandi was simple. It was a three-day affair. On the morning of the first day we were all briefed simultaneously, then mixed up, so each one landed a partner of a different nationality. I had an Italian art director who did not speak a word of English! One American art person tore his hair because he got a French copywriter.

The top floor of the JWT building (six-storeyed, if I recollect) was at that time empty except for wall-to-wall carpeting and the radiators emanating heat (it was winter and snowing outside). The eight of us were let loose in this space with our pads, pencils and brushes. The teams were not permitted to talk to one another but had to get down to their campaigns. So we lolled about on the carpet, keeping a safe distance between us so that our ideas would not clash.

The teams could not leave this space the entire three days. Coffee, tea and meals were sent up at intervals while we plunged into frenetic creativity. Because I was an 'outsider', I was permitted to go home in the evenings, thereby missing what happened after hours. On the third day we were expected to rise again from our creative depths and make our presentations.

The panel consisted not just of the creative director on the Kraft UK account, but also some Kraft big brass who flew in specially from Chicago for the presentation. It made my hair curl to think I would have to present to these great ones. I pleaded with Jill to return from her shoot in time to make the presentation but she answered, reasonably enough, "It's your campaign, you present it. Even if I come back in time, I'll sit at the back and cheer lustily."

As it turned out, the whole exercise went off well. The American art person went the *soft, fat cheese* way with some super space-age razzle dazzle stuff that kept us in splits. The others presented great ideas that broke the language barriers. My Italian and I went the *bread and cheese* route: Philly and Buns, Philly and Bagels, Philly and Baguettes, Philly and Pizza, Philly and Brun . . . that sort of thing. I was very nervous; it was the first time I was presenting a campaign on 'foreign soil'!

I tried to remember to talk distinctly and not wave my arms about. Like the last time I presented to a client back home. I had described a film idea with great gusto and hand waving. When I was through the client said, "I didn't understand a word of that, June, but go ahead anyway!"

Now, ten thousand miles away from good old Mumbai and the back-up of my colleagues, it was sink or swim. I gritted my teeth and thought of Gandhi. I launched into my theme. I delivered my little scenarios in what I thought were accents French, Jewish and Italian, accompanied by much arm-waving a la India! Today I cannot quite recall the ads, except that we had chosen situations like *at the races with Philly and buns*, presented in my best Cockney, dropped 'aitches' and all. The audience was kind enough to laugh.

The Kraft panel was extremely appreciative of the creative work our motley teams had produced in under 72 hours. The atmosphere was friendly and informal. The judges were hard put to decide which campaign to go with. Months later they still could not decide. Perhaps that is why Philly cheese is not being eaten with 'brun' and 'gutlis' in India. As yet.

Presentation and selling skills improve with time and practice.

Defending Your Work

1. Listen carefully.
2. Make notes of the objections.
3. Marshall your reasons.
4. Stay cool.
5. Wait for silence and attention.
6. Take each point singly.

7. Give counter-arguments clearly and succinctly.
8. Be respectful.
9. Be open to changing your mind.
10. Try and see the other point of view.
11. Give in gracefully if you have to.
12. Be prepared to re-work the campaign.
13. Keep your temper.

Defending your work is a vital part of a copywriter's role. If you cannot defend your ideas, some good stuff may go down the tube. On the other hand, you must be flexible enough to see another's viewpoint, to recognise a better idea than your own. Agency life, like life itself, is a matter of give and take. Rules and guidelines are everywhere, but not everyone keeps them. But until you become an expert at your craft, it is wiser to stick to the guidebook.

How the Bible Helped Me Prepare Under Pressure

Tim Sebastian of the BBC is often heard saying that the hardest type of interview is the off-the-cuff interview. The same could be said of this type of presentation. Sometimes you may be called upon to deliver a speech or rise to the occasion with little time to prepare. *Do not panic*. The training and discipline of years will not desert you in times of crisis. Just breathe a prayer and summon your inner reserves.

This happened to me at the HTA creative directors' conference in 1989 (mentioned in the chapter on Brainstorming and the Big Idea). The short speech on 'Being a Leader', which won me an impromptu award, was inspired by Bible verses. Very briefly, this is how the presentation went. I spoke into a collar microphone and used a few acetate sheets on an epidiascope.

The theme was 'Leadership'. Earlier, we had been addressed by several 'leaders' in their fields. They included Jaitirth (Jerry) Rao, the then CEO of Citibank, Alfred D'Souza of the Stopgaps choir, C L Proudfoot of ACC, the head of an *ashram*, and a bigwig from the police. So I took off from there . . . .

VISUAL	AUDIO
Blank screen	When Ivan asked me to join HTA Madras he said, "June, I want you to be a leader." I became very nervous. Till then, all I had been leading was a quiet life in Poona. *SFX:* Polite laughter So as soon as I joined the Madras Office
1. (Handwritten Words) LISTEN/LEARN	I set about learning what makes a leader. One of the first things I had to do was learn to LISTEN. I listened to the copy-writers. I listened to the art directors. I listened to the account executives. I listened to the telephone operator and found out where I could buy fresh fish after church on Sunday. In this way I got to know a great deal about the people in my department and place of work. This helped me to deal with the problems that arose at work, even the tricky ones.
2. (Handwritten Words)	The second thing I learned as a leader was to get a sense of the Big Picture . . . an Overview.
OVERVIEW looks over/overlooks	This meant, not just looking over the shoulders of my colleagues in the department, but overlooking human errors and weaknesses.
3. (Written Words)	The third quality of a leader is Valour—this means in effect having
VALOUR Courage to stand up/to stand down	the courage to stick by your convictions . . . and the grace to admit that you were wrong, if need be.

	Visual	Audio
4.	(Handwritten Words) Empathy to be able to step into someone's shoes without stepping out of your own	Last, but not least, a leader must empathise with people. I define empathy as being able to step into someone else's shoes . . . without stepping out of your own!
5.	Sketch of Summit Logo Creative Department 1989 (diagram)	This is what the Madras creative department looks like. The green circles are the copy strength, the red circles are the art people, the blue circles stand for film, av, finishing artists, photography, and we are all held up by dear Mr Ramabhadran, my secretary. *SFX:* Much laughter (as Mr VRR is the oldest member of the office and an institution)
6.	(Handwritten words) HTA-Madras and Others at the Trough Lintas/Mudra/O&M R K Swamy/Artig/Sista's/ Rediffusion "Where no oxen are, the trough is clean. But much increase comes by the strength of an ox." —*Proverbs 14:4*	(Here I spoke of the competition HTA faced in Madras, their strengths and weaknesses, and our own.)
7.	"He who deals with a slack hand becomes poor, but the hand of the diligent makes one rich." —*Proverbs 10:4* HTA Madras Rs 80,000,000 Number One Because we tried harder.	(An account of our performance over the year, and how we had grown from a Rs 20 million to a Rs 80 million office in a mere three months.)

	VISUAL	AUDIO
8.	NEW BUSINESS India Cements, Sun-Polymer, Solidaire, Citibank, Chemplast, Ashok Leyland. ". . . always pursue what is good both for yourselves and for all." —*1 Thessalonians 5:15* "You shall increase my greatness." —*Psalm 71:21*	(This section outlined not just what we had achieved, but also dealt with future plans and objectives.)
9.	HTA-Madras STATE-OF-THE ART "We are hard pressed on every side, yet not crushed; we are perplexed, but not in despair." — *2 Corinthians 4:8*	(Here is an impassioned plea for more H.O. resources for this office, which at that time was the weakest and struggling to keep its head above water.)
10.	"Let all that you do be done with love." —*1 Corinthians 16:14* ■ Prayer meeting ■ Creative review ■ Operative systems ■ Clean channels	(Spoke about the operational style in creative; the weekly meetings which started with spiritual reading and a few minutes meditation; the monthly creative review; the work-flow systems—and keeping the communication channels free of rust.)
11.	". . . whose hope is the Lord . . . shall be like a tree planted by the waters, which spreads out its roots by the river . . . nor will cease from yielding fruit." —from *Jeremiah 17:7–8* ■ more informality ■ higher levels of creativity ■ talent spotting/development	(Plans, hopes, dreams and aspirations for the next year.)

VISUAL	AUDIO
▪ participation in workshops and seminars ▪ more inter-office exposure ▪ creative cosmopol-itanisation and contemporarisation!	
12. TRIBUTE TO A LEADER "She makes linen garme-nts and sells them . . . . Strength and honour are her clothing; She shall rejoice in time to come." —*Proverbs 31:24,25*	(I ended with a small but sincere tribute to the General Manager, a young woman.) *SFX:* Silence. Followed by standing ova-tion.

One thing about ad people; they are are so very generous and spontaneous. I shall treasure the remarks made to me by my peers from the other offices that day, even more than the impromptu token award which I shared with my team.

It is moments like this which makes the grind worthwhile.

(All the verses are according to the *New King James Bible.*)

Workout

1. You are given three minutes free air time on TV, just after Simi Garewal's half-hour chat with celebrities. Just as the music fades out, you come in. You have to raise funds for the Latur earthquake victims. No props, just you and your voice. How would you get the viewer to listen to you? AND donate generously?
2. Assemble a group of friends and neighbours and convince them to switch to Dentium toothpaste. Promise not to take up more than half an hour of their time!

26

Presenting to the Client

The dress rehearsal is over.

D-Day is here.

All the blood, sweat, toil and tears of the last few weeks or days or months lead up to the grand finale when the agency has to show its mettle to the clients.

Account supervisors and executives grab ties and put on coats, the creative team don clean jeans and creaseless kurtas.

The agency is buzzier than ever—until the contingent departs for the *meeting of great minds* . . . .

Then secretaries sit back and sigh, and wait for the phone call that says 'thumbs up' or 'no go'.

Most important presentations are made on the client's turf. That is when the agency has to work to sell its ideas. Sometimes the client (or prospective client) is invited over to the agency. This could be when the agency is wooing the client, as in a new business pitch. There is a certain protocol which attends client presentations, not so evident in the dress rehearsal.

It is up to the agency Big Dads to decide who goes on when—that is called *strategy*. They have been up half the previous night plotting and planning. Normally, Client Servicing starts the ball rolling. Then it is the turn of Creative, followed by Media, then Research, and finally Finance and Budget to wrap up the deal.

The Formal Presentation

Young writers are not usually invited to participate in major client presentations. But there is no harm in being a fly on the wall of the conference room where the meeting is being held. So take your seats in 'the gods' and watch the Play unfold.

Curtain Opens on Act I

(Morning: Conference room in client's office)

The scene is set.

Conference table shines. Glasses of water. Pens, pencils, notepads. Briefs bound and placed before each chair. Projectors in place. Charts, laptops, other paraphernalia.

Client enters from right.
Agency enters from left.
Take their places facing one another.
Smiles and handshakes all round.
Tension in the air.

Someone says, "Well, shall we begin?"

Someone else says, "Just give us a sec, the projector (laptop, or electric cord) . . . slight snag . . . ."

Nervous laughter, but friendly.

Act I Scene I

(The same)

The agency presenter stands up.

Rustle of paper as everyone looks at the agenda.

Agency man outlines the purpose of the presentation. Lays the groundwork for selling the ideas that follow. Of course, he does not reveal the idea. Anticipation is a part of good salesmanship. Remember the magic words: sell sell sell.

He refers back to the Agency Brief. The sales targets. The marketing objectives. The advertising goals. The advertising task. The clients tacitly agree. After all, they have put their signature to the Brief.

This is just recall.

He talks about the product. Evaluates its strenghts and weaknesses from the consumer's viewpoint. In short, he sets the stage for Creative.

If client has something to say, he says it.

It is best to clear up any possible misunderstanding about the Brief at this stage. Mostly minor.

Presenter sits down. Everyone looks expectantly at the creative team.

Act I Scene II

(the same)

Creatives take the floor.

This is the main course—got to sell both steak and sizzle! Begin with the consumer profile. Pick out the target audience. Analyse the product benefits in terms of consumer needs.

Build steadily up to the proposition. With or without the aid of charts/slides.

Client listens with interest.

This is the *creative thinking*—they have to understand it so that they can judge the final campaign accurately.

The revelation of the Big Idea is the moment of truth.

Creatives can do it in one fell swoop—or string it out. Depends on what tactic is warranted.

Watching the client and being sensitive to the mood helps. It also depends on how the Creatives have prepared their strategy. Sometimes they could change tactics in midstream.

Take a shortcut, or spend more time on certain layouts.

Creatives unveil the Big Idea.

Explain how it is the solution to the problems outlined earlier by Client Servicing.

Show some alternative approaches.

Media and Client Servicing watch the performance with their fingers crossed. This is the real McCoy, this is what brings home the bacon. They cheer the Creatives along with their mouths shut.

Layouts are presented.

The TV commercial is shown.

The radio spot is played.

The POP displayed.

Everyone takes a good long look.

Creatives explain how the Big Idea can be effectively employed in all media. Translatability. Understandability. Reproduceability. Saves-you-costability.

Client lets it all sink in slowly.

Agency waits for the reaction.

Client smiles and nods. Appreciates the hard work agency has put in. So far so good.

They congratulate the Creative team on the excellent work.

Creatives look modest and leave the room amidst mild applause.

Someone suggests lunch.

THE CURTAIN FALLS

Curtain Opens on Act II

(The same conference room—after lunch)

The table has been cleared, the creative work put neatly aside for client to look at again later.

Media and Account Servicing sit facing the Client at the table.

Media presents its plans and schedules—which newspapers, magazines, theatres, towns, where and when.

Who to reach and how many times. Client has to really pay attention to these facts and figures. They spell money.

Budget is discussed.
Media costs are discussed.
Production costs are debated.
The need for research is discussed.
The budget is finalised.
Method of payment is decided.

Client promises to revert on final creative decision.
Everyone shakes hands.

THE CURTAIN FALLS AGAIN

Act III

(Life in the agency carries on.)

There is a saying in theatre circles that there are no good third acts. So we will end our drama here.

The Informal Presentation

While creative work is the *raison d'etre* of an agency, all sorts of other activities are carried on simultaneously. Not the least of these are the informal meetings between agency and client. Across the table. On the phone. Via e-mail/fax. Over a drink in the evening. People are constantly interacting, with one goal in mind. To do business. To sell ideas. To elicit briefs. To extract payments. To clear up misunderstandings. To promote goodwill. To discuss legal problems. To finalise dates.

Informal meetings and interaction are the lifeblood of agency-client relationships. Meetings may be horizontal, vertical or diagonal among staffers. Suit and tie are forsaken for the rolled up shirt sleeves approach. Every agency has its own culture and method, and so does every advertiser. The wheels of communication have to be kept well-oiled. The show must go on.

Some hairy stories are told about day-to-day client presentations. One client was (in)famous for hurling the layouts and documents at account executives if he was annoyed by the work presented. Needless to say, the agency finally parted company with this individual. Another client, who was MD of his own company, making a certain kitchen utensil, loved holding day-long meetings in his oversized office. He would talk for hours on end, with the creative work spread out in front of him, going through every line of copy, nitpicking, changing commas, while at least five senior managers of the agency sat around him in silence, clenching their teeth. Ultimately, the agency relinquished the account as being a losing proposition.

Another client had a habit of putting his legs up on the table while he talked with the agency team, even if there were women present. When I had occasion to be there once, I gently swivelled around in my seat till I had my back to him. He took the hint and the legs came down. Well, it takes all types.

Most clients are a decent bunch.

The New Business Pitch

Some agencies take the stand that they will not pitch for accounts. Their work speaks for itself. Also, they do not want to make speculative presentations based on inadequate or hypothetical information. But in today's competitive world, and considering the inflation rates, this is changing. One has to run in order to stand still. Agencies go after accounts. How much time and money they want to invest in chasing clients probably depends on what they hope to gain by way of billings.

Besides, accounts also leave an agency for one reason or other, and so a constant equilibrium must be maintained.

The New Business presentation is not much different from the formal presentation. However, the emphasis is slightly different. The agency has to sell itself, and show the client how and why it thinks it is qualified to handle the client's business. Here too, the agency has done its homework. If they feel the client's creative work can be improved, they might proffer a campaign as bait.

Most agencies have a showreel of their accomplishments, their resources, their personnel, or at least a self-introducing brochure. This is regularly updated.

A few agencies also have a House Journal for private circulation among their employees and clients. This too is a wonderful way to build morale, as well as to strengthen the client's faith in the agency. Self-promotion is a part of sales promotion. And why not. Faint heart never won fair business.

Agencies, like any other brand in the market, also make positionings statements about themselves. This is reflected in their working (tone of voice), the type of accounts they handle (brand image) and their clients list (target audience).

Some agencies are creative hotshops/boutiques.
Some are work horses, competent and hardsell.
Some are marketing oriented.
Some are like universities.
Some are creative and businesslike.
Some are financial/public issue oriented.
Some are professionally-managed.
Some are proprietor concerns.
Some are permutations and combinations of the above.

The industry is large enough and flexible enough to offer something for everyone. Take a look around the market. Name five agencies that are top-of-mind. How do you think they have positioned themselves? What sort of accounts do they have? Which type of client do you think they will attract? Copywriters must keep their ears and eyes open, and their mouths frequently shut, in order to evolve into advertising persons. The more you know, the more it shows.

Since advertising is basically a people business, the best way to acquire information—and thus knowledge—is from the people who make up the business.

Starting with those you interact with daily in your own agency, master the art of getting along with people, and you will go far towards mastering your craft as a copywriter.

A good ad should be like a sermon: it must not only comfort the afflicted, it must afflict the comfortable.

—Bernice Fitz-Gibbon in *Elyse and Mike Sommer Similis Dictionary,* Gale Research Company, p. 12

27

Getting Along in the Agency

People are the main assets of an advertising agency. And consistently good creative ideas are an agency's products. The happier and more satisfied its people, the higher the productivity. That is why man-management is a priority in an ad agency. A recent trend with big agencies is the introduction of a Human Resource Development department. This has become practically a science in itself, as management recognises that employee satisfaction does not stem from a fat pay packet alone. For optimum performance, the employee's body, mind, spirit and psyche have to work in sync as far as possible.

This chapter is not about HRD,. valid and very, very important though it is. It is about how to become a better—and hence happier—copywriter by showing you where to go for what you need. Books, references, libraries, files, back-up systems, all the data you need to access, has first been put there by people. When in doubt, go to people.

The Golden Rule: Go to People

Get oriented: meet your fellow workers.
Go around all the departments.
Ask questions.
Be a pest.
Take notes. Listen. Learn.
Keep writing.
Make notes.
Never trust your memory.
Learn about Media.
Learn about Billings.
Learn what client servicing does.
Visit the studio.
Talk to the art directors.
Talk to the visualisers.
Talk to the illustrators.
Talk to the typographers.
Visit the print shops.
Talk to the film people.
Talk to the TV people.
Visit sound-recording studios.
Visit film-making units.
Be interested in everything.
Master at least one thing.

People Management

(or how not to step on corns)

You may wonder what this has to do with writing copy, but if you want to get the best work out, remember that creating a campaign is teamwork. If you are stuck for an idea, you could find yourself asking people for help. Anyone can come up with a good idea—an account executive, your art director, one of the secretaries. People never mind being asked, and if you are on good terms with them, they will spare the time. Just something someone says could give you an idea to help you out of a rut.

The same goes for getting your work out on time. Diplomacy is the name of the people game—particularly in agencies where egos are particularly tender and tension runs high. One account supervisor was avoided like the plague because he had a nasty habit of grabbing people by the neck and banging their head against the wall if he was dissatisfied with the way things were going. This is not the way to get good work out of creative—or other—people!

Higher up the ladder, egos bruise more easily than way down at the bottom. So tread softly, or you will tread on someone's corns. Prima donnas are tolerated sometimes if their work is spectacular, or if they are otherwise very nice guys or dolls. But like high-spirited racehorses, they make the others feel nervous, so the work does not exactly go smoothly.

In most agencies the atmosphere is informal. Everyone is on a first-name basis. But it is safer to say Mr X or Mrs Y unless asked otherwise. Even after 25 years, I could never call Subhas Ghosal anything but Mr Ghosal. Once I overheard Gerson da Cunha say, "Subhas, how is it everyone calls you Mr Ghosal, but even the peons in Lintas call me Gersonji ?"

Getting Along

Getting Along with the Boss

What does he expect of you? Study your boss, discover his weaknesses and strengths. Think of ways to be a helper, not a hindrance. Be respectful but not familiar. Grow a thick skin; learn to take rejections and corrections. In fact, learn, learn, learn. You are being paid to do a job, do it as well as you can. Most bosses appreciate honesty and sincerity. If you have a grievance, share it with your boss first. He might be able to sort it out before the world gets to know of it. It is also advisable not to go over his head to his boss—unless absolutely necessary. You could make an enemy for life. Every agency has a management style and corporate culture. Aim to fit in—if you cannot, move on. Nobody will blame you.

It must be tough to know you know more than your boss, and still have to do things his way. I sympathise with people like this. It takes some skill to get your boss to come round to your ideas without making him feel small.

Getting Along with Client Servicing

We have touched on this before, but it is worth repeating that client servicing people have the toughest job in the agency—to be the buffer between the client and the creatives. They have to take the flak from both sides. So be a little understanding of their plight. In their lowest avatar, client servicing guys are mere postboys, but at their best they can be dynamic contributors to the creative process and great administrators.

Getting Along with the Art Department

Remember they are your other half. Learn their language and speak it, form friendships, eat lunch with your visualisers and avoid copywriter cliques. Ask intelligent questions, offer to go to the printers with them.

It pays to get along with people, especially in the world of advertising. Ad people are among the most likeable and sensitive in the world. They are also the kindest, most helpful, cheerful and humorous. They are mostly chatty and goodnatured. No wonder the advertising profession is the most sought after.

Remember to

Greet the doorman when you come in.

Tip the tea boy.

Be nice to secretaries.

Smile at everyone.

Stay on the good side of the 'little people' (they are the ones who run the shop).

Be cordial with your superiors but don't get too close—the same fire that warms can also burn.

Always help anyone who comes to you for help—if you can.

Never encourage gossip/backbiting/dumping. Some people love to air grievances, which are generally non-existent.

Keep out of politics.

Keep your nose clean.

Keep your cool.

People are an agency's main assets. People make the product of an agency: Big Ideas. People sell these ideas to the clients. People translate the ideas into realities (press, TV, film).

For a lot of people realities are profits after tax.

Believe it or not,
Clients are people.

Once I saw an ad which said, "You find the nicest people on a Honda."

Wrong. You find the nicest people in an ad agency.

So Who Cares?

"Advertising people are people who care. They care about the professional development of their craft. They care about the responsibility of advertising to fulfill its growing role in reducing the cost of sales. They are deeply troubled by the misunderstanding about the purpose, function and benefit of advertising that exists in some high and influential places, and, to a degree, in the minds of some who might benefit most by the more enlightened use of advertising's force.

"They are concerned about attracting the right kind of young and searching minds to the business of advertising and about improving the advanced academic training needed to prepare them. Men and women in the advertising and communications industries have a deep concern for the welfare and the advancement of their fellows. There is a close bond, a fraternal emotion, between them."

These words were written more than 30 years ago by Frederic C. Decker, publisher of Printer's Ink (USA) and vice-president of Vision Inc. He became publisher of the 75-year old marketing and advertising magazine in September 1960. Decker was a co-founder of *Guideposts* magazine in 1947, and served as its MD for five years. After that he joined *Christian Herald Magazine* as associate publisher.

People who need people are the luckiest people in the world.

—Barbra Streisand

28

The End of the Road

What happens when the party is over? What becomes of copywriters as they mellow (not yellow!) with age? It always comes as a pleasant surprise to me to know that some famous personalities in our times began life as copywriters. Here are a few:

Murray Bail:	Australian award-winning fiction writer
Fay Weldon:	English novelist
Shobha De:	Indian writer and author
Rahul Bose:	Actor, TV presenter, theatre personality
Satyajit Ray:	International film-maker
Shyam Benegal:	Film-maker
Kabir Bedi:	Actor

Less well-known are some former copywriters I know who have become

- a full-time minister of his church
- a vintage car mechanic
- a yoga teacher and *sanyasin*
- a vocational counsellor
- a recluse
- a performing flautist

Most copywriters are content to practise their craft lovingly and faithfully till retirement day, when they bid a tearful farewell to their colleagues, while clutching Long Service Awards. But there are many who decide to change horses mid-stream. Some opt out of the business altogether to do something different, pursue an alternative profession or follow a dream. The more ambitious ones move within an agency into client servicing and hope to become MDs and CEOs, either of the agency or their own shops. Some leave the mainstream to become freelancers and creative consultants. Many copywriters moonlight at more than one job.

Creative people will always yearn to express their creativity in some form or other. If agency life satisfies this urge they generally stick around. If not, they look for greener pastures. But basically, professional copywriters continue to practise their craft in some form or other.

Saying Goodbye

Leaving an agency is an art in itself. I would always like to be remembered with affection by my last agency ("Nothing so became her as the manner of her leaving"!). When Ivan Arthur asked me to rejoin HTA as creative director, he said to me, "I looked up the files for your resignation letter. It prompted me to ask you to join us again." I think I had written a rather mushy piece about leaving the 'old ship' where I had spent so many satisfying years. People leave for a variety of reasons—not all of them pecuniary.

If you are leaving for 'better prospects' as they say, do so graciously. Give your agency enough time to find someone to replace you—or at least to adjust to your future absence. Sometimes you feel tempted to resign just to find out whether you will be missed—a little flirtation is permissible, I suppose. I recall putting in my resignation for the first time at HTA when I was offered a more lucrative position with another big agency. The deal was all but signed—and Mr Ghosal had to be informed.

It was an incredible hour I spent with him. He talked about this, that and the other, gently probing the reasons for my leaving. He was so gracious and charming, and appreciative of all that I had done for the company and how much they valued me, I ended up in tears, I was so moved! Never once did he mention the matter of money, nor did he offer me a raise to make me stay on. I decided to stick with HTA and had to face the rather embarrassing task of informing the other agency I would not be joining them. In the event, Mr Ghosal kept his word about "making it up to me", and I got a raise in salary the next month. What a man!

The second time I resigned from HTA, however, he let me go easily, "The bride returns to the father's house". And back to Lintas I went at their request.

Sometimes things do not go so smoothly. You have to make a decision for yourself. Personal reasons may come up. Perhaps you take a long hard look at how things are in the agency and read the writing on the wall. You have come to a dead end in your career climb. Gender cards may be stacked against you. There is no more room at the top. Or may be you are just suffering from a dose of battle fatigue. A change would be healthy. Gerson da Cunha gave me some sound advice, "Job hop while you are young. Then when you find the agency whose culture suits you, stick with it." In today's rapidly mobile world, I do not know if there is place for such wisdom. But anyway, it is offered.

On Keeping a Portfolio

Most working copywriters are so immersed in their professions, they do not think in terms of saving their campaigns or keeping a record of their work. As a copywriter you are as good as your last campaign.

If you are active and high profile, people in the industry will automatically hear of you and your market value will be accordingly determined and job offers will keep coming your way.

Still, competition being what it is, it is advisable that copywriters keep a portfolio of their work. It could be done either in the form of actual pulls in an 'album' . . . or the work can be xeroxed or photographed. In any case, it should be easily accessible if required. Most employers like to have a look at a portfolio. Today, there are video cassettes, compact discs, etc. Everything is computerised. Why not your portfolio?

Fear of Failure

Now we have come to the end of our journey together. I hope you have enjoyed this book as much as I enjoyed writing it. Before we say *au 'voir*, let me share a few true stories about failure.

True Story Number One

Many a year ago the Chesebrough-Pond's company entrusted India's leading agency with the job of organising their three-day annual sales conference in Madras. The agency was accustomed to this sort of thing and had many successes in the previous years, so the copywriter who was masterminding the project was sure that this one too would win plaudits from the clients who were a generous bunch. She thought of a wonderful theme—computers—about which she knew little or nothing, and made some grand designs for the decor which she gave to the Madras carpenters to construct.

On the day, some large boxes measuring 6' x 5' x 6' were delivered to the hotel where the conference was being held. They were the carpenter's idea of computers, each larger than a fair-sized water tank!

Anyway, these were placed strategically in front of the hall, and the lights, which were to blink on and off, strung across them. The salesmen trooped in and took their seats expectantly. Little did they know what was to come. Behind the scenes, the agency engineer fell down in a faint from too many late nights and overdose of coffee, so the lights did not come on. The man who was to dress as the robot and do a dance to space age music arrived in a costume which looked like something out of the Wizard of Oz. He had to do his dance behind a white sheet with a lamp behind it, so the audience could only see a strange silhouette moving grotesquely on the blank screen. The music that accompanied the dance was flown down from Mumbai, on a small cassette recorder which emitted a tinny sound.

The audience sat in stony silence as all this corny stuff went on. There was no clapping. The copywriter in charge was wishing the earth would open and swallow her up. In the first row of the audience, the top brass of Ponds, Mr Ghosal of HTA and Mr Gerson da Cunha of Lintas squirmed in pain.

Finally the ordeal was over. The salesmen left to partake of the dinner, which was a hundred times more palatable than what they had just been subjected to. Mr Ghosal found the copywriter weeping among the abandoned computer boxes. He gave her a wry smile and said, "At least they liked the advertising campaign".

The copywriter wept some more.

It was her first taste of failure, and no one was blaming her.

She felt rotten. But it taught her a lot of things.

Anyone can fail.
Things can go wrong.
People are understanding.
Learn from failures.
Do better the next time.
Never take anything for granted.
Check. Double check. And check again.

True Story Number Two

India's second largest agency has the task of releasing the Hindustan Lever Chairman's Annual Speech. This is a full-page, fine-print effort. The job must be perfect. No less a person than the creative group head is entrusted with the job of proof-checking this magnum opus. She accepts the assignment with alacrity and a certain trepidation. She reads and rereads the proofs at least half a dozen times. There are no mistakes.

When the speech appears in all the leading newspapers, the Chairman phones Mr Padamsee. There are three spelling errors! A sealed white envelope reaches the creative head's desk. She opens it with trembling fingers. There is a single sheet of paper with these words in Alyque's familiar hand:

What is the meaning of this sorry saga?

It is the second major failure of her otherwise magical career. She betakes herself to his office and offers to resign from the agency. Alyque lets her off with a reprimand and a promise to look into the matter of hiring an experienced proof-reader just for this onerous task. The agency recalls the offending ad from the dailies and releases a fresh speech—without mistakes—at its own cost.

Failure is part of the game.

Accidents will happen. Sometimes you can check and check and check again—and still something goes wrong.

Do not despair.

Get up and walk.

You still have feet, right?

True Story Number Three

This book almost never got written.

Just as I had finished the first draft on the computer, and was about to save and transfer it onto a floppy, I pressed some wrong buttons. Four years' labour got wiped out in under a second. Everything. And I did not have a printout.

The neighbours came and tried to retrieve. The computer engineer came and tried to retrieve. Friends from Delhi telephoned instructions how to retrieve. No go. The entire work had disappeared. It was not to be found even in the Recycle bin.

I went to pieces. Howled for 24 hours. Decided to call Ranjan Kaul of Response Books and tell him I quit. It was 23rd March 1999. He was expecting the draft by 30th March.

The next day I went about collecting my files and books, prior to putting them away forever. My heart was wooden.

And then I saw a couple of chapters I had written years ago lying among the papers. The pages were old and dog-eared.

I picked them up. I sat down at the computer again.

I prayed. And began to key in.

On March 30th 1999, Mr Ranjan Kaul was sent the draft for the first 10 chapters of this book. They were nothing like what I had written the first time round. *They were better.*

And finally, I am so privileged to let that un-ordinary man mentioned in My preface, have the last word.

An Open Mind

by Ram Ray

It there is one thing I genuinely abhor it's a closed mind. The day you think you know it all, you'll be brain-dead. Advertising is one profession in which you have to stay very much alive mentally.

You can master every tool of the trade, soak in every theory. But there's no formula yet to guarantee success. You're forever in search of those elusive quanta that make people tick. Research can provide pointers, but they are approximations really.

What worked yesterday won't necessarily work today. We have no Hubble telescope, no cyclotron to map and analyse the ever-changing human psyche.

So I put a high premium on *gut feel*. Always have, always will.

Gut feel plays a great part in creating brilliant advertising. But it is not a matter of individual quirks deciding on what's good or bad. In mass communication you can't get too esoteric on that.

If you do some close analysis of some really classic campaigns, you'll find they engage and appeal to a whole range of human senses: your aesthetic sense, your sense of humour, your culturally determined sense of values, your sense of self. . .

And as ephemeral as the medium is, it does give you moments of great pleasure.

Like reading June's book. It's a gentle book, but it has all the fundas. It has a souffle touch, and it is not preachy. It's a unique book on the craft of copywriting. There is no other book of this kind in India, and probably very few in the world! Wannabe writers: keep an open mind and do the exercises suggested . . . my gut feel is they could help you write a top campaign or two . . . of this century!

* * *

PRAISE THE LORD

Appendix

Top 100 Advertising Campaigns of the Century

1. Volkswagen, "Think Small", Doyle Dane Bernbach, 1959.
2. Coca-Cola, "The Pause that Refreshes", D'Arcy Co., 1929.
3. Marlboro, The Marlboro Man, Leo Burnett Co., 1955.
4. Nike, "Just do it", Wieden & Kennedy, 1988.
5. McDonald's,"You deserve a break today", Needham, Harper & Steers, 1971.
6. DeBeers "A Diamond is forever", N.W. Ayer & Son, 1948.
7. Absolut Vodka, The Absolute Bottle, TBWA, 1981.
8. Miller Lite beer, "Tastes great, less filling", McCann-Erickson Worldwide, 1974.
9. Clairol, "Does she, or doesn't she?", Foote, Cone & Belding, 1957.
10. Avis, "We try harder", Doyle Dane Bernbach , 1963.
11. Federal Express, "Fast talker", Ally & Gargano, 1982.
12. Apple Computer, "1984", Chiat/Day, 1984.
13. Alka-Seltzer, Various ads, Jack Tinker & Partners, Doyle Dane Bernbach, Wells Rich, Greene, 1960s, 1970s.
14. Pepsi-Cola, "Pepsi-Cola hits the spot", Newell-Emmett Co., 1940s.
15. Maxwell House, "Good to the last drop" Ogilvy, Benson & Mather, 1975.
16. Ivory Soap, "99 and 44/100% pure", Procter & Gamble Co., 1882.
17. American Express, "Do you know me?", Ogilvy & Mather, 1975.
18. US Army, "Be all that you can be", N.W. Ayer & Son, 1981.
19. Anacin, "Fast, fast, fast relief", Ted Bates & Co., 1952.

20. Rolling Stone, "Perception Reality", Fallon McElligott Rice, 1985.
21. Pepsi-Cola, "The Pepsi Generation", Batton, Barton, Durstine & Osborn, 1964.
22. Hathaway Shirts, "The man in the Hathaway Shirt", Hewitt, Ogilvy, Benson & Mather, 1951.
23. Burma-Shave, Roadside signs in verse, Allen Odell, 1925.
24. Burger King, "Have it your way", BBDO, 1973.
25. Campbell Soup, "Mmm mm good", BBDO 1930s.
26. US Forest Service, Smokey the Bear "Only you can prevent forest fires", Advertising Council, Foote, Cone & Belding.
27. Budweiser, "This Bud's for you", D'Arcy Masius Benton & Bowles, 1970s.
28. Maidenform, "I dreamed I went shopping in my Maidenform bra", Norman, Craig & Kunnel, 1949.
29. Victor Talking Machine Co., "His master's voice", Francis Barraud, 1901.
30. Jordan Motor Car Co., "Somewhere west of Laramie", Edward S. (Ned) Jordan, 1923.
31. Woodbury Soap, "The skin you love to touch", J. Walter Thompson Co., 1911.
32. Benson & Hedges 100s, "The disadvantages", Wells, Rich, Greene, 1960s.
33. National Biscuit Co., Uneeda Biscuits' Boy in Boots, N.W. Ayer & Son, 1899.
34. Energizer, The Energizer Bunny, Chiat/Day, 1989.
35. Morton Salt, "When it rains it pours", N.W. Ayer & Son, 1912.
36. Chanel, "Share the fantasy", Doyle Dane Bernbach, 1979.
37. Saturn, "A different kind of company, A different kind of car", Hal Riney & Partners, 1989.
38. Crest Toothpaste, "Look Ma! No cavities!", Benton & Bowles, 1958.
39. M&Ms, "Melts in your mouth, not in your hands", Ted Bates & Co., 1954.
40. Timex, "Takes a licking and keeps on ticking", W.B. Doner & Co. and predecessor agencies, 1950s.
41. Chevrolet, "See the USA in your Chevrolet", Campbell-Ewald, 1950s.
42. Calvin Klein, "Know what comes between me and my Calvins? Nothing!".

43. Reagan for President, "It's morning again in America!", Tuesday Team, 1984.
44. Winston cigarettes, "Winston tastes good—like a cigarette should", 1954.
45. US School of Music, "They laughed when I sat down at the piano, but when I started to play!" Ruthrauff & Ryan, 1925.
46. Camel cigarettes, "I'd walk a mile for a Camel", N.W. Ayer & Son, 1921.
47. Wendy's, "Where's the beef?", Dancer-Fitzgerald-Sample, 1984.
48. Listerine, "Always a bridesmaid, but never a bride", Lambert & Feasley, 1923.
49. Cadillac, "The penalty of leadership", MacManus, John & Adams, 1915.
50. Keep America Beautiful, "Crying Indian", Advertising Council/ Marstellar Inc., 1971.
51. Charmin, "Please don't squeeze the Charmin", Benton & Bowles, 1964.
52. Wheaties, "Breakfast for champions", Blackett-Sample-Hummert, 1930s.
53. Coca-Cola, "It's the real thing", McCann-Erickson, 1970.
54. Greyhound, "It's such a comfort to take the bus and leave the driving to us", Grey Advertising, 1957.
55. Kellogg's Rice Krispies, "Snap! Crackle! and Pop!", Leo Burnett Co., 1940s.
56. Polaroid, "It's so simple", Doyle Dane Bernbach, 1977.
57. Gillette, "Look sharp, feel sharp", BBDO, 1940s.
58. Levy's Rye Bread, "You don't have to be Jewish to love Levy's Rye Bread", Doyle Dane Bernbach, 1949.
59. Pepsodent, "You'll wonder where the yellow went", Foote, Cone & Belding, 1956.
60. Lucky Strike Cigarettes, "Reach for a Lucky instead of a sweet", Lord & Thomas, 1920s.
61. 7 UP, "The Uncola", J. Walter Thompson, 1970s.
62. Wisk detergent, "Ring round the collar", BBDO, 1968.
63. Sunsweet Prunes, "Today the pits, tomorrow the wrinkles", Freerg Ltd., 1970s.
64. Life cereal, "Hey, Mikey", Doyle Dane Bernbach, 1972.
65. Hertz, "Let Hertz put you in the driver's seat", Norman Craig & Kummel, 1961.

66. Foster Grant, "Who's that behind those Foster Grants?", Geer, Dubois, 1965.
67. Perdue Chicken, "It takes a tough man to make tender chicken", Scali, McCabe, Sloves, 1971.
68. Hallmark, "When you care enough to send the very best", Foote, Cone & Belding, 1930s.
69. Springmaid sheets, "A buck well spent", In-house, 1948.
70. Queensboro Corp. Jackson Heights Apartment Homes, WEAF, NYC, 1920s.
71. Steinway & Sons, "The instrument of the immortals", N.W. Ayer & Son, 1919.
72. Levi's Jeans, "501 Blues", Foote, Cone & Belding, 1984.
73. Blackglama-Great Lakes Mink, "What becomes a legend most?" Jane Trahey Associates, 1960s.
74. Blue Nun Wine, Stiller & Meara Campaign, Della Femina, Travisano & Partners, 1970s.
75. Hamm's Beer, "From the Land of Sky Blue Waters", Campbell-Mithus, 1950.
76. Quaker Puffed Wheat, "Shot from guns", Lord & Thomas, 1920s.
77. ESPN Sports,"This is Sports Center", Wieden & Kennedy, 1995.
78. Molson Beer, Laughing Couple, Moving & Talking Picture Co., 1980s.
79. California Milk Processor Board, "Got Milk?", 1993.
80. AT&T, "Reach out and touch someone", N.W. Ayer, 1979.
81. Brylcreem, "A little dab'll do ya", Kenyon & Eckhardt, 1950s.
82. Carling Black Label Beer, "Hey Mabel, Black Label!", Lang, Fisher & Stashower, 1940s.
83. Isuzu, "Lying Joe Isuzu", Della Femina, Travisano & Partners, 1980s.
84. BMW, "The ultimate driving machine", Ammirati & Puris, 1975.
85. Texaco, "You can trust your car to the men who wear the star", Benton & Bowles, 1940s.
86. Coca-Cola, "Always", Creative Artists Agency, 1993.
87. Xerox, "It's a miracle", Needham, Harper & Steers, 1975.
88. Bartles & Jaymes, "Frank and Ed", Hal Riney & Partners, 1985.
89. Dannon Yoghurt, Old People in Russia, Marstellar Inc., 1970s.
90. Volvo, Average life of a car in Sweden, Scali, McCabe, Sloves, 1960s.

91. Motel 6, "We'll leave a light on for you", Richard Group, 1988.
92. Jell-O, Bill Cosby with kids, Young & Rubicam, 1975.
93. IBM, Chaplin's Little Tramp character, Lord, Geller, Federico, Einstein, 1982.
94. America Tourister, The Gorilla, Doyle Dane Bernbach, late 1960s.
95. Right Guard, "Medicine Cabinet", BBDO, 1960s.
96. Maypo, "I want my Maypo", Fletcher, Calkins & Holden, 1960s.
97. Bufferin, Pounding heartbeat, Young & Rubicam, 1960.
98. Arrow Shirts, "My friend, Joe Holmes, is now a horse", Young & Rubicam, 1938.
99. Young & Rubicam, "Impact", Young & Rubicam, 1930.
100. Lyndon Johnson for President, "Daisy", Doyle Dane Bernbach, 1964.

Source: The Advertising Century, *Advertising Age,* [on-line].

References

Baker, Stephen (1979), *Systematic Approach to Advertising Creativity,* McGraw-Hill Book Company Inc., New York.

Bernbach, William (1989), *Bill Bernbach Said,* DDB Needham Worldwide.

Britt, Stuart Henderson (1973), *Marketing Manager's Handbook,* Dartnell Corporation, Chicago.

Burnett, Leo, *100 Leo's,* Leo Burnett Company, Chicago, Illinois.

Fitzhenry, Robert I. (1993), *The Fitzhenry Whiteside Book of Quotations,* Fitzhenry, Whiteside Ltd., Toronto.

Glim, Aesop (1945), *How Advertising is Written and Why,* Dover Publication Inc., New York.

Joyce, Walter (1963), *Advertising Today/Yesterday/Tomorrow,* McGraw-Hill Book Company Inc., New York.

Lord Leverhume (William Hesketh Lever) (1981), *Oxford Dictionary of Modern Quotations,* Oxford University Press, Oxford.

Lutz, William (1974), *The Age of Communication,* Goodyear Publishing Company Inc., California.

O'Toole, John (1981), *The Trouble with Advertising,* Chelsea House, New York.

Ogilvy, David (1971), *Confessions of an Advertising Man,* Ballantine Books, New York.

Ogilvy, David (1985), *Ogilvy on Advertising,* Vintage Books, New York.

Pliskin, Robert (1963), Quoted in Stephen Donadio (1992), *The New York Public Library: Book of Twentieth Century American Quotations,* Stonesong Press, New York.

Reeves, Rosser (1971), *Reality in Advertising,* Shoaib & Sunder Publishers, Bombay.

Sandage, Charles H. (1972), 'Some Institutional Aspects,' *Journal of Advertising,* Vol. 1.

Simpson, James B. (1964), *Contemporary Quotations,* Vail-Ballon Press, Binghampton, NY.

St. John of the Cross (1979), *The Collected Works of St. John of the Cross,* ICS Publication, Institute of Carmelite Studies, Washington DC.

Watkins, Julian Lewis (1959), *The 100 Greatest Advertisments,* Dover Publications Inc., New York.

Index